IMAGES
of America

STAR LAKE

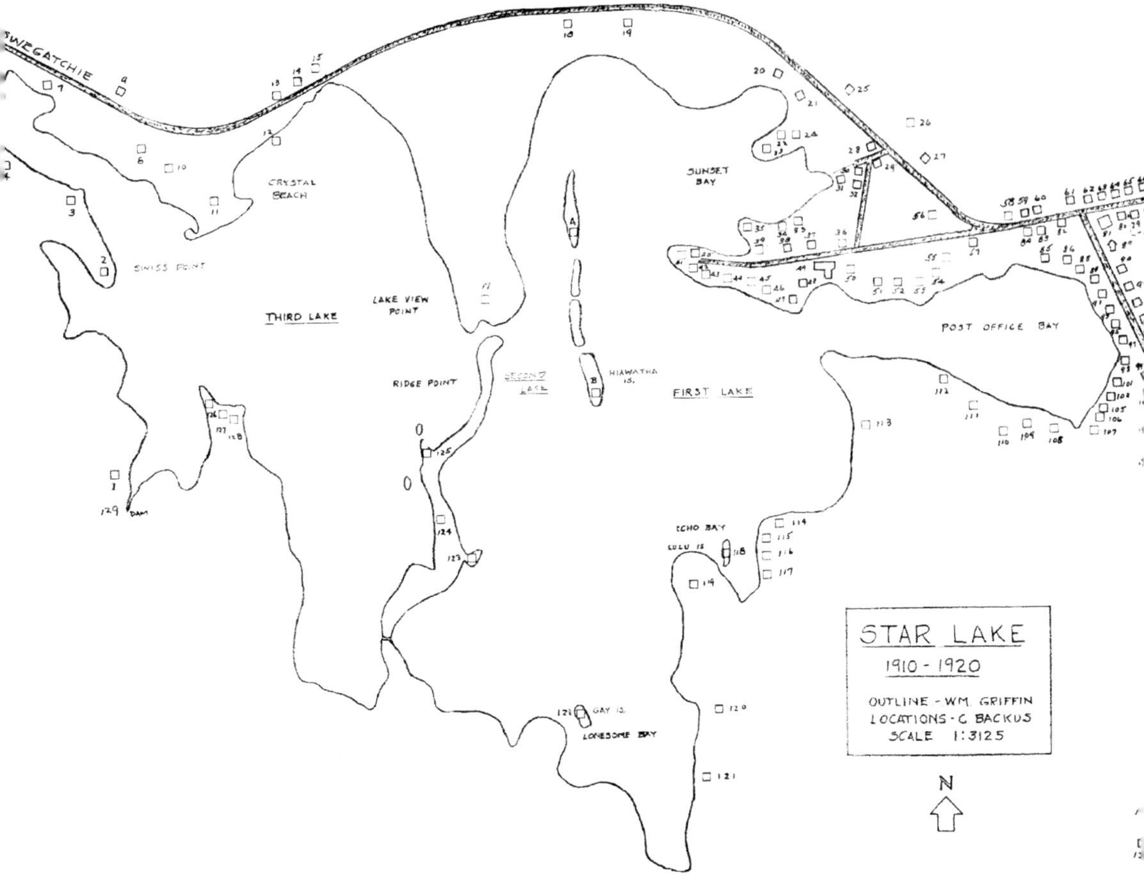

This map of Star Lake shows the locations of known structures between 1910 and 1920.

On the cover: Shown is one of the many rustic bridges on Star Lake around the beginning of the 20th century.

IMAGES
of America

STAR LAKE

Shawn R. Bauerschmidt

ARCADIA
PUBLISHING

ISBN 978-0-7385-4454-0

Published by Arcadia Publishing
Charleston, South Carolina

Printed in the United States of America

Library of Congress Catalog Card Number: 2005935042

For all general information contact Arcadia Publishing at:
Telephone 843-853-2070
Fax 843-853-0044
E-mail sales@arcadiapublishing.com
For customer service and orders:
Toll-Free 1-888-313-2665

Visit us on the Internet at www.arcadiapublishing.com

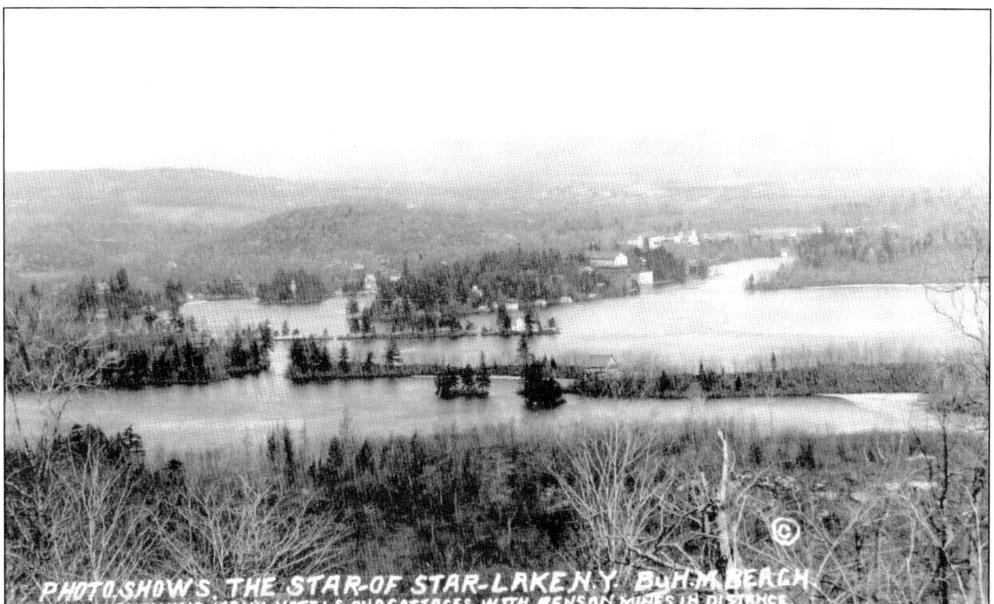

This panoramic view of Star Lake was taken from the top of Maple Mountain by photographer H. M. Beach around 1910. Many of the local hotels and cottages can be seen in this photograph. Benson Mines can be seen in the far distance.

Contents

Acknowledgments		6
Introduction		7
1.	The Village	9
2.	The Hotels	25
3.	The Star Lake Inn	41
4.	Star Lake Cottages	63
5.	Camps and Other Cottages	73
6.	Recreation and Personalities	111

ACKNOWLEDGMENTS

This book would not have been possible if it were not for a group of select people who spent time with me remembering the early days of Star Lake. They provided incredibly vivid facts, stories, and materials related to their time at the lake. In particular, I would like to thank Cecelia Henri, Christopher Wiles, Bert Benson, Jared Cooper, George Perrson, Jean Grimm, Eileen Schuyler, Leon Zois, John Sayles, and Ada Kilbourne.

I would also like to thank the St. Lawrence County Historical Association and Susan Smeby for allowing me access to their Star Lake photograph collections. The St. Lawrence County Historical Society has an incredible research facility, and the staff is second to none.

Last but not least, I thank my family: my wife, Kristin, who has been extremely supportive and understanding during the months I was immersed in the research for this book; and my parents, Robert and Irene Bauerschmidt, who at an early age instilled in me an appreciation for history for which I am truly grateful.

INTRODUCTION

In 1791, Alexander Macomb, who had gotten rich as a merchant in the American Revolution, purchased over three million acres of land from the state of New York. This tract of land included much of northern New York, including St. Lawrence County. Macomb's endeavor as a land speculator was a failure, as his sales of land failed to keep pace with the due dates for payments to the state. He was taken to debtor's prison in 1792 over a $300,000 debt and never regained his fortunes.

Eventually, the land was resold to a group of land speculators represented by Judge John Fine of Ogdensburg. Elias Teall was contracted by the speculators to establish the first settlement in 1823. The speculators reasoned that if Teall was successful, other settlers would be encouraged to move to the area and that, in turn, would make the land more valuable. Teall built a mill near the mouth of Little River but stayed for just three short years. In 1828, James Haile attempted to settle the area with one or two other families. He also established a small sawmill on the Oswegatchie River, but he left the area in 1833, after the other settlers abandoned him. Finally in February 1834, Amasa Brown contracted with Haile's land speculators to try his hand in settling the area. Within a few months, Brown built a permanent house and moved his family into it. He operated a successful sawmill on the Oswegatchie River, and by 1843, there were 43 people of voting age living in the newly formed town of Fine.

At this time, Star Lake was still an unsettled area located between the townships of Fine and Clifton. It was originally named Big Lake to distinguish it from nearby Twin Lakes and then was called Pointed Lake because of its distinctive looking bays and peninsulas. In 1878, it was renamed Star Lake.

The first person to settle the Star Lake area was Joseph Backus in 1858. He built the first permanent residence on what is now Youngs Road, near Kinney Hill. Other early Star Lake families include the Walkers, Griffins, Dellapents, Foleys, Colbys, Forneys, Kilbournes, Bensons, and Marshalls.

In 1882, the primary occupations in Star Lake were farming and working in the lumber industry. Ezra Colton built the first hotel overlooking Star Lake in 1882. The hotel was later sold to Foley and Lyman and renamed the Star Lake Hotel. At this time, the stagecoach was the only form of transportation available to tourists and businesspeople. The dirt roads made travel difficult, time-consuming, and very uncomfortable. It was not until 1888, when the Carthage and Adirondack Railway opened a depot in Oswegatchie, that the hotel industry in Star Lake began to flourish. Wealthy tourists and cottage owners from the cities could now board a train and arrive at an Adirondack destination within hours instead of days. The railways heavily promoted the Adirondack experience with printed hotel advertising booklets and pamphlets. Within a few short years, Star Lake became known as a popular summer resort area in the western Adirondacks.

Most of the images used in this book depict the heyday of Star Lake, during the time period of 1890 to 1940. Although most of the hotels, stores, and other commercial buildings are gone, many of the original cottages along the 12 miles of shoreline remain. People still return to Star Lake every summer for the same reasons that they did 100 years ago. It is a great place to relax in the fresh air, crystal clear water, and beautiful scenery.

To give readers an idea of what it was like to stay at the Star Lake Inn around the turn of the century, here is a letter dated July 23, 1912.

Dear Hedwig,

Was glad indeed to hear from you. I have not written a single lengthy letter since I've been here, but this will be a bit longer as you know enough about the place to be sufficiently interested.

In the first place, one dresses four times a day here—and all one's spare change goes to tips. We tip the waiter a dollar between us every three days—give five cents to the bellhop everytime one of them brings hot or cold water and also the chambermaids. The head waitress too rings in. All the waitresses here are school teachers and the proprietors, head clerks, etc are high school principals. Our waiter happens to be a foreigner.

There are 150 guests registered here. Everyone is sociable and two or three times a week we have special doings. For instance, last Thursday night we had a beef steak party out in the woods. A chef broiled the meat in an open oven and the guests ate it with their fingers. We had a corn roast too, and Congress and Blue Label flowed merrily. Later we danced. There is dancing every night. Saturday night we had a sweater party—a lot of Vaudeville stunts in the ballroom and later a spread. This was held in honor of seven New York boys who were going to leave the next day.

I have a steady friend Mr. Isaacs, who has taken me to everything. We at the Inn, never join in the village affairs, as we have all kinds of recreation here. We even get our mail here. It is a sort of substation and it's always an exciting time, especially at night. Mr. Isaacs and I are going on the Maple Mountain trail some morning before we leave. Tomorrow we are going to Cranberry Lake, at last, at last.

I saw Frank Adler this morning. I suppose you know his girl Lucia Hull went back on him. He is stopping at the Sunnyside Inn. Yes, I've been to Young's farm twice. It is 2 ¼ miles from the village—in fact I went this afternoon. The weather is always cool. It poured all day yesterday.

How are you? Now that the cool weather has set in, you'll be much better as the hot weather is enough to drive anyone to drink. I can't write anymore. Everyone is chatting in the lobby and my friend and I am going strolling. It isn't serious—just a passing summer fancy. Will call you immediately upon my return.

Much love,
Elaine

One

The Village

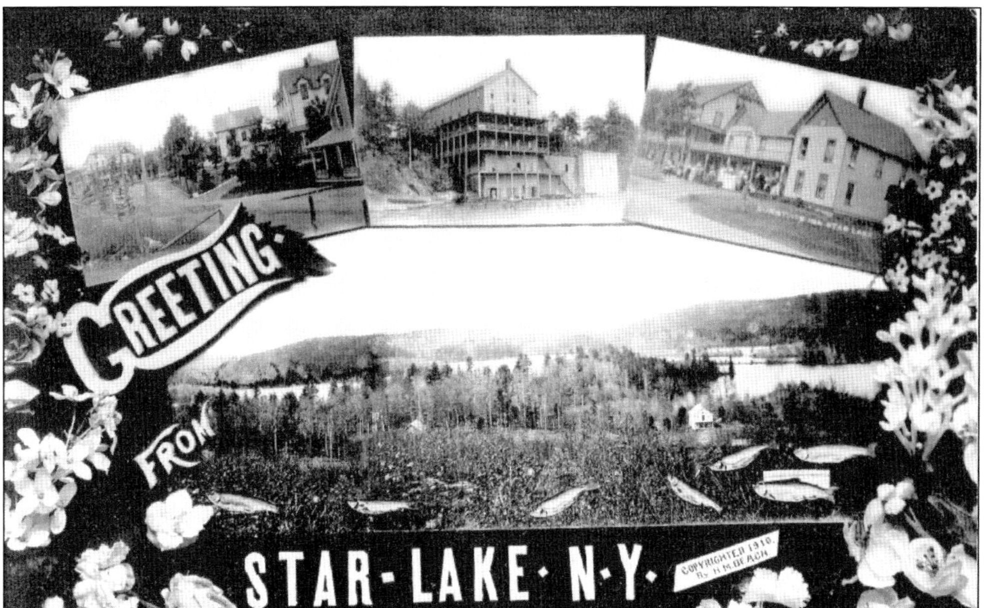

This multi-view photo postcard of Star Lake was produced around 1910 by the prolific postcard maker H. M. Beach of Remsen, New York.

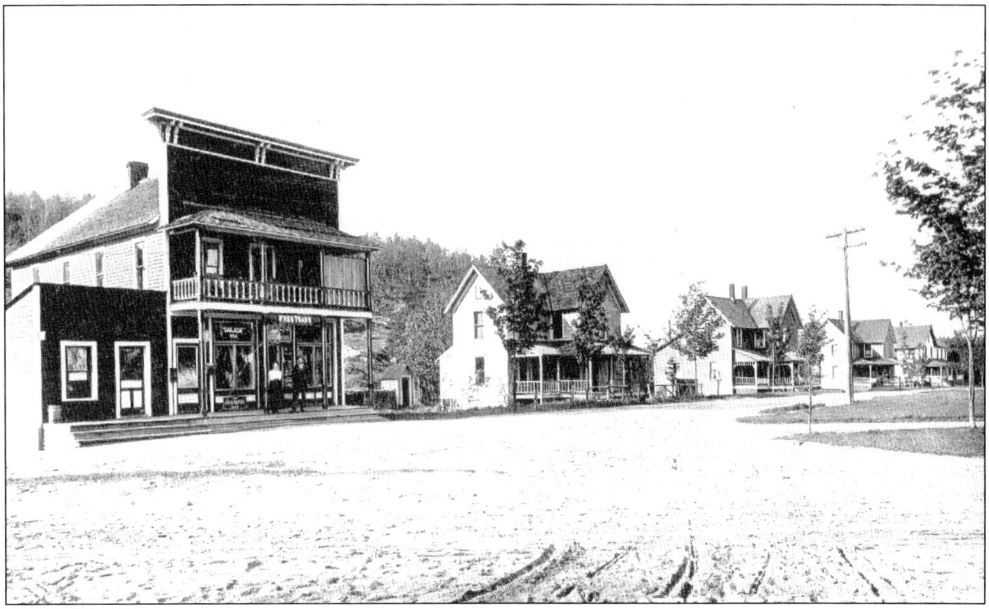

Fred and Anna Tears stand outside their newly acquired store around 1910. The Tears family purchased the store from Harry Slack in 1909. Harry Slack remained postmaster from 1907 to 1915, and Tears Store continued to be the official site of the Star Lake Post Office. Fred Tears was postmaster in Star Lake from 1930 to 1934.

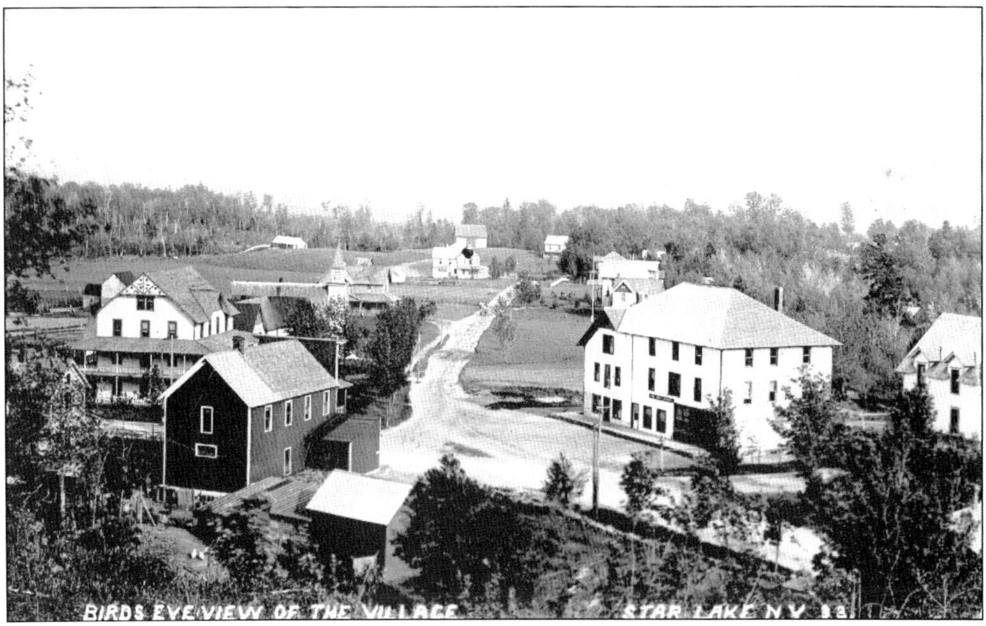

This bird's-eye view of the village was taken from the top of Bald Mountain looking south toward Youngs Road around 1910. The large Kinney barn can be seen on the hill. In the back of Tears Store, chickens can also be seen.

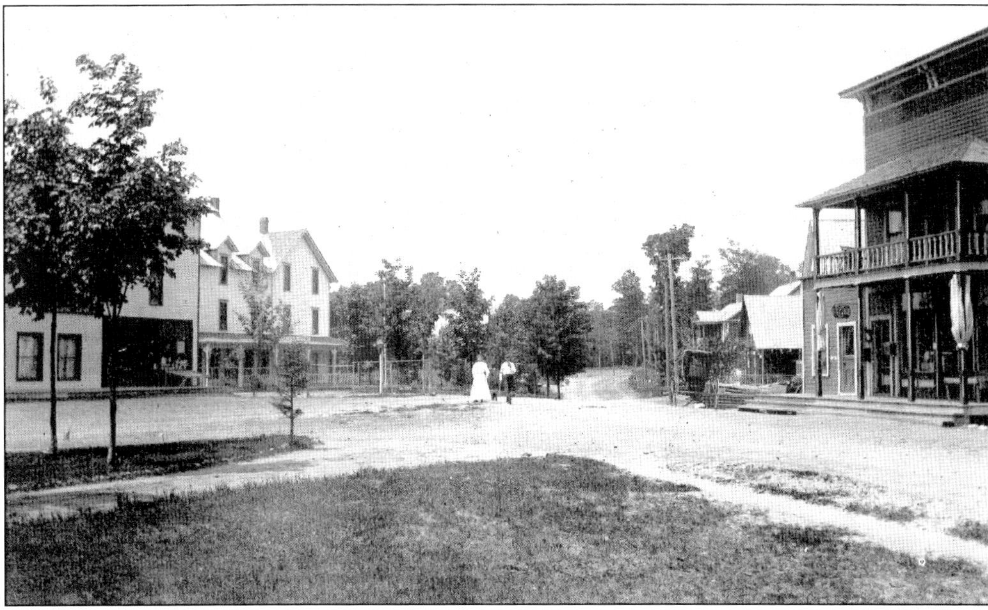

This view of Main Street was taken looking west around 1908. Slack's Store, which later became Tears Store, can be seen to the right with an oval post office sign hanging from the front porch. Harry Slack was the postmaster of Star Lake during this time period.

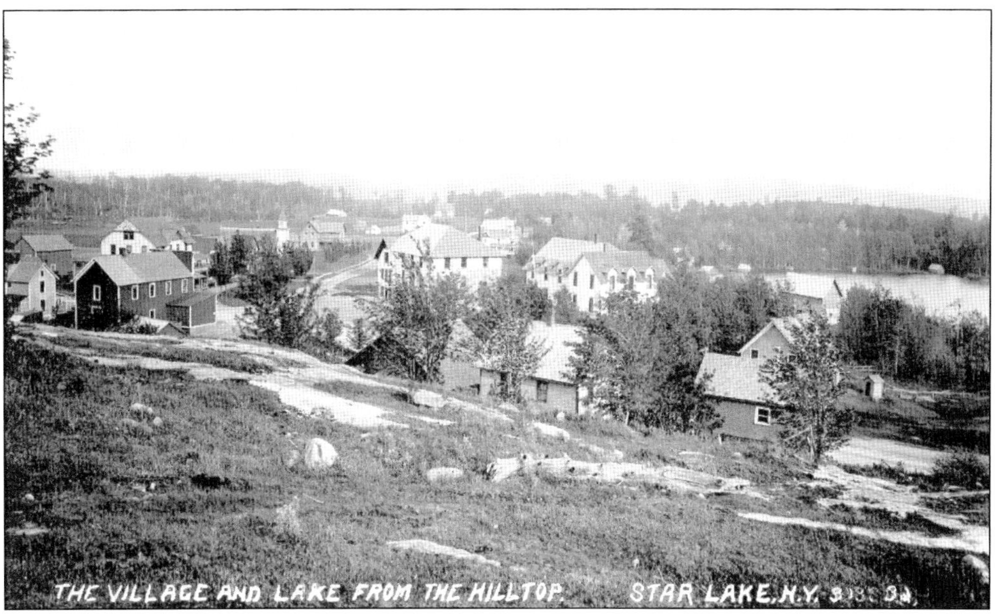

The village of Star Lake is seen from Bald Mountain around 1910. Bald Mountain and surrounding forest areas near the village were barren or covered with dead tree stumps from the previous forest fires.

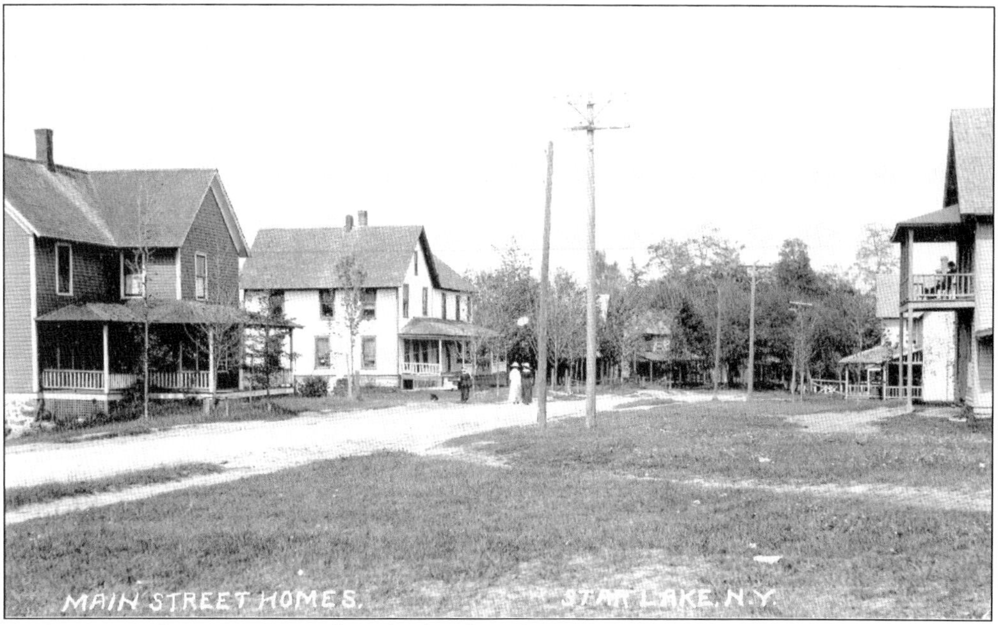

Looking east, these two views show both sides of Main Street. Just a few of the Victorian-era homes are still in existence. This dirt road was the main route of travel to get to and from Benson Mines.

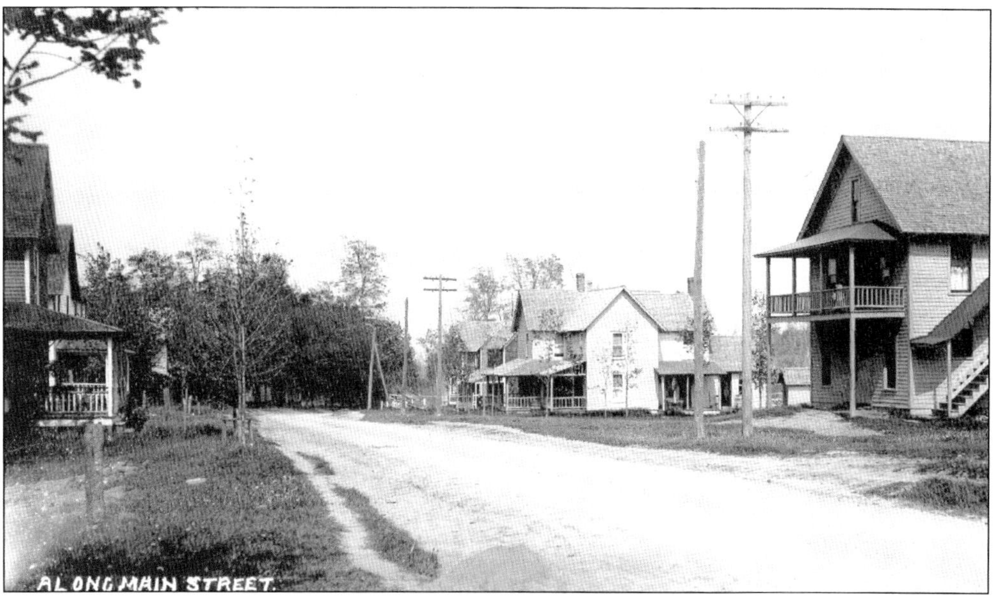

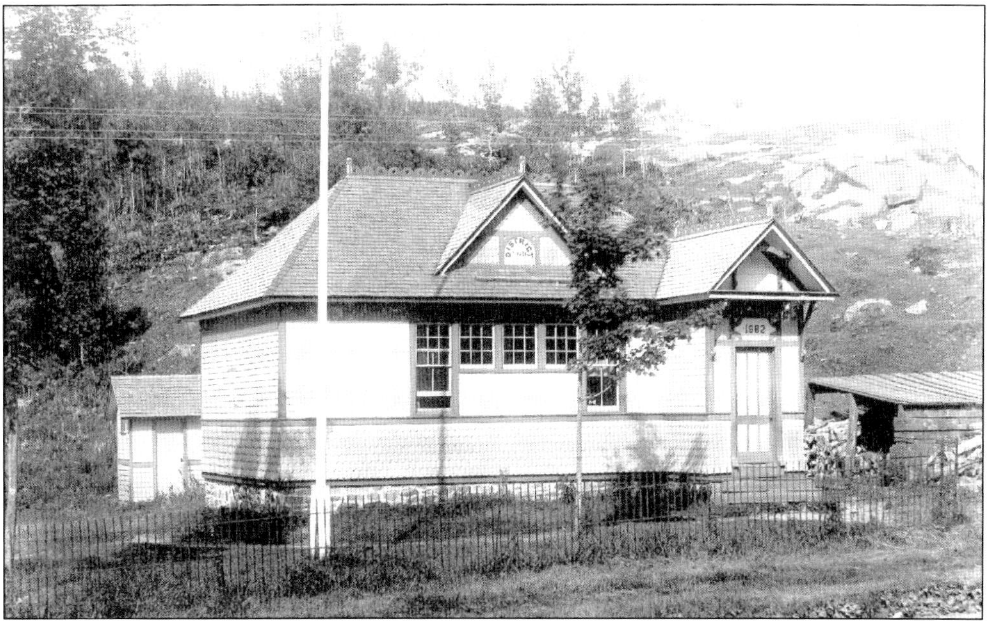

These two views show the Star Lake District No. 9 schoolhouse prior to the addition being built and after. The woodshed was located to the right of the entrance, and the outhouse was located near the back of the building. The school was constructed in 1882, and the addition, which doubled the building's size, was completed in 1892. The dates of completion were displayed over the entrance doors. A small library was also added during the 1892 construction. General Marshall was a teacher at this schoolhouse for many years.

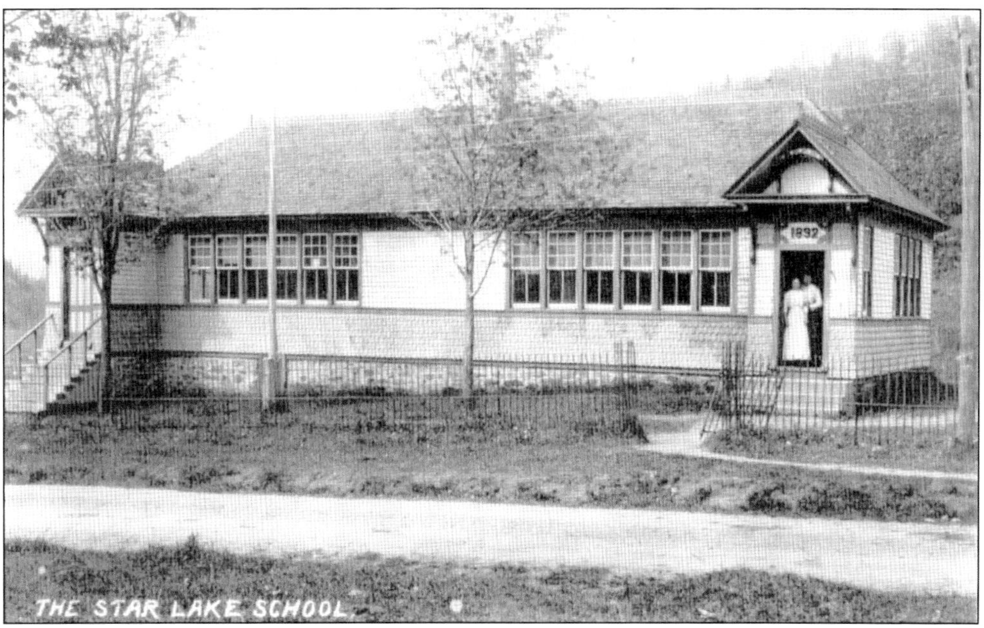

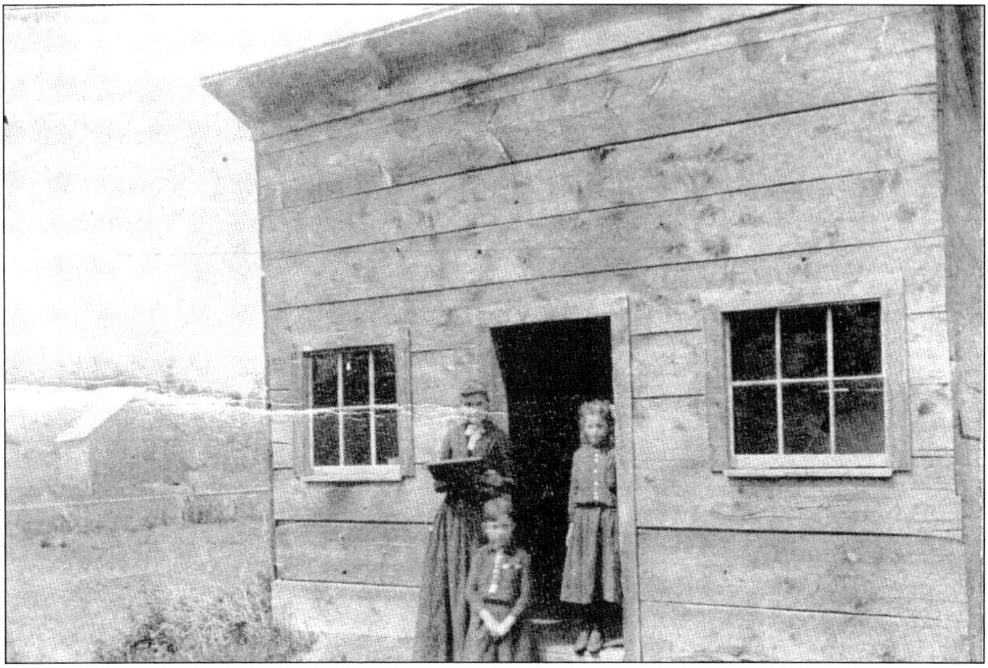

The very first schoolhouse, built in Star Lake around 1878, looked more like a shed than a school. The primitive one-room building had a wood-burning stove in the center of the room and benches along the side walls for students to sit on.

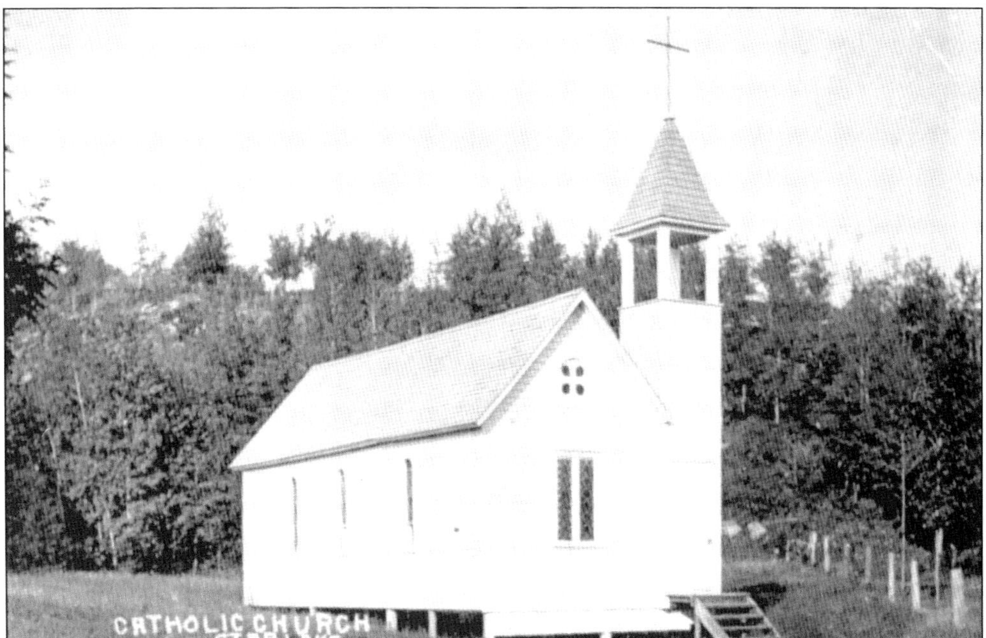

The first Catholic church in Star Lake is pictured around 1907. This church was located where the current firehouse now stands. The building was later bought by Bernard Redmond of Evans Mills and moved across the road near Potter's Grocery Store. The building, less the steeple, was then remodeled and used as an ice-cream parlor for many years.

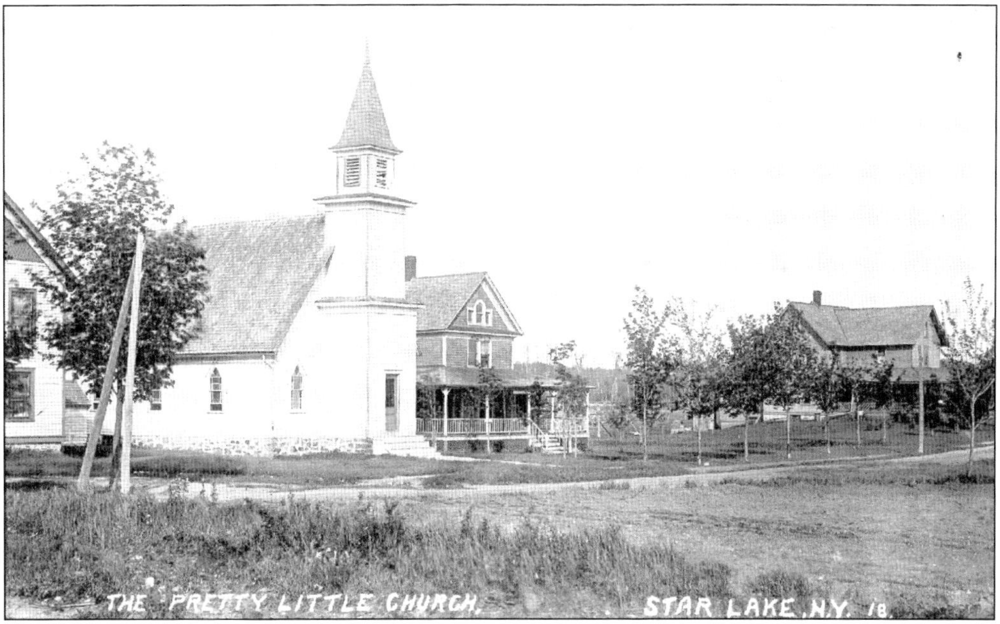

The original Star Lake Presbyterian Church was built in 1893 and later burned in 1938. This replacement building was built in 1943 and still can be seen on Youngs Road. It was later converted to an A-frame structure.

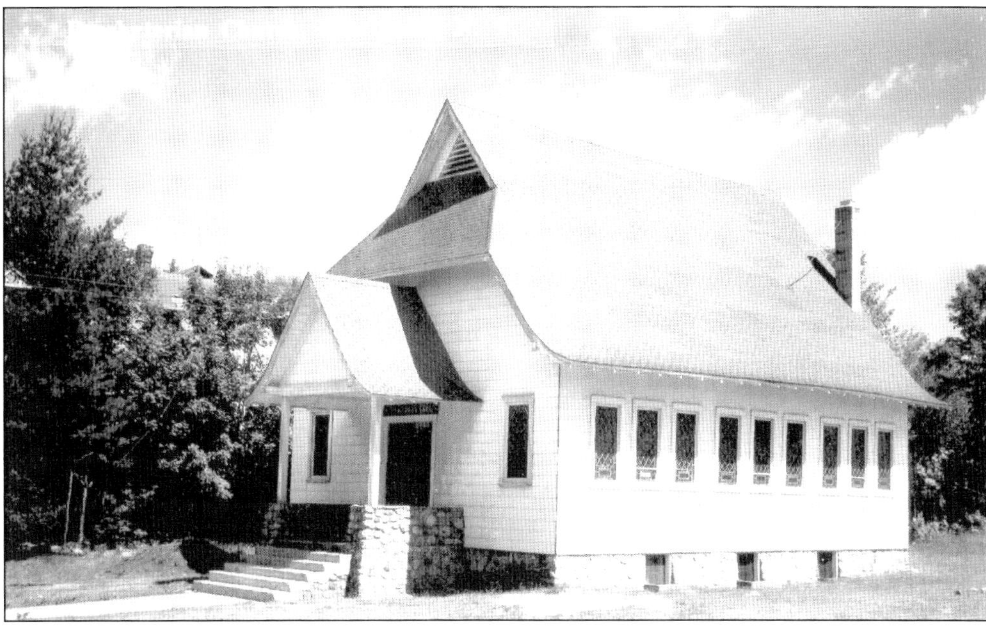

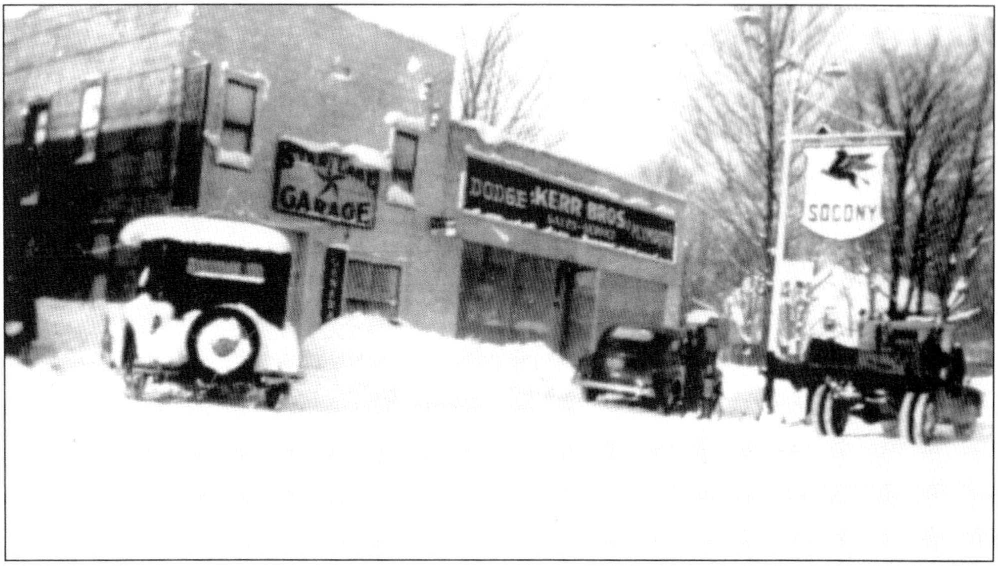

In 1931, Ralph and John Hartwell Kerr owned and operated the Kerr Bros Plymouth and Dodge automobile dealership, in addition to the Star Lake Garage. In the 1940s, they also sold Jeep vehicles and appliances. This was the first store in Star Lake to sell television sets.

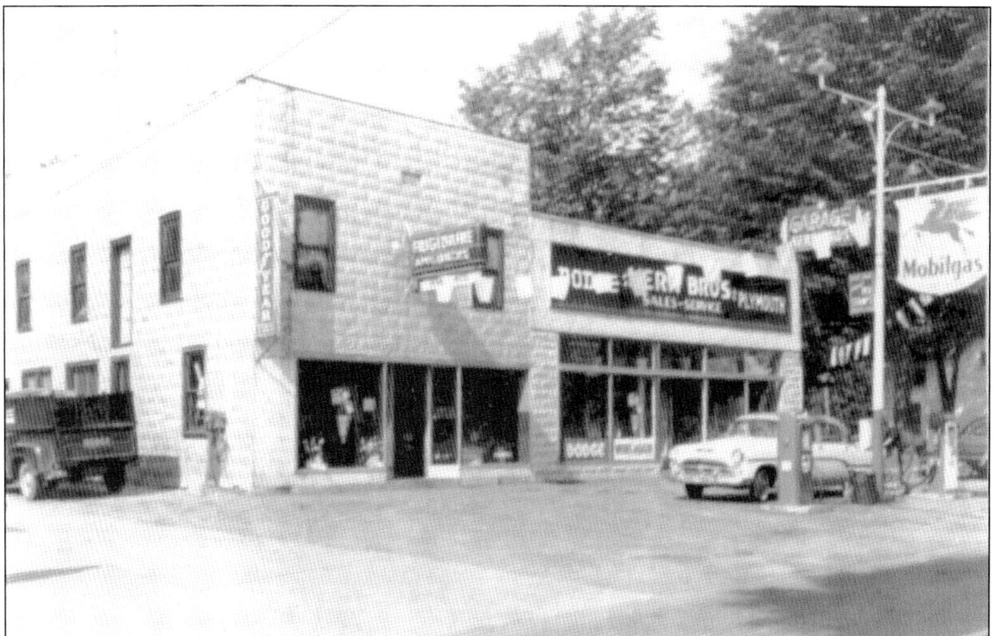

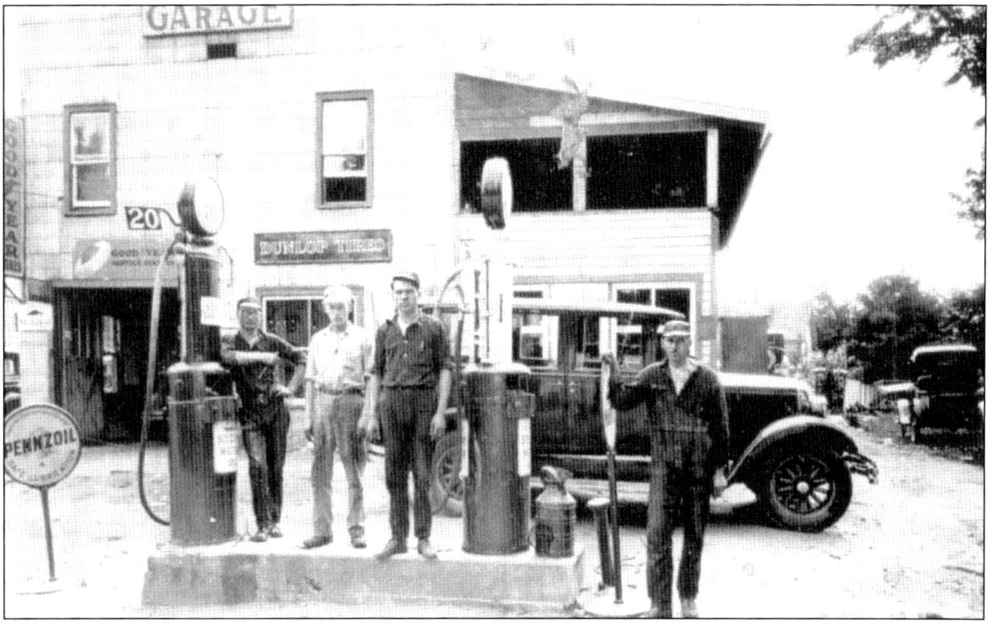

This view of Kerr's Star Lake Garage dates from the 1920s. The station sold Socony gasoline, Goodyear tires, and a variety of oil and lubricants. The town's fire truck was stored in the garage at this time, and the fire siren was located on top of the garage.

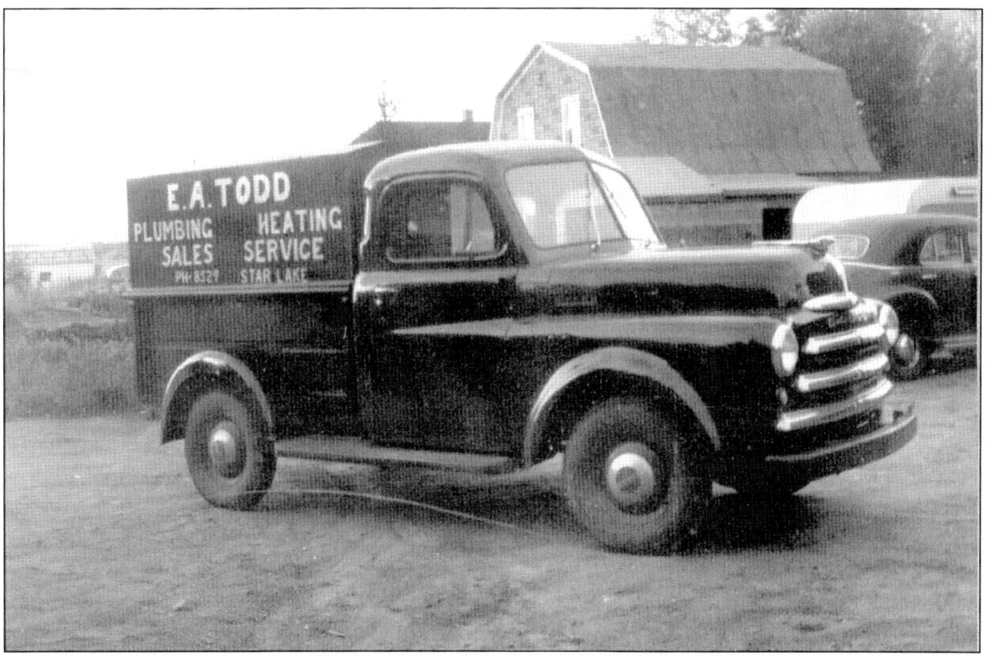

Ernie Todd established the E. A. Todd Plumbing & Heating Company upon returning from the war in 1947. Todd serviced the Star Lake Inn and many of the camps and cottages around Star Lake. He later opened Todd's True Value hardware store, which is still located on Main Street.

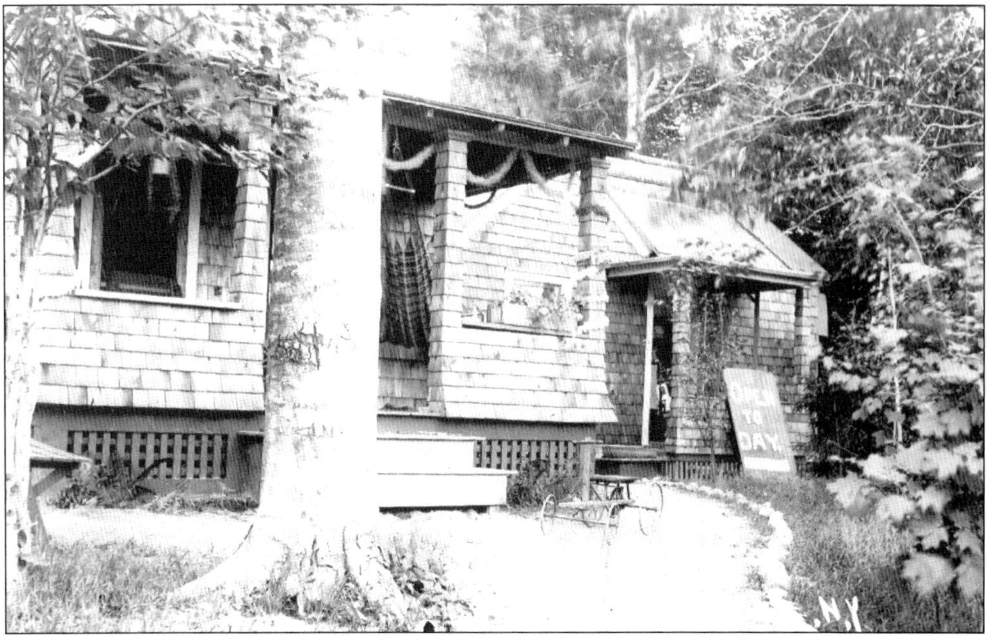

This view of C. E. Runions's photograph studio dates from around 1910. The studio was located on Main Street and specialized in portraits, as well as the manufacturing of photo postcards. The Runions family had many small photograph studios throughout the western Adirondack region. The Star Lake studio was only in business a few years.

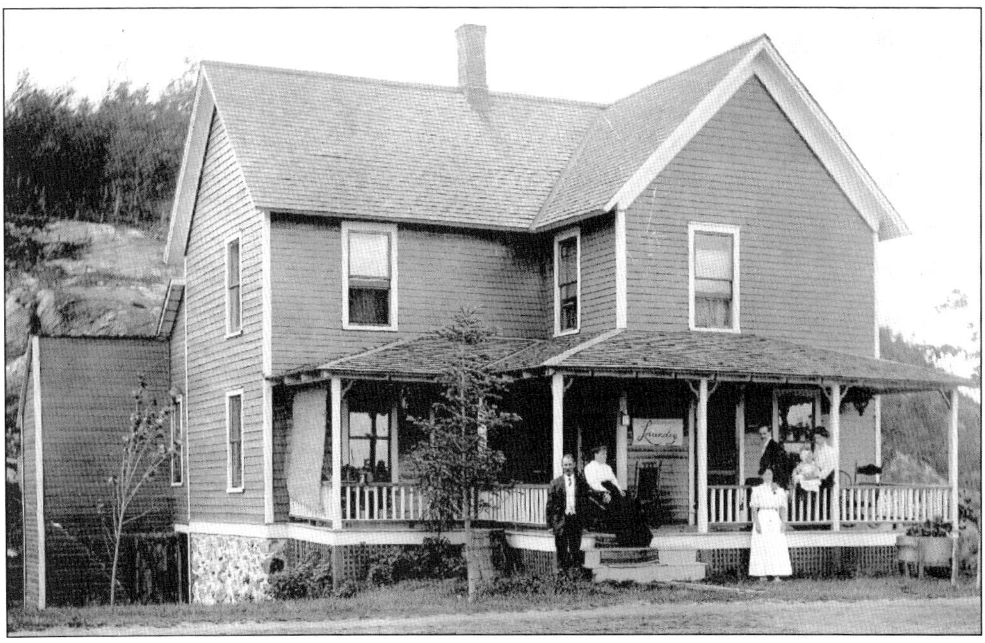

Typical of the entrepreneurial spirit of the town, some of the locals would advertise for laundry services. Members of this family ran their laundry business right out of their Main Street home, catering to the many hotels, sportsmen, and business travelers.

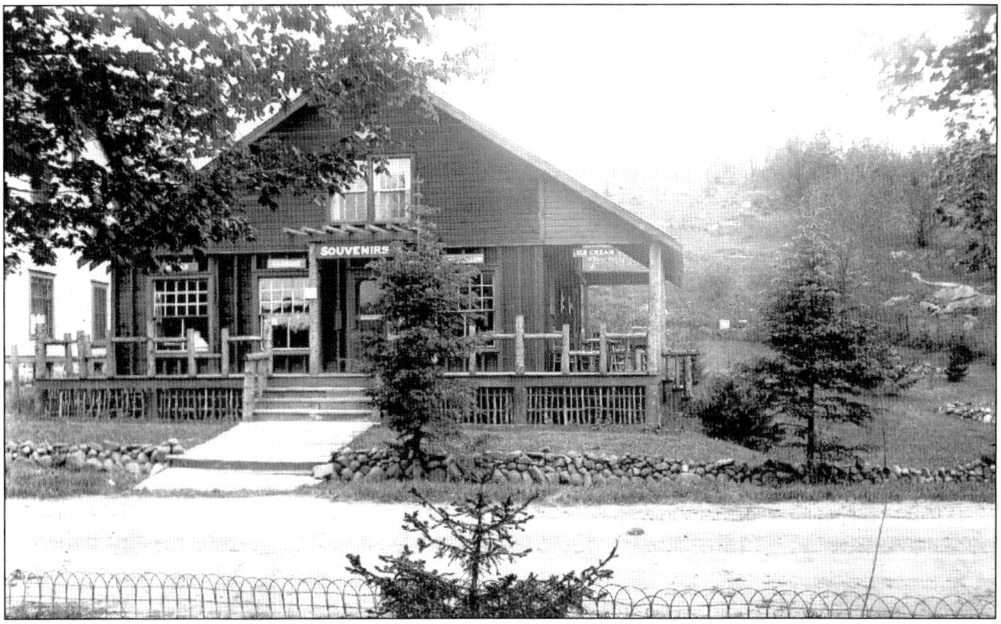

The Swastika souvenir store is pictured around 1910. The swastika logo on the front of the building is actually Native American and stands for "whirling logs." Owned by Claude Reimer and later by Gerald Marshall, the business sold ice cream, postcards, souvenirs, and candies. The building is now a private residence on Main Street.

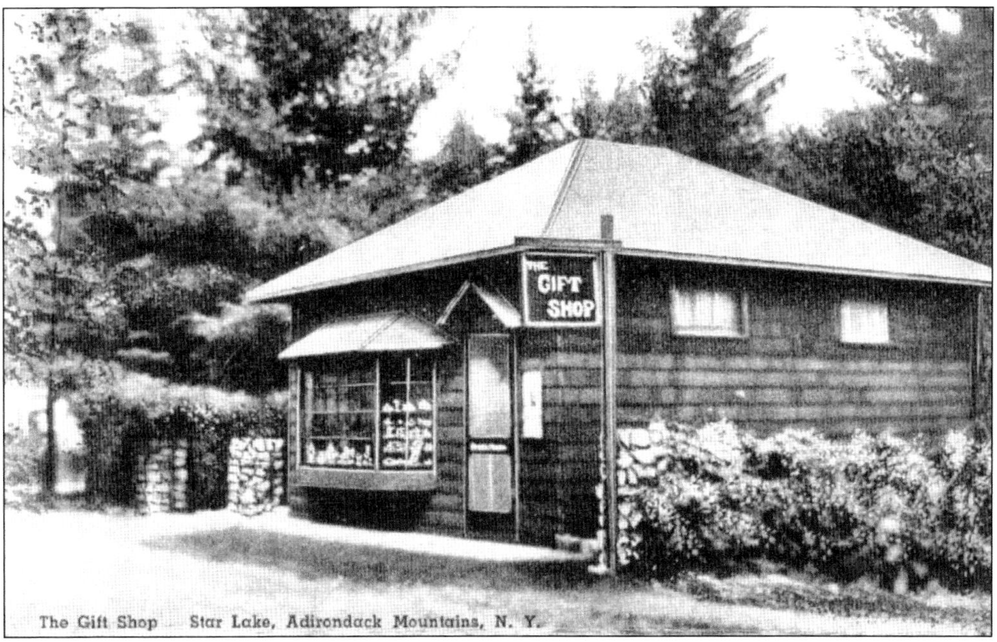

The Gift Shop was built in the 1920s by Claude Reimer. He sold souvenirs, cameras, and film in the small shop, which still can be seen along Main Street today. Kodak film was 20¢ per pack, prints were 5¢ each, and postcards cost 6¢ each. The Gift Shop was later sold to retired school teacher Gerald Marshall, who was also the local podiatrist at the time.

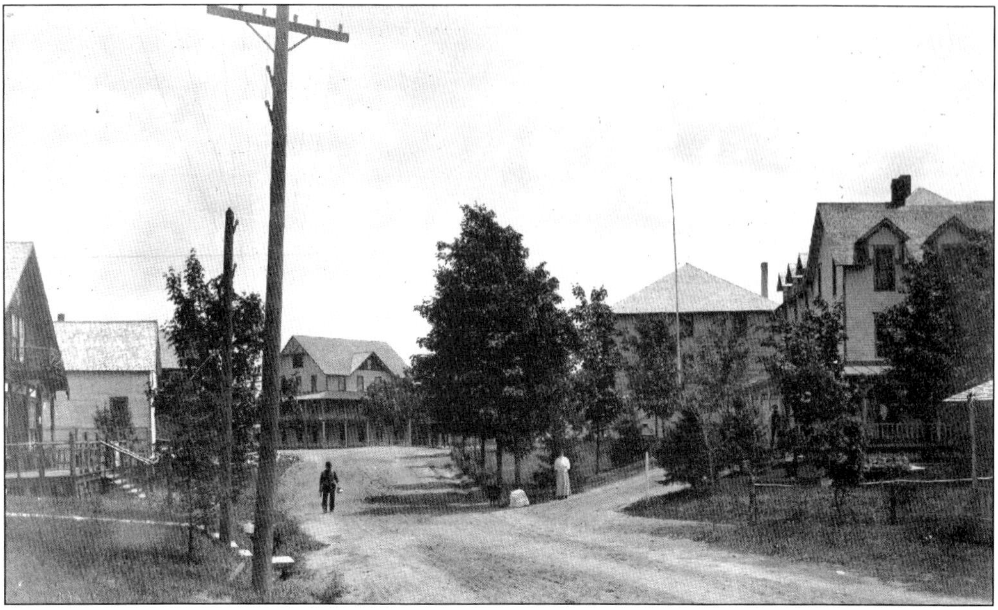

This c. 1910 view shows the three large hotels located in the village of Star Lake. From left to right are Sunnyside Inn, New Central Hotel, and the Lake View House.

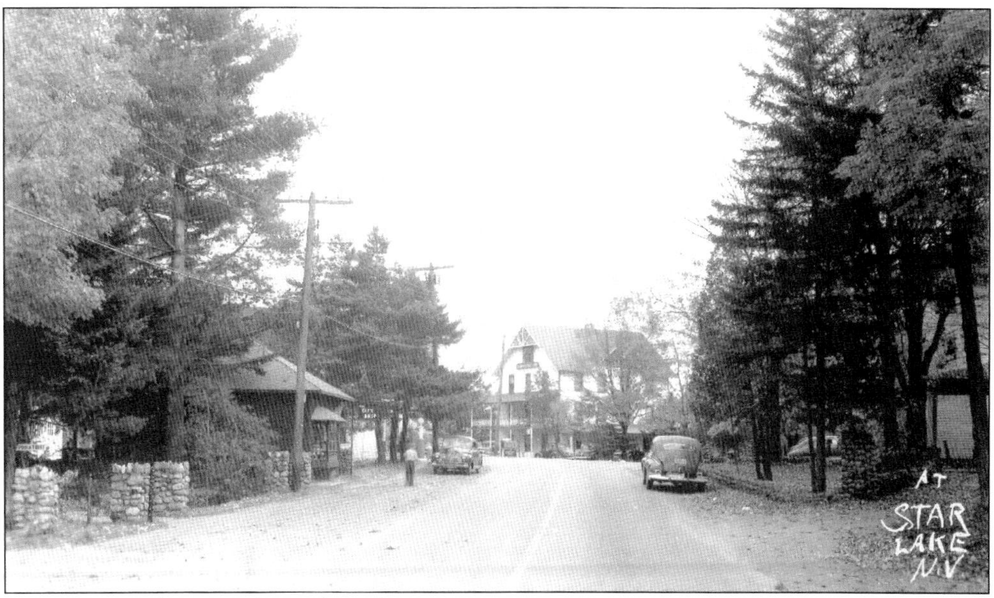

Looking east, this view shows the village of Star Lake around 1930. Gerald Marshall's Gift Shop and the Sunnyside Inn can be seen. At this time, Marshall was using the main building behind the shop as an office for his podiatry business. The podiatrist sign can be seen in the lower left.

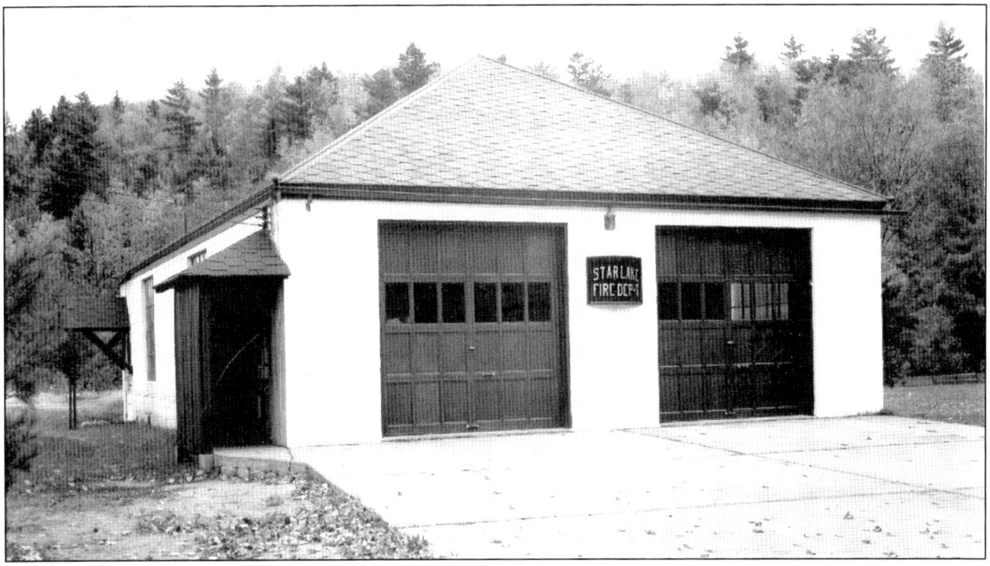

Pictured around 1940 is the very first fire department building in Star Lake. Andy Garbreana was elected as the first fire chief of Star Lake. John M. Sayles, owner of the Star lake Inn, donated the building lot, which was adjacent to the schoolhouse lot.

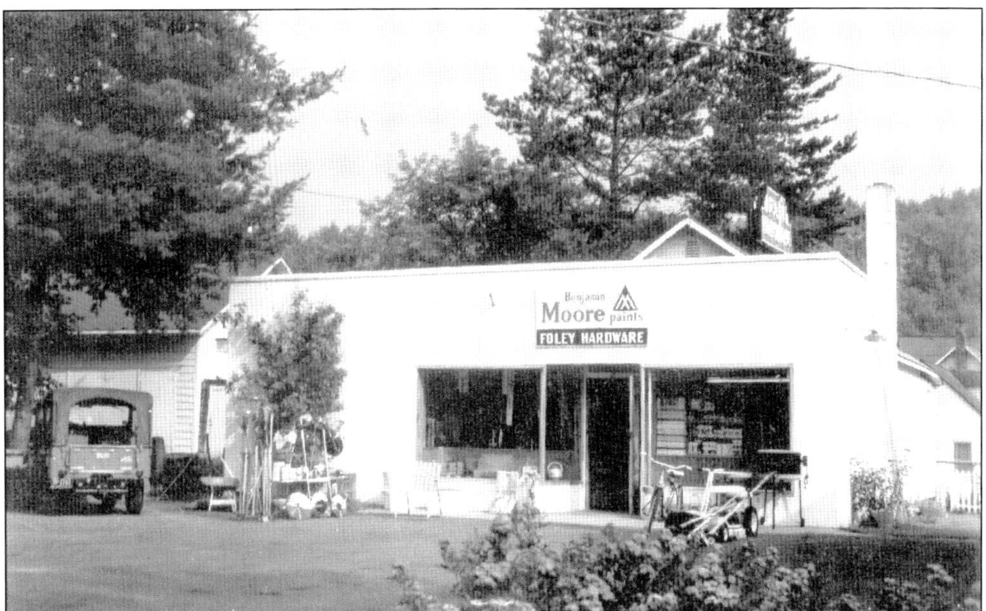

Daniel Foley Jr. opened up the Foley Hardware Store in 1949 in back of Hawley's funeral home. In addition to hardware, the store sold fishing tackle, guns, sporting goods, and plumbing and electrical supplies.

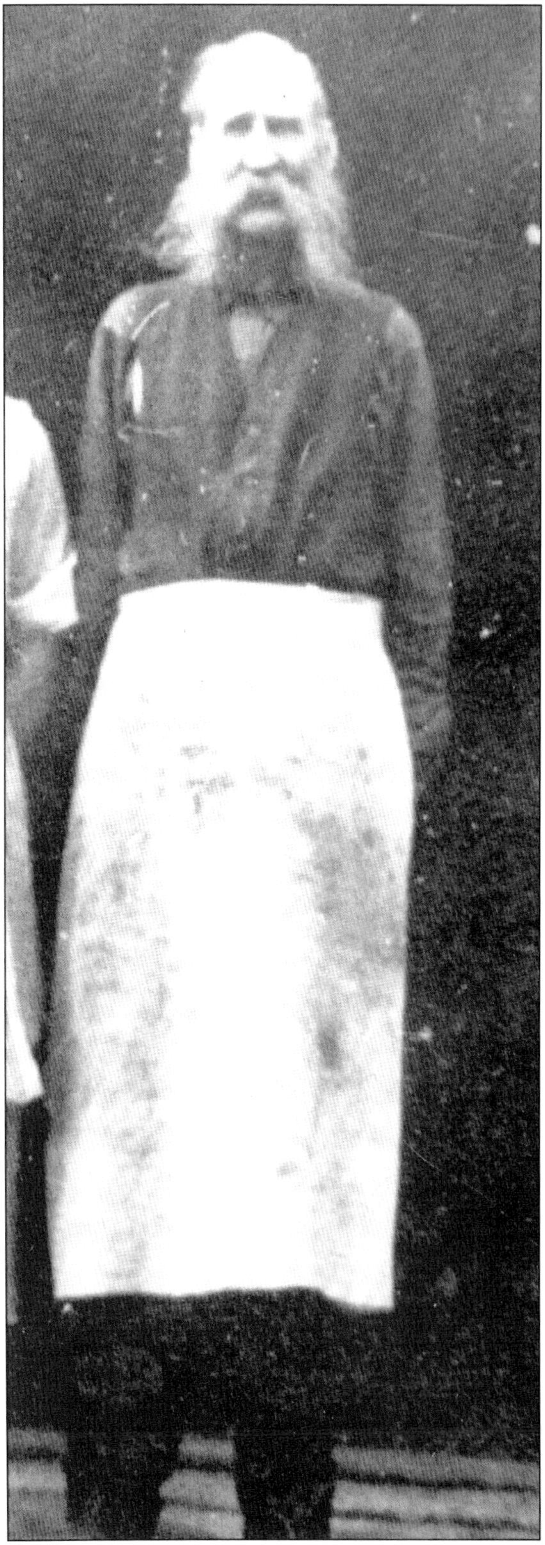

Local businessman Fred B. Potter owned Potter's Grocery and Meat Market, which was located across from the golf course on what is now named Potter Avenue. He was easily recognizable with his long white side whiskers. Born in 1857, Potter grew up as a farm boy in Michigan. At the age of 20, he became a cowboy on the western plains. In a 1937 newspaper article, Potter reminisced about his early days as as western cowboy. In the late 1870s, he had contacts with Wild Bill Hickok, Calamity Jane, Buffalo Bill, Bat Masterson, and other western notables. He later settled in Star Lake with his only son, Charlie.

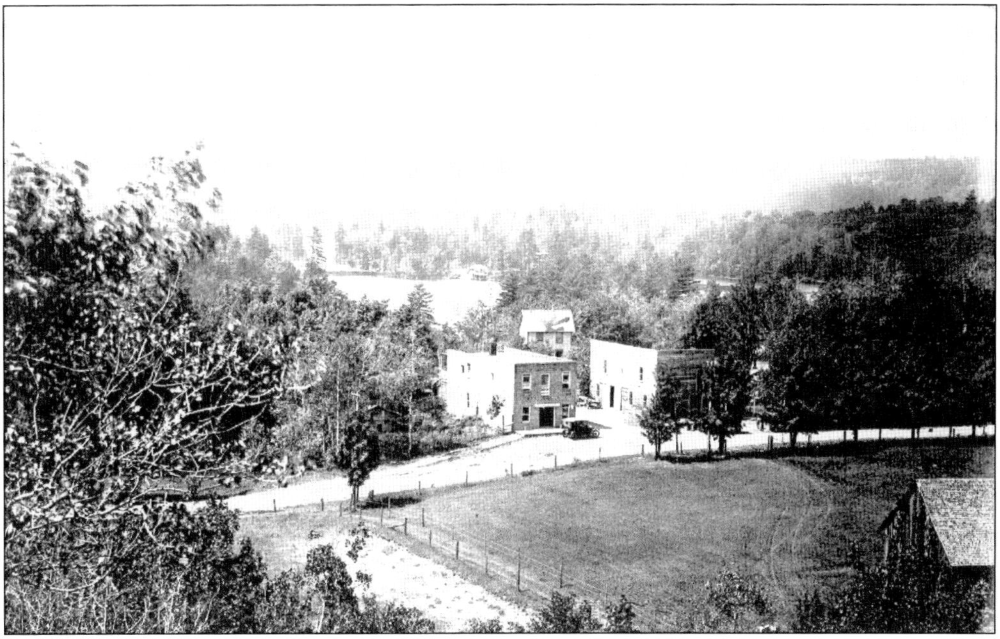

Potter's Grocery Store and Kerr's Garage can be seen in this view. Fred Potter would make an annual late fall trip to Rochester with a huge load of Christmas trees to sell. In turn, he would buy a fresh load of fruits and vegetables from the Rochester merchants and provide for local residents fresh produce through the long winter months.

This view looks down on the Potter Block from the nearby hilltop around 1910. Sam Spain's barn can be seen across the street.

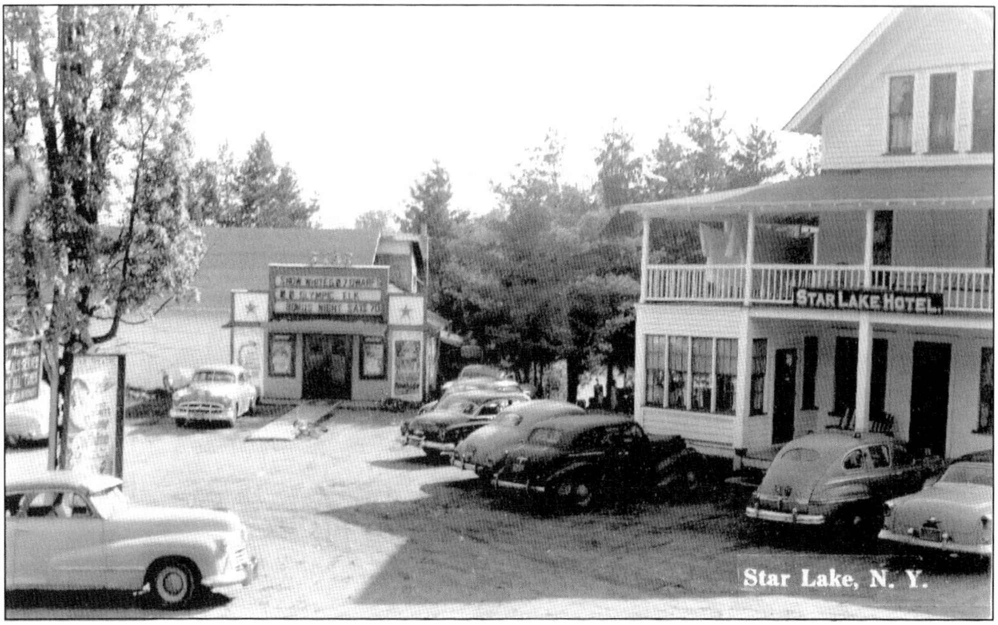

The Star Theatre opened for business in 1948. It was owned and operated by Bernard Lydamore. It was later converted to a roller-skating rink and then torn down.

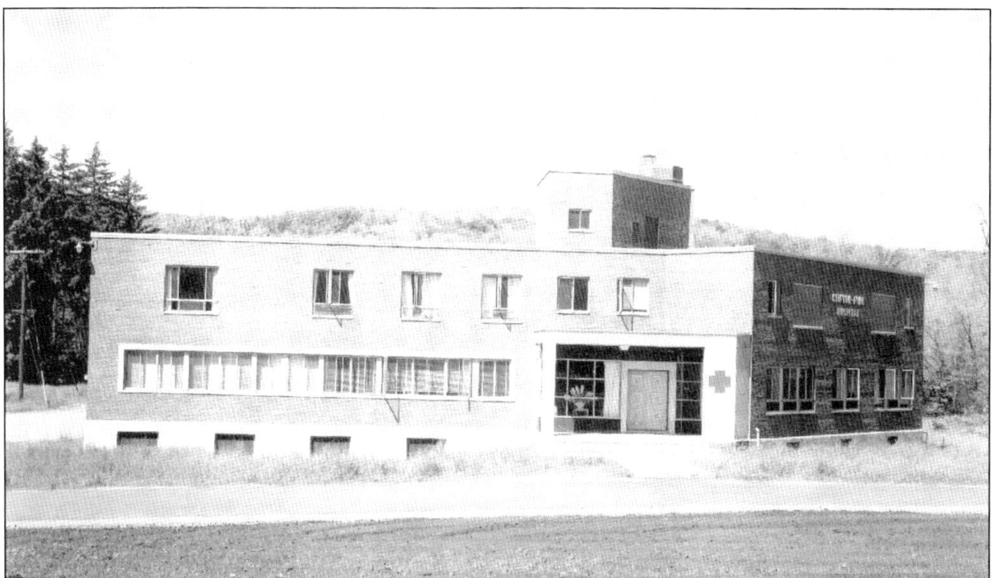
The 30-bed Clifton-Fine Hospital was completed in 1951 at a cost of $350,000. It was considered a major achievement at the time for a small rural community to have such a state-of-the-art medical facility.

Two

THE HOTELS

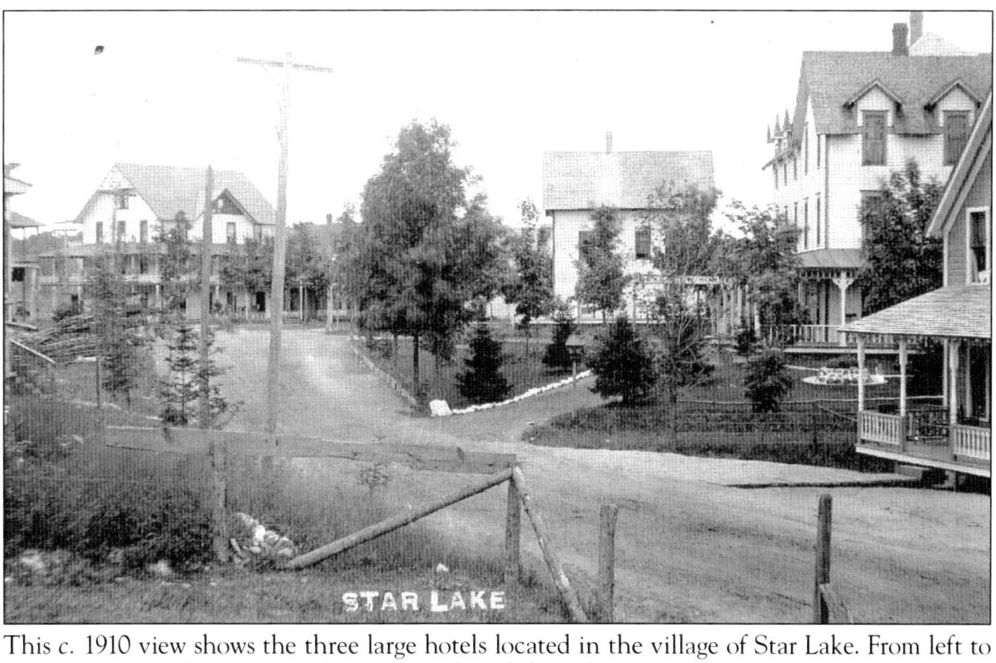

This *c.* 1910 view shows the three large hotels located in the village of Star Lake. From left to right are Sunnyside Inn, New Central Hotel, and the Lake View House.

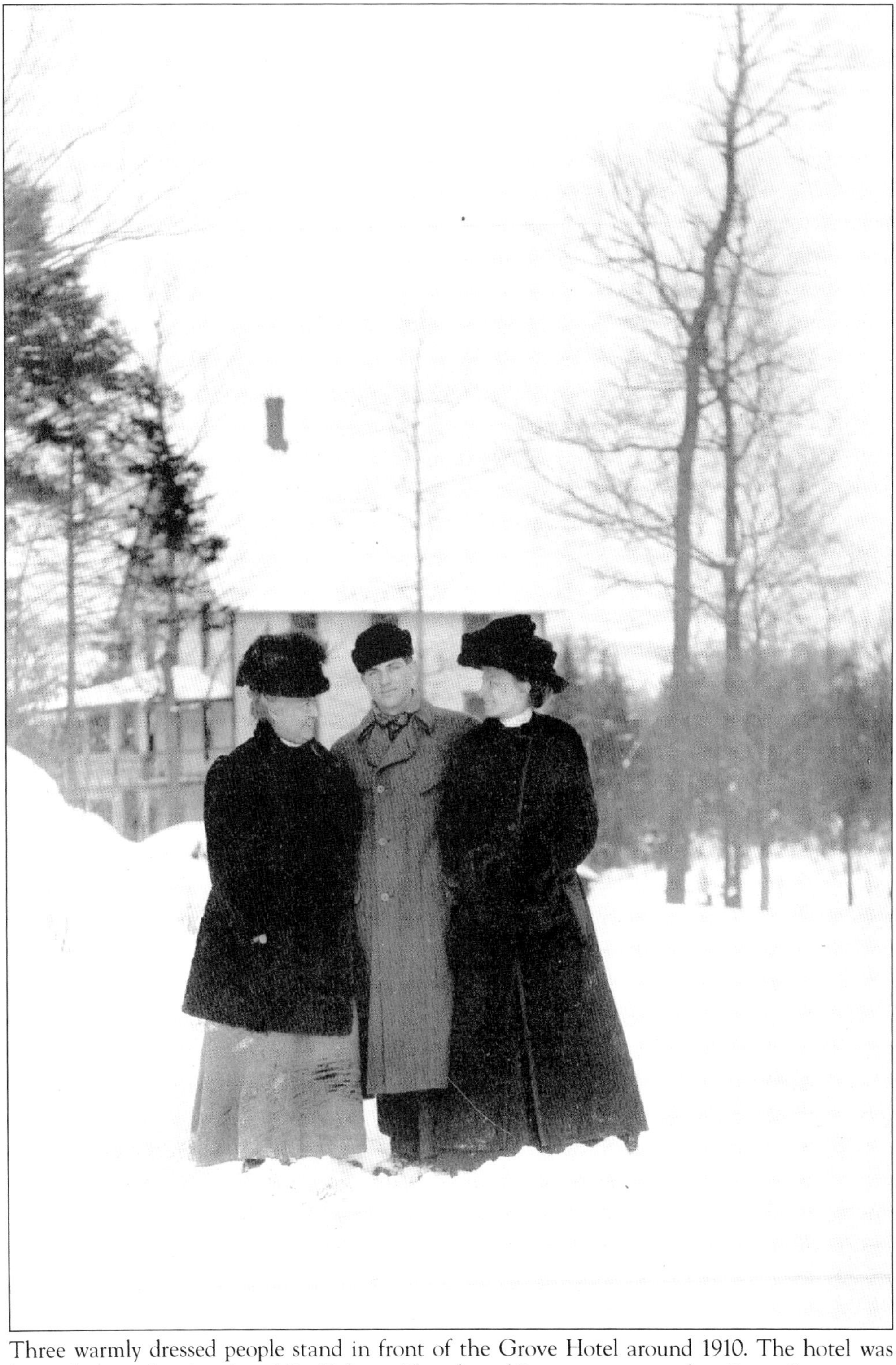

Three warmly dressed people stand in front of the Grove Hotel around 1910. The hotel was located where the abandoned St. Huberts Church and Rectory now stand on Route 3.

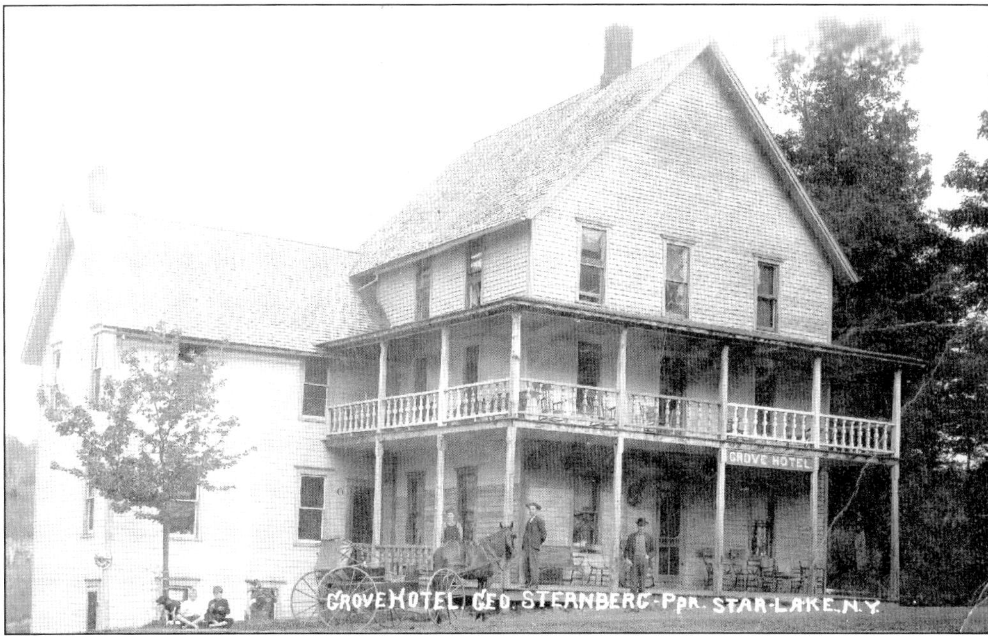

These two views of the Grove Hotel date from around 1910, when George Sternberg was the proprietor. The Grove Hotel was built by Michael Brainard, who was the brother of Anna Tears. The Grove was unique in that it was situated in both the towns of Clifton and Fine. When local authorities decided about whether or not alcoholic beverages would be allowed to be sold, if one town went dry and the other stayed wet, the bar was moved to the other side of the hotel.

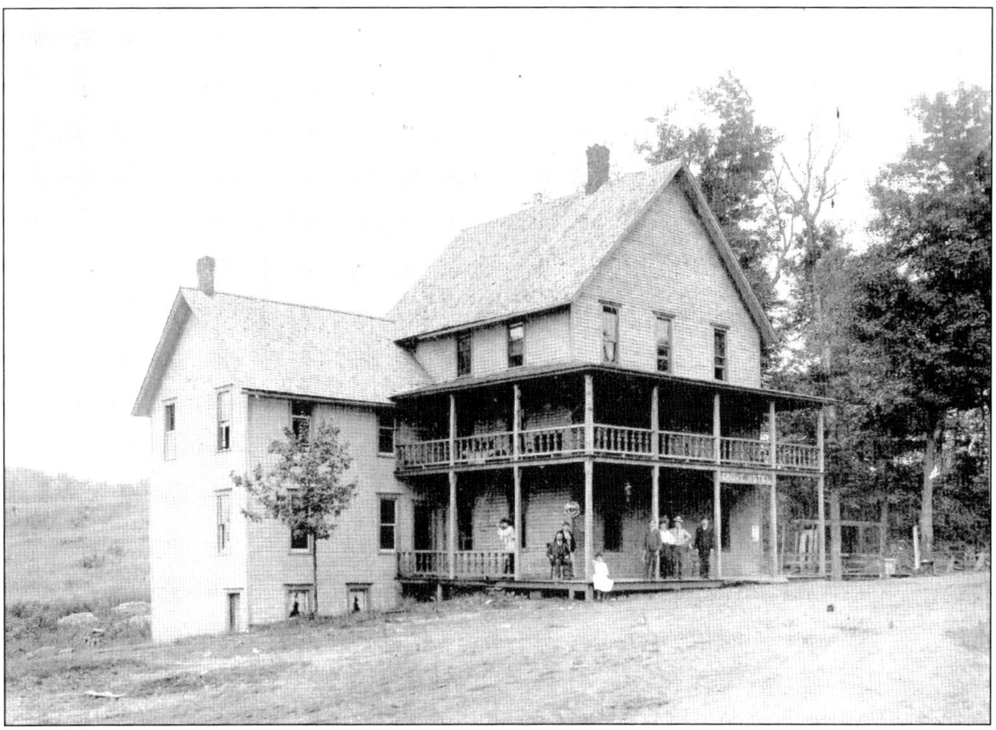

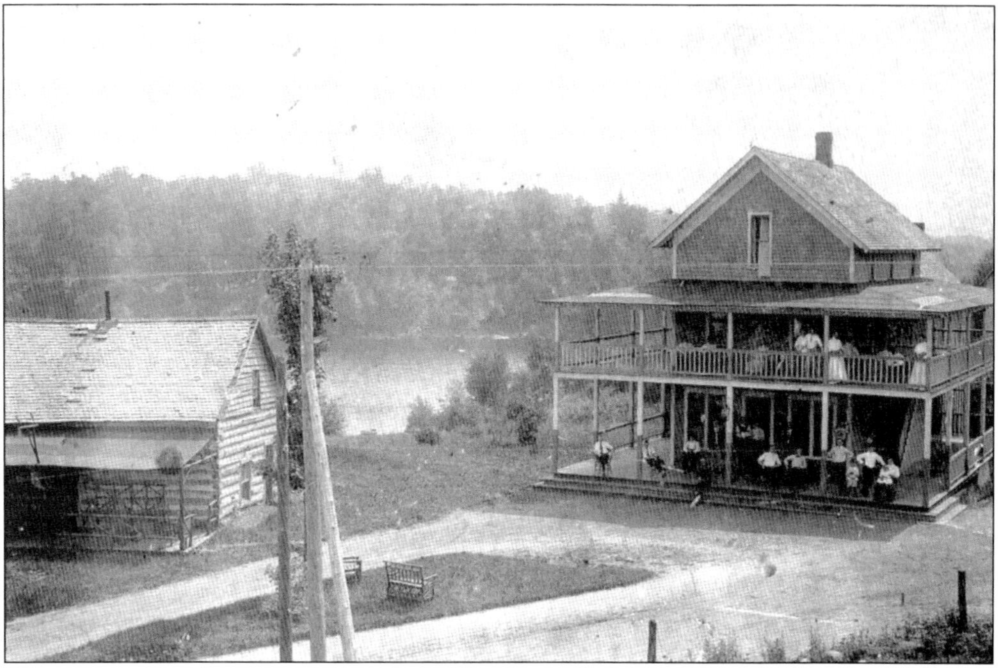

These two c. 1908 views show Foley's Star Lake Hotel and the log cabin annex. The second floor of the hotel was used as the summer dining room and was connected to the summer kitchen, located in the upstairs of the outbuilding. The top floor held the rented rooms of the hotel.

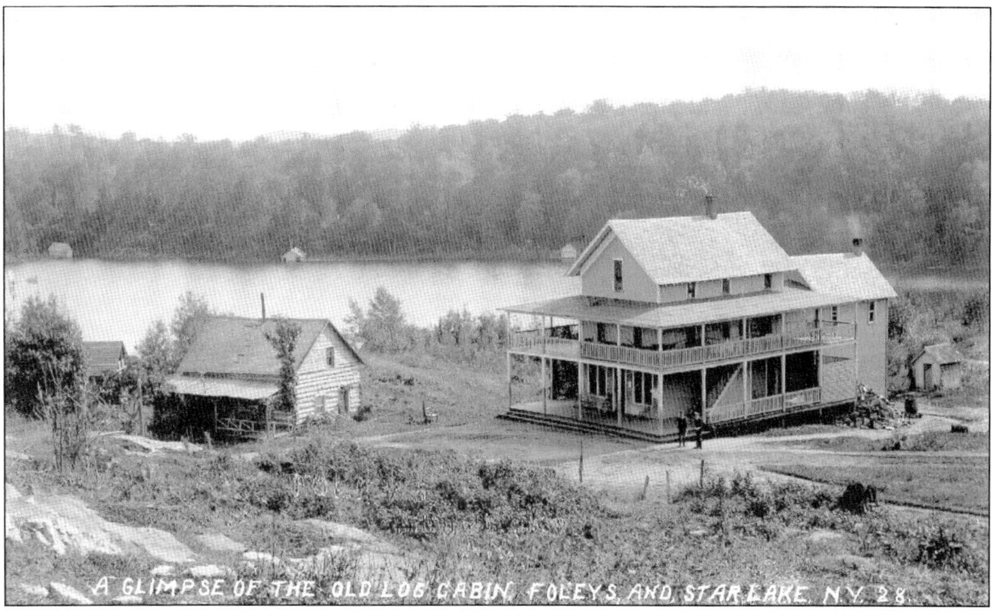

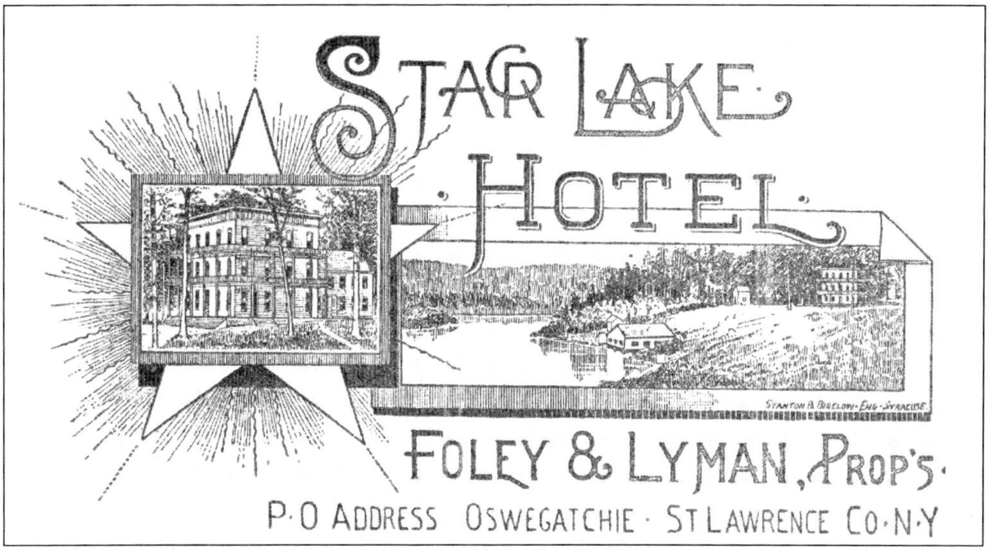

This is the original advertising card for Daniel Foley and Bart Lyman's Star Lake Hotel from around 1887. It advertised pure water and fresh air, boat livery, and teams or guides furnished when desired. Room and board were $2 to $3 per day and from $10.50 to $22.50 per week. This hotel burned to the ground on October 13, 1897. It was later rebuilt by Daniel Foley Sr. in 1901.

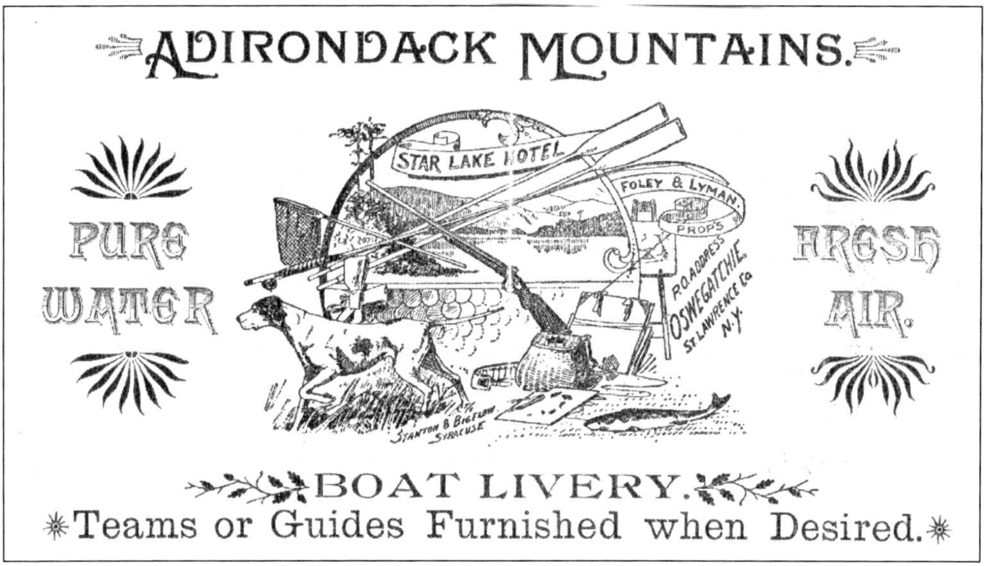

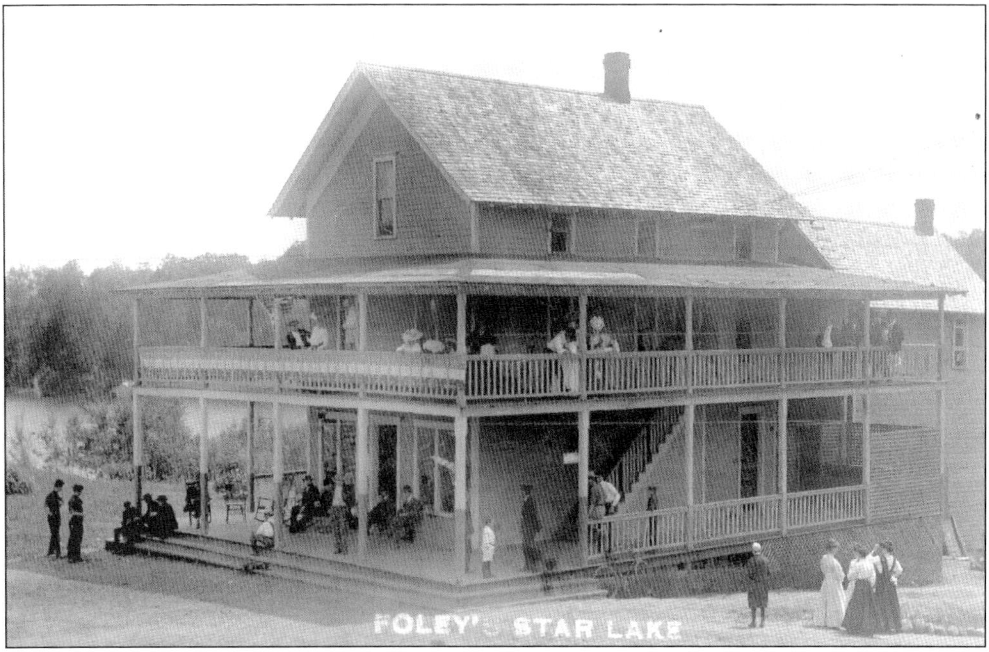

Groups gather to get ready for the annual Field Day celebrations at Foley's Star Lake Hotel around 1908. The hotel was a popular destination for the summer residents during that weekend. Residents and vacationers could choose any or all of the following events for an admission price of 25¢ per event: supper at 5:00 p.m., boxing at 7:00 p.m., band concert at 8:00 p.m., and the dance at 9:00 p.m.

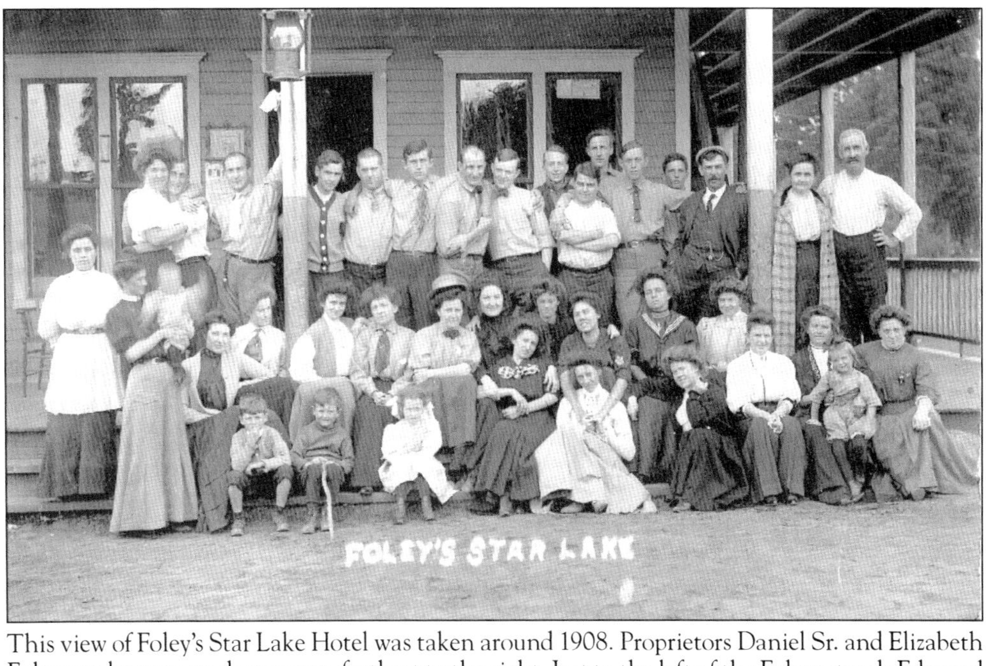

This view of Foley's Star Lake Hotel was taken around 1908. Proprietors Daniel Sr. and Elizabeth Foley can be seen on the top row, farthest to the right. Just to the left of the Foleys stands Edmund Pendleton, the third postmaster of Star Lake. Daniel Foley Sr. was the second postmaster and served from 1897 to 1899.

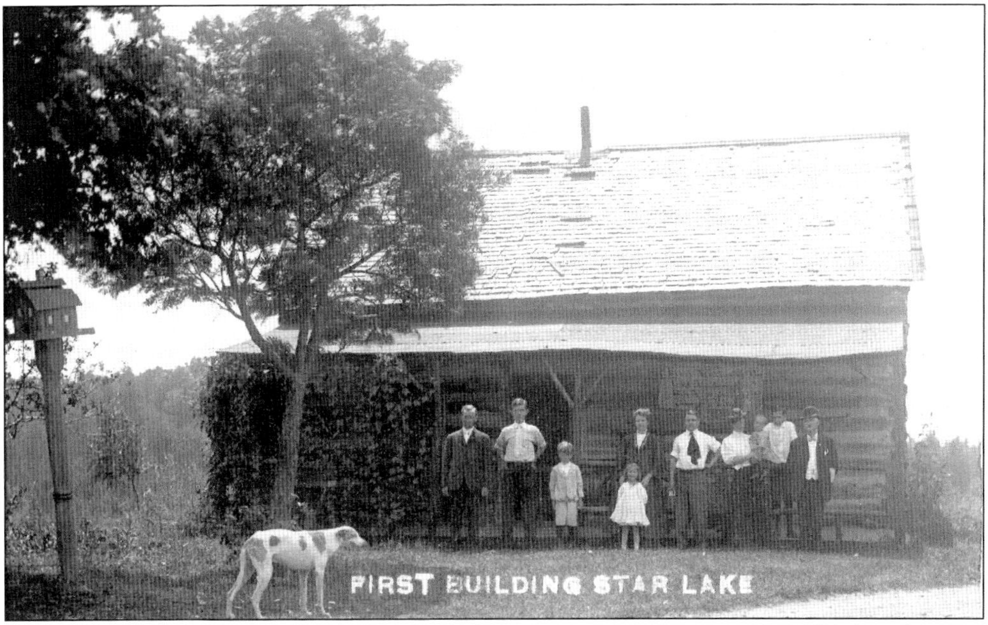

These front and side views of the Soper log cabin camp were taken around 1905. The cabin was built around 1866 by Civil War veteran Sylvester Soper and is believed to have been the first summer vacation home built on the lake. The cabin was later sold by Soper to George Grannis, president of the Carthage & Adirondack Railroad. It was later purchased by the Foleys and used as an annex to the Star Lake Hotel. It was furnished with iron beds and all modern conveniences of the time. It was located just to the east of where the Star Lake Hotel once stood overlooking Post Office Bay. Today, it would have been located very near where the Clifton-Fine Community Center now stands.

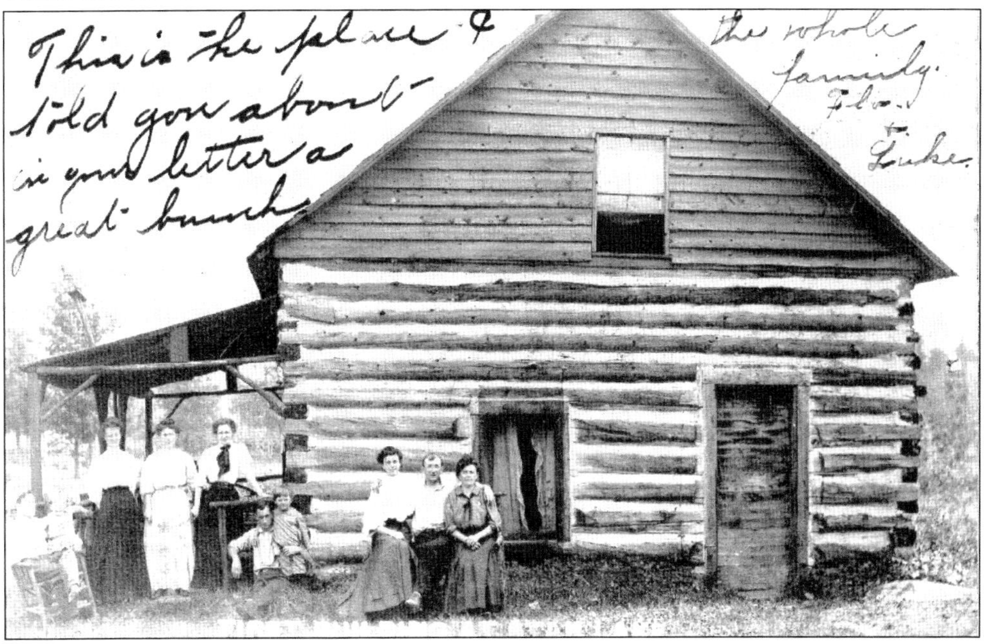

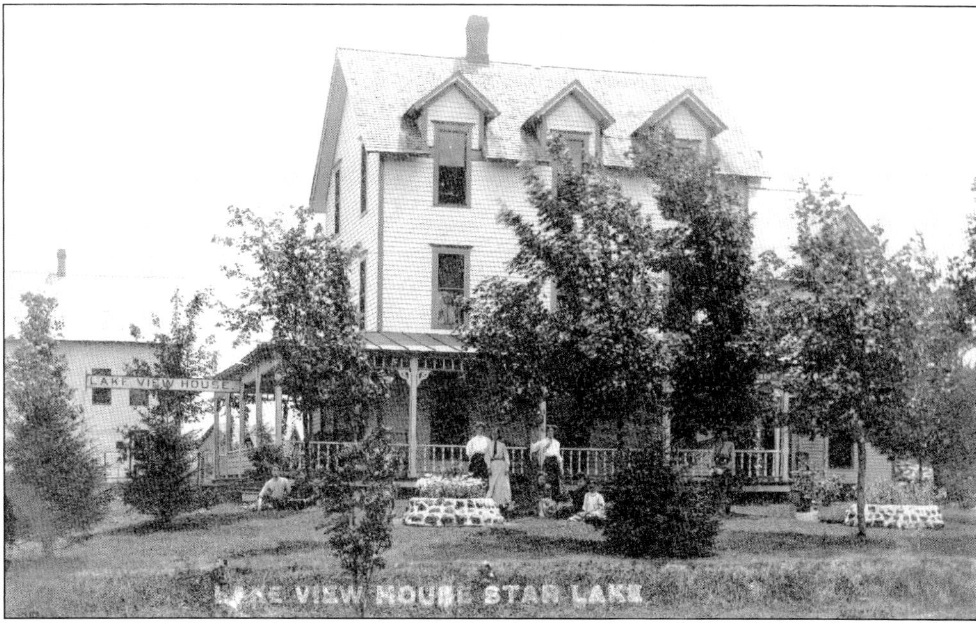

The Lake View House was built in the 1890s by Dr. Hurlbut of Norwood. He later sold it to William Corey, who later sold it to Ruth Patterson in 1913. After Ruth Patterson's death in 1949, her daughter sold the Lake View to Clark Malady. The hotel still stands on Main Street in the village, although the porch and roofline have been removed and modified through the years.

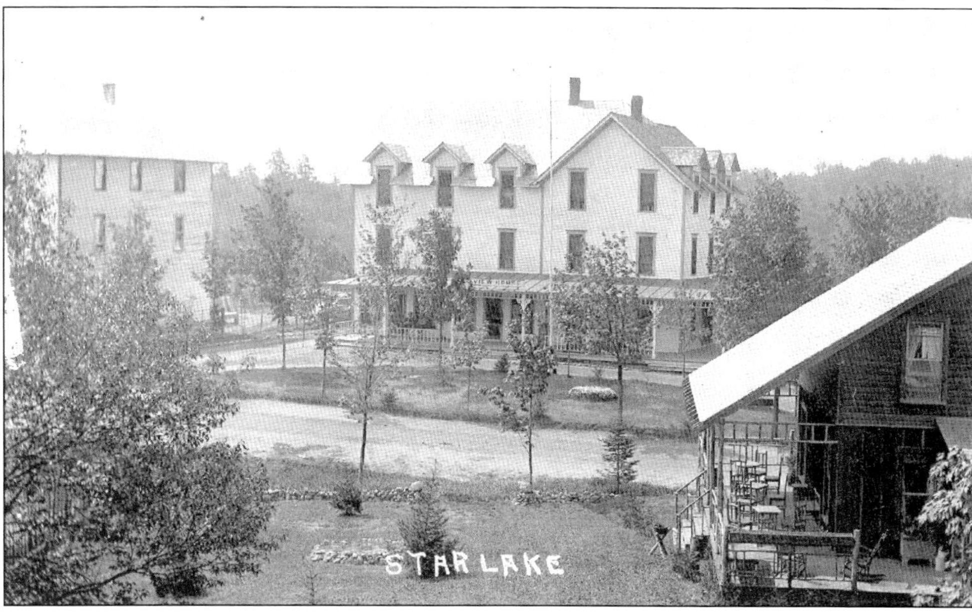

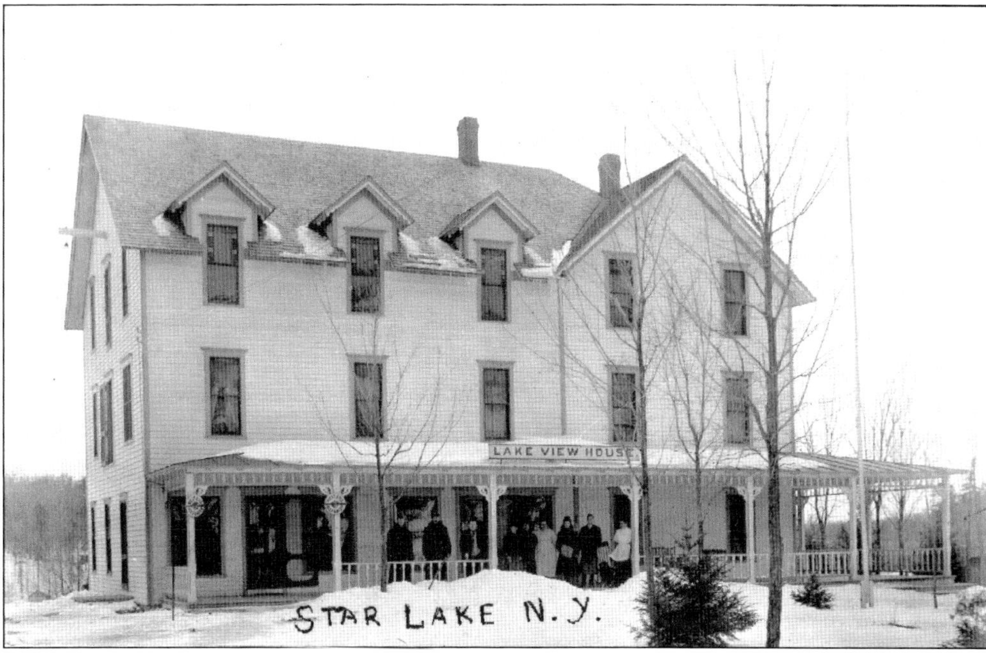

The Lake View House's bar was located to the east side of the porch. The large back bar was removed from the old Benson Mines Hotel. Prior to prohibition in 1920, West End ales and lager from Utica were favorite choices amongst patrons. Several of the West End Brewery porcelain advertising signs can be seen hanging from the porch in the early photographs.

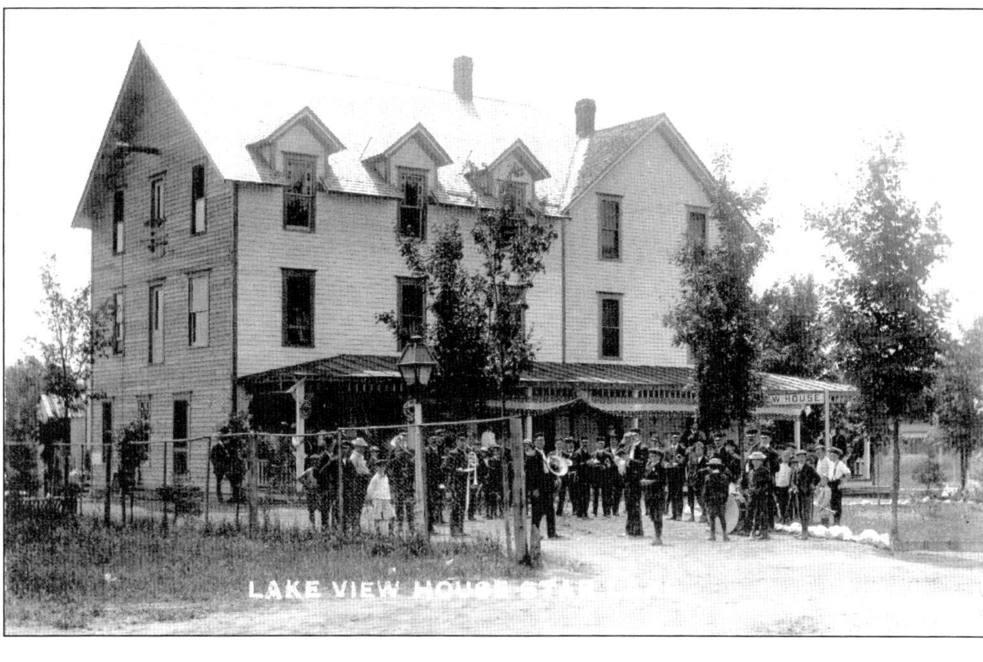

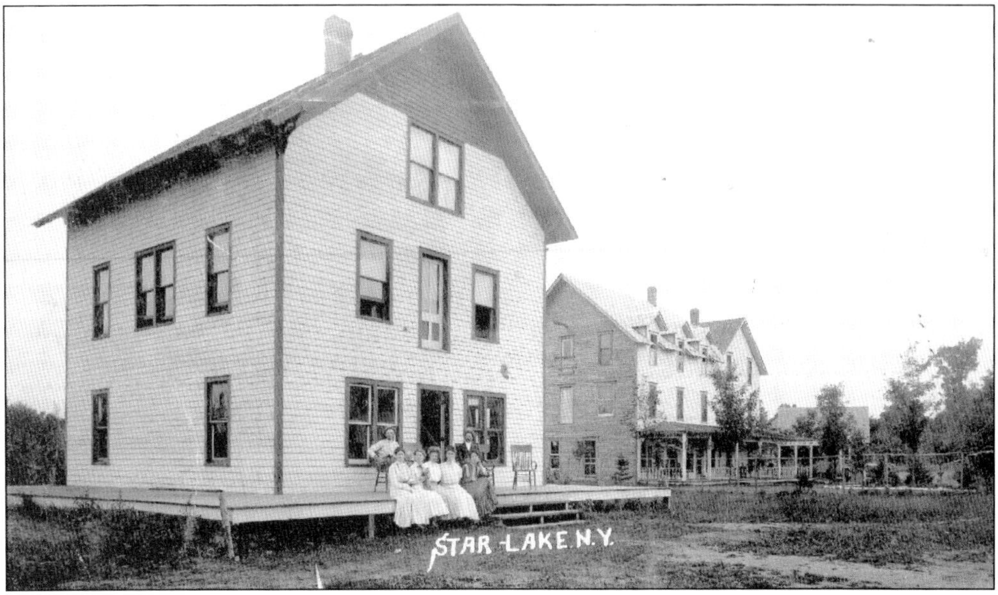

These two views show the New Central Hotel, as it was originally called, between 1907 and 1912. It was located to the immediate left of the Lake View Hotel. The addition to the right of the hotel was originally used as a small dry goods store. The hotel section also served alcohol prior to Prohibition. Through the years, the hotel section had many businesses, including a barbershop, a post office, and an upstairs dance hall. The dry goods store eventually became a soda fountain called the Star Lake Sugar Bowl.

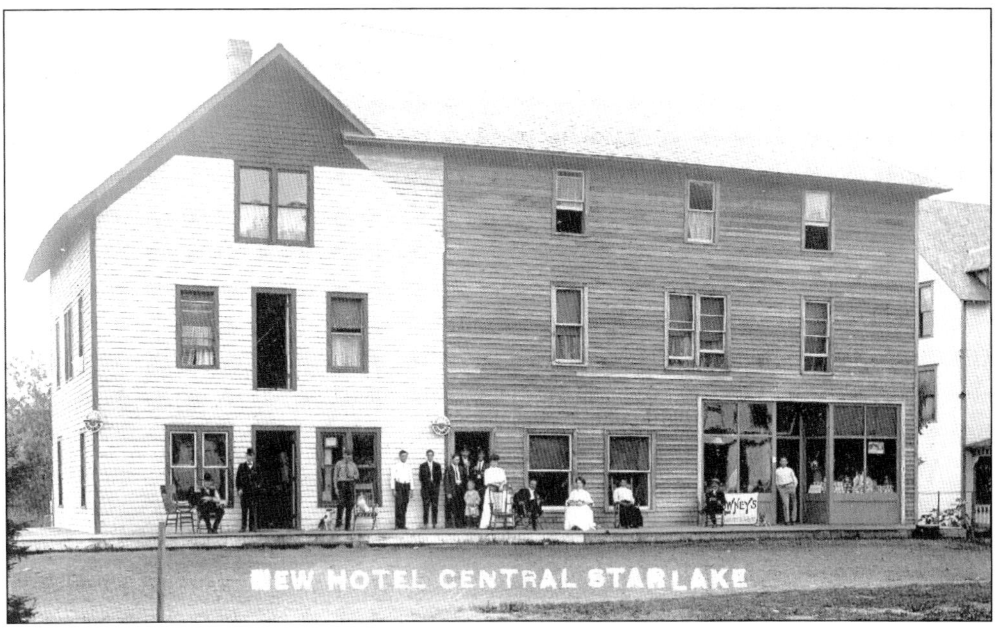

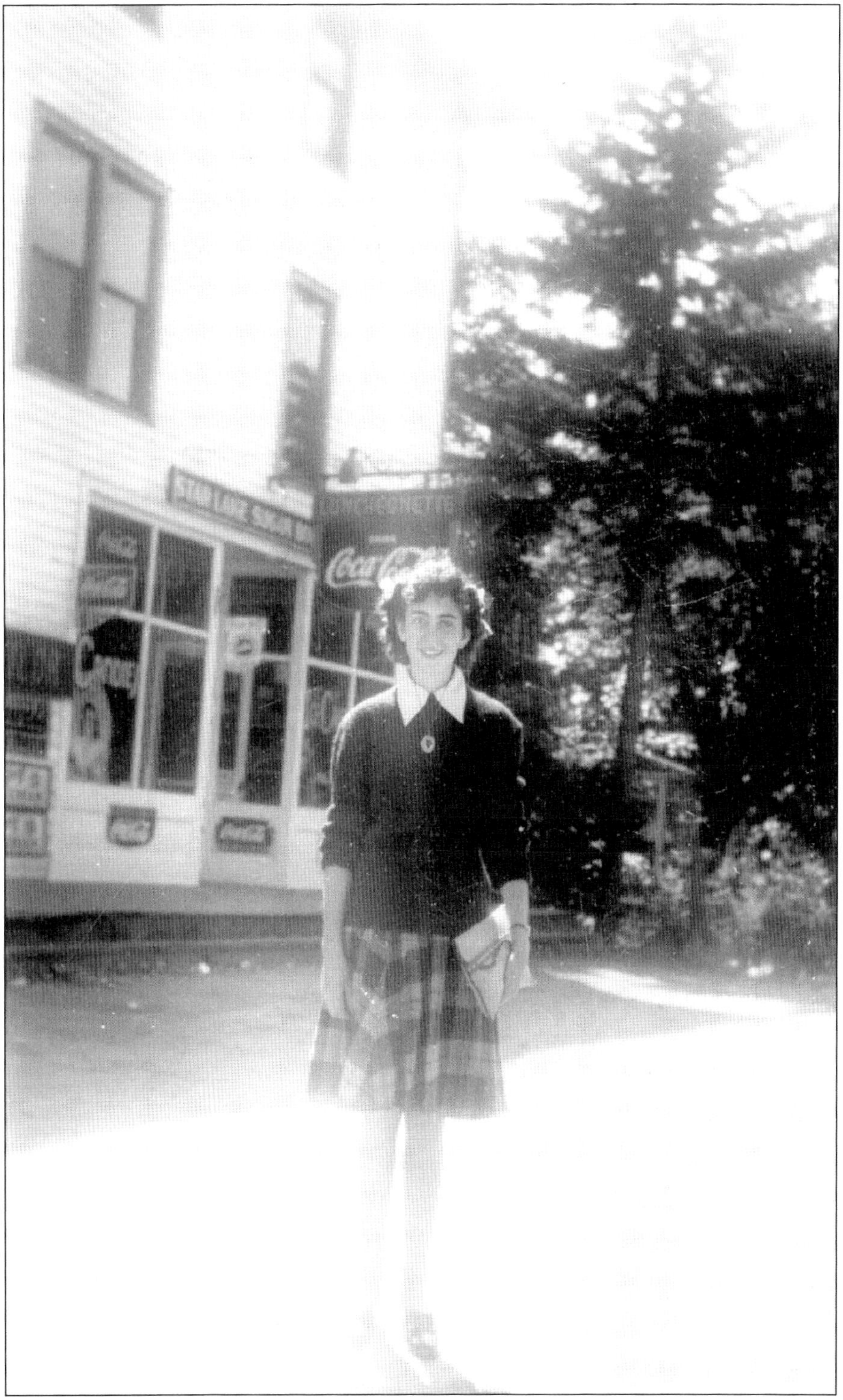

Cecelia Henri stands in front of the Star Lake Sugar Bowl around 1938. This was the local soda fountain in town, serving ice cream, malts, candy, and sandwiches.

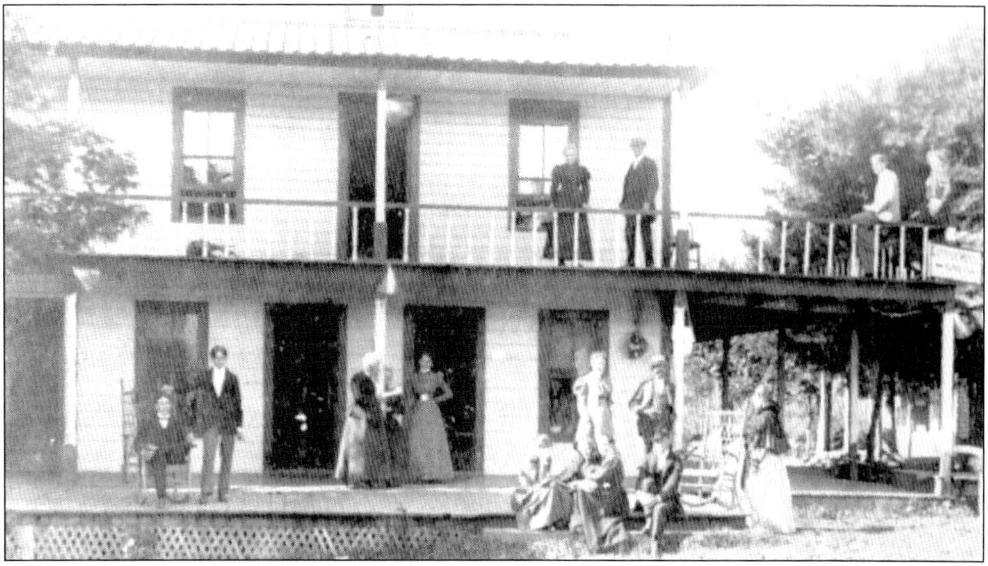

This view shows the Cottage Hotel around 1900. This hotel was built by Frank Redway and was later sold to Frank Goutrement of Carthage. It was destroyed by fire shortly after this photograph was taken. Edwin Young later rebuilt the new Cottage Hotel on his property at the end of Youngs Road.

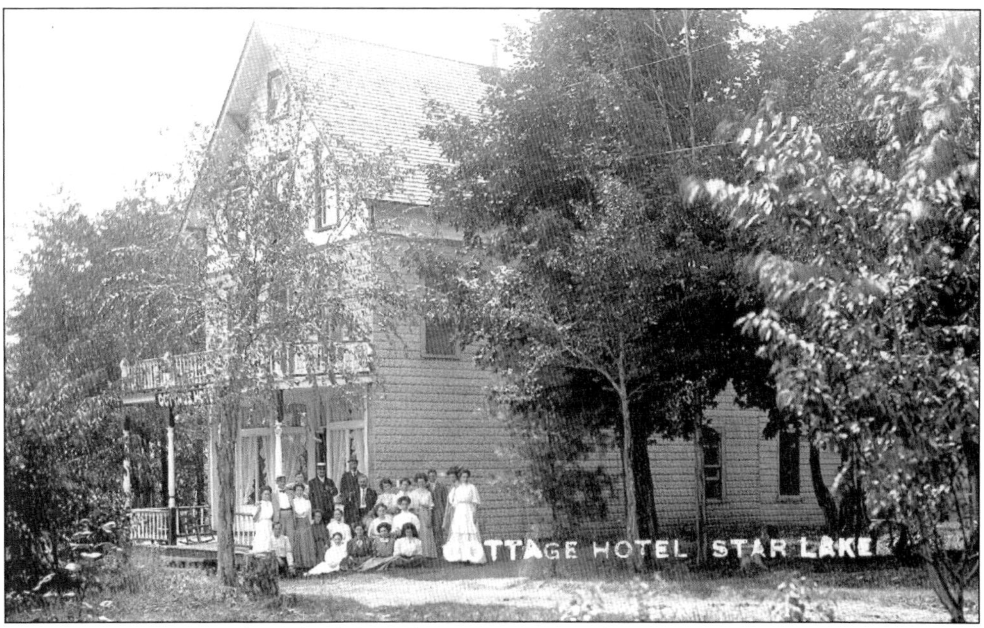

The new Cottage Hotel was built by Edwin Young around 1910. It was located at the very end of what is now Youngs Road. The original Cottage Hotel was built by Frank Redway and was located on Potter Avenue. It burned to the ground in 1900.

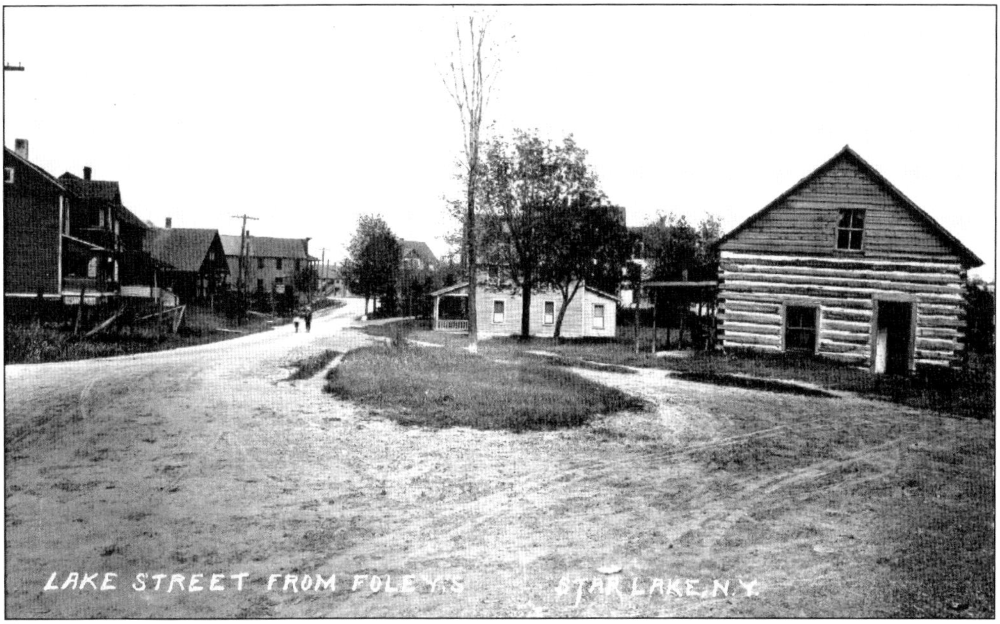

This early view of Main Street looks east from the front of Foley's Star Lake Hotel around 1907. Two young children can be seen walking down the middle of the road. The only means of transportation available at this time were in a horse and buggy, on a bicycle, or on foot.

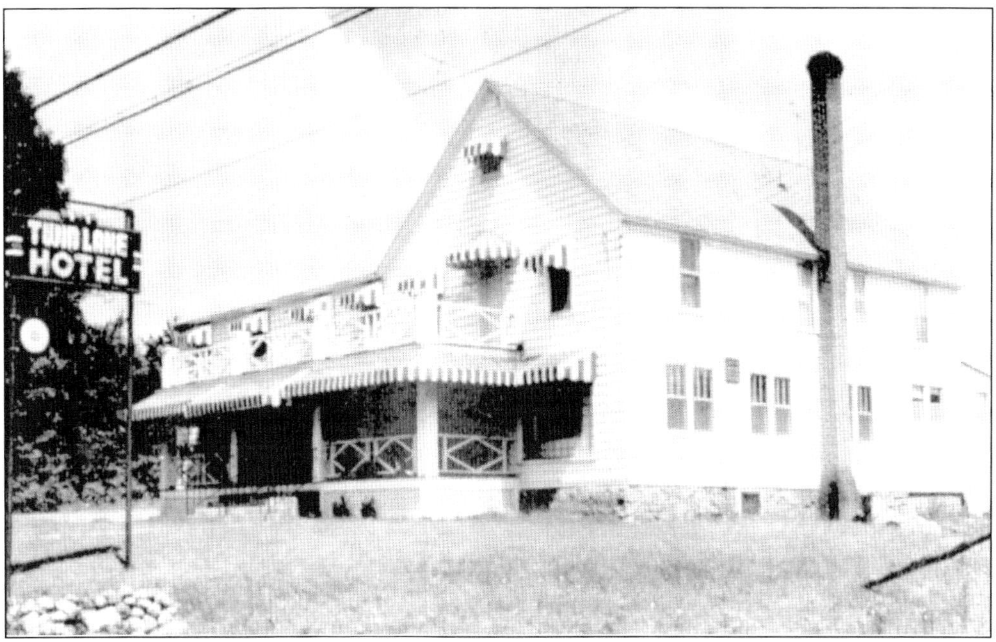

The Twin Lakes Hotel was established in 1940 by Mable Rubyor. It was then purchased in the 1940s by Margaret Duchano. The hotel rented up to 10 rooms until the 1970s. The hotel is now a restaurant and is still run by Duchano's granddaughter.

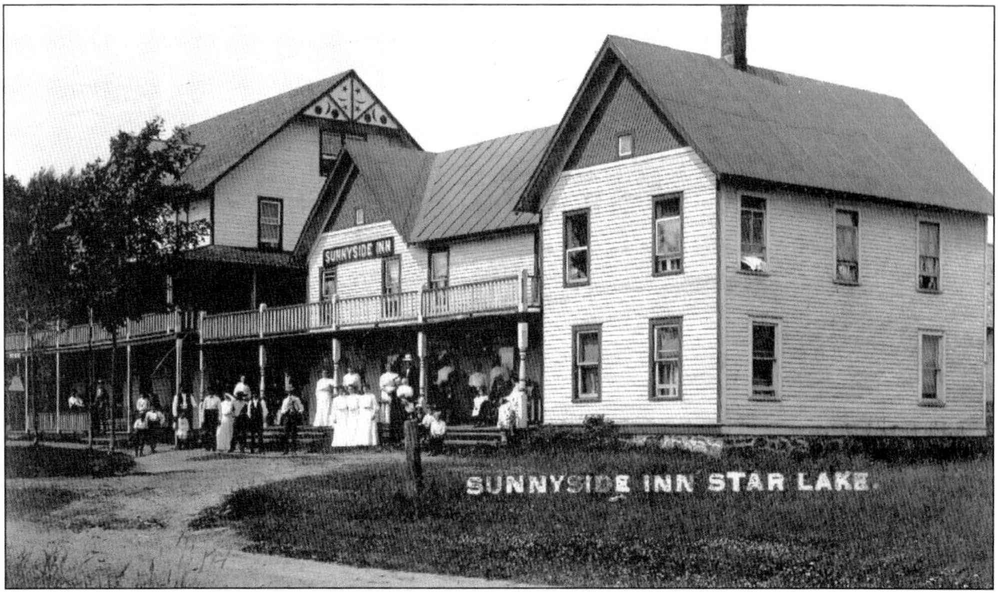

The Sunnyside Inn was built by the Walker Brothers around 1890 and was located on the corner of Main Street and Youngs Road where the gas station stands today. The south wing of the inn was built by George Walker as his home. A few years later, a young man named Andrew Astrello came to Star Lake to try and cure his tuberculosis illness with the fresh Adirondack air. He was, in fact, cured after being given just six months to live, and he decided to make his home in Star Lake. He bought the Sunnyside Inn and ran it until the death of his wife, Jennie, in 1938. He later partnered with Carolyn Gertz, who then sold it to Vernon Keene in 1940. Eventually condemned, the inn was torn down in 1959.

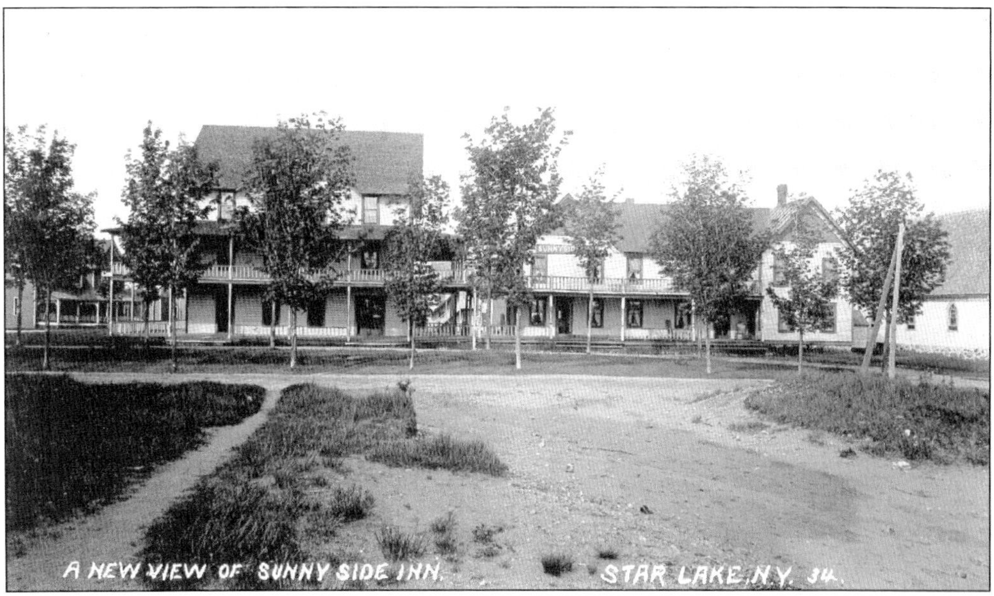

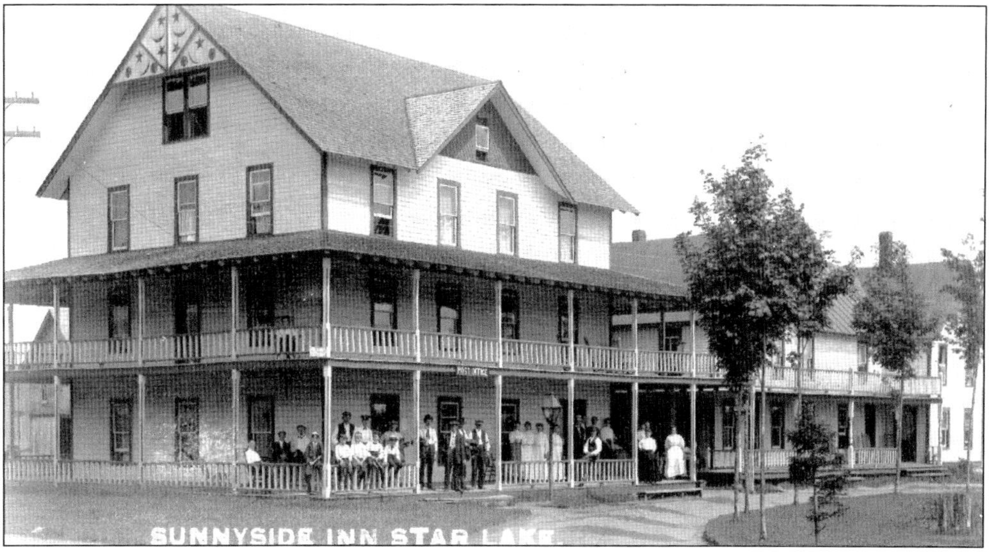

Andrew Astrello was appointed postmaster of Star Lake in 1905, after acting postmaster Edmund Pendleton was accused of embezzling $100 from the government coffers. Astrello located the post office inside the Sunnyside Inn. The post office sign can be seen hanging from the side porch. This postcard was postmarked "Star Lake, NY—July 19, 1906," most likely by Astrello himself.

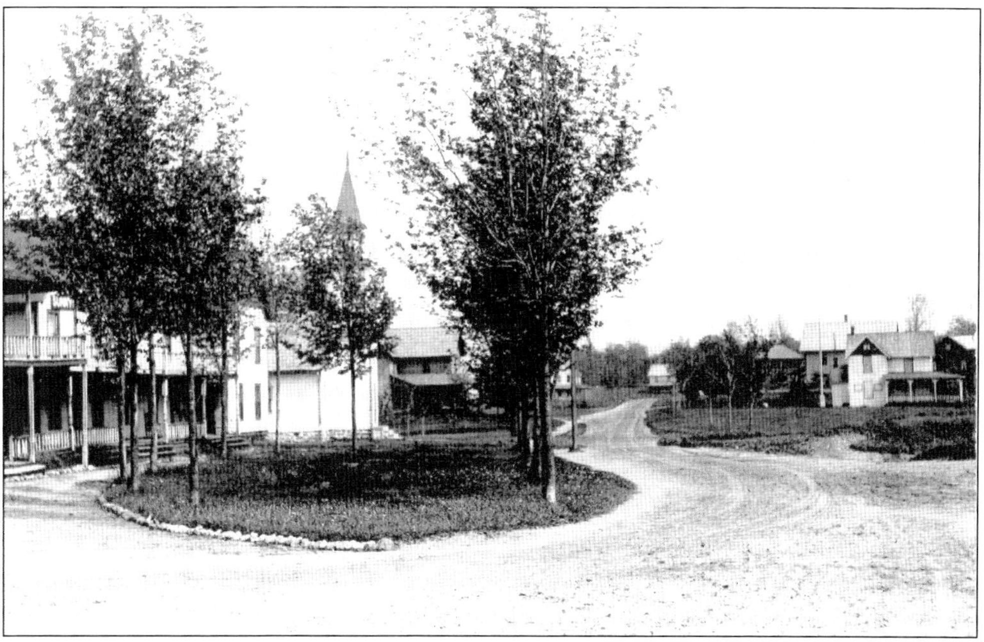

This view of Main Street was taken from Tears Store, looking toward Youngs Road around 1910. The circular driveway in front of the Sunnyside Inn can be seen on the left.

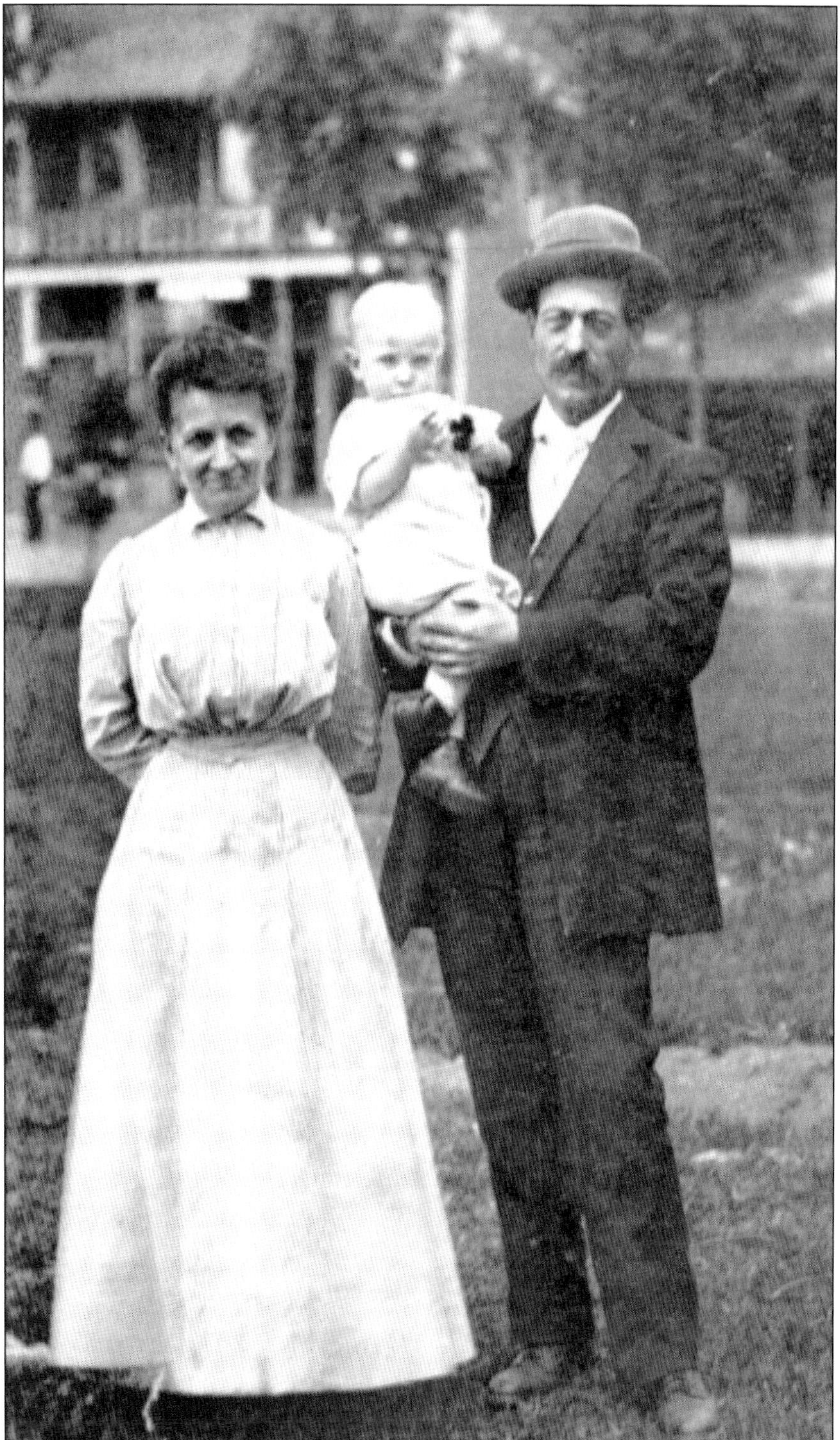

Andrew Astrello, his wife, Jennie, and a child stand in front of the Sunnyside Inn around 1910.

Three

THE STAR LAKE INN

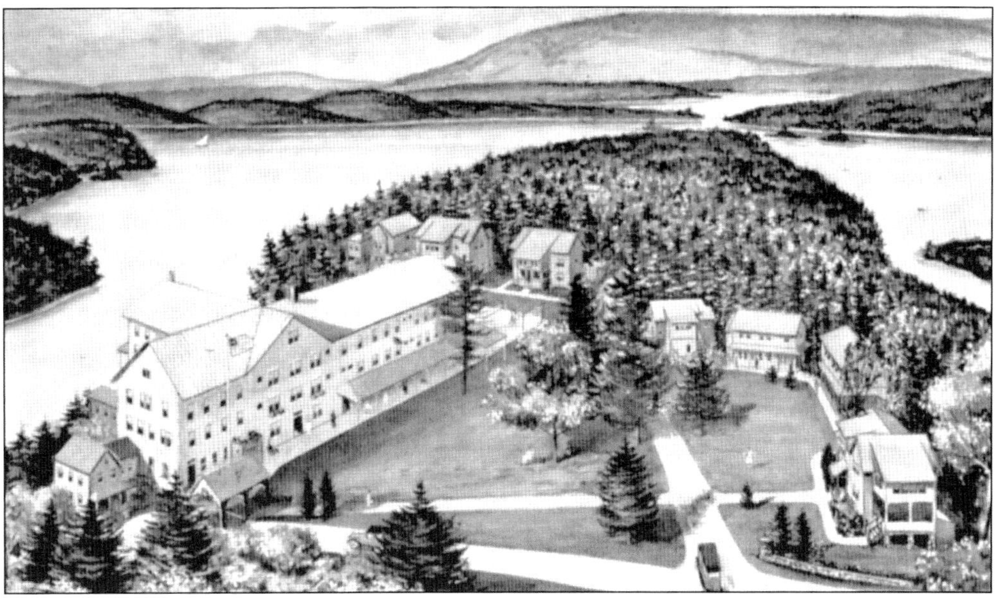

This is an artist's rendering of the Star Lake Inn and surrounding colony of satellite cottages around 1925. In total, there were 18 satellite cottages rented by the inn. The cottages varied in size from four rooms, suitable for one or two families, to twelve rooms, which could be broken up into suites. Eight of the cottages had maid and hotel services available, and three of the larger cottages were equipped for full housekeeping, with servants quarters attached. All were fully furnished and included the same amenities as the inn.

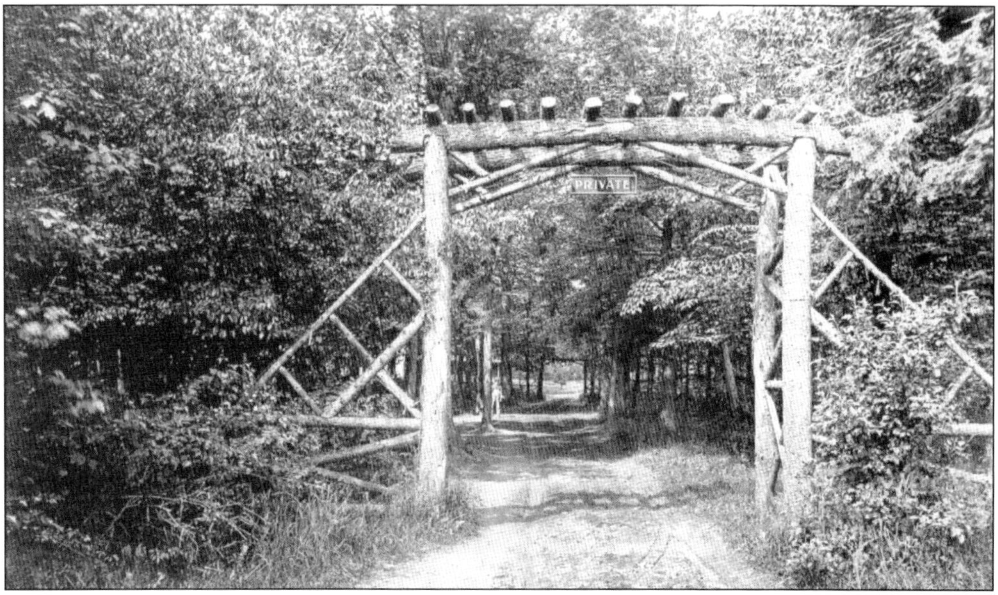

These were the original two entrance gates to the Star Lake Inn around 1910. Guests arriving via horse-driven surrey would first travel through the outer rustic gate, proceed through Justin Park, and finally travel through the main entrance gate to the inn.

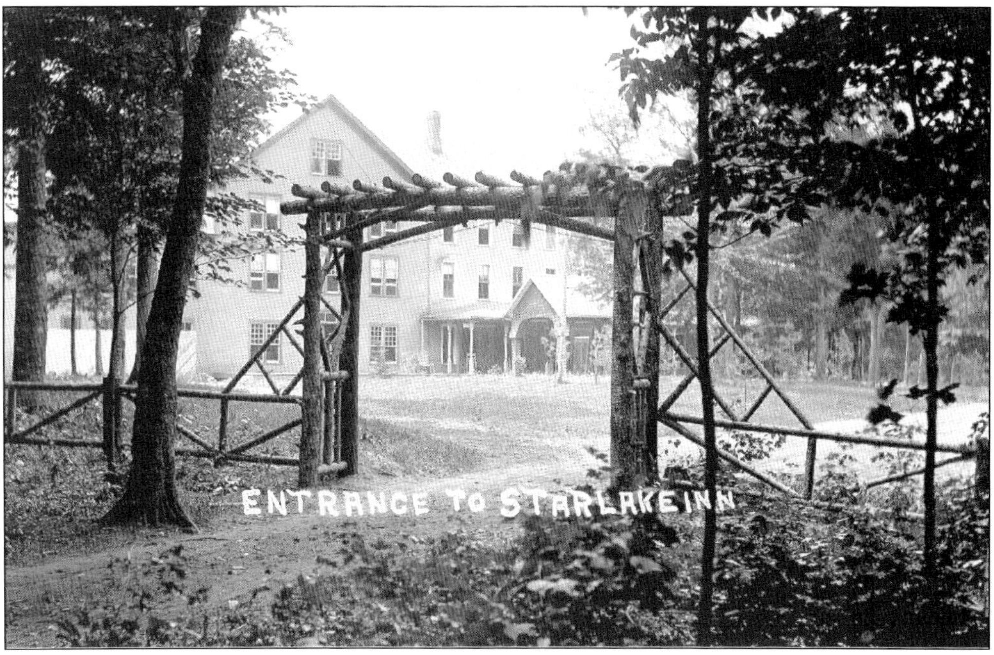

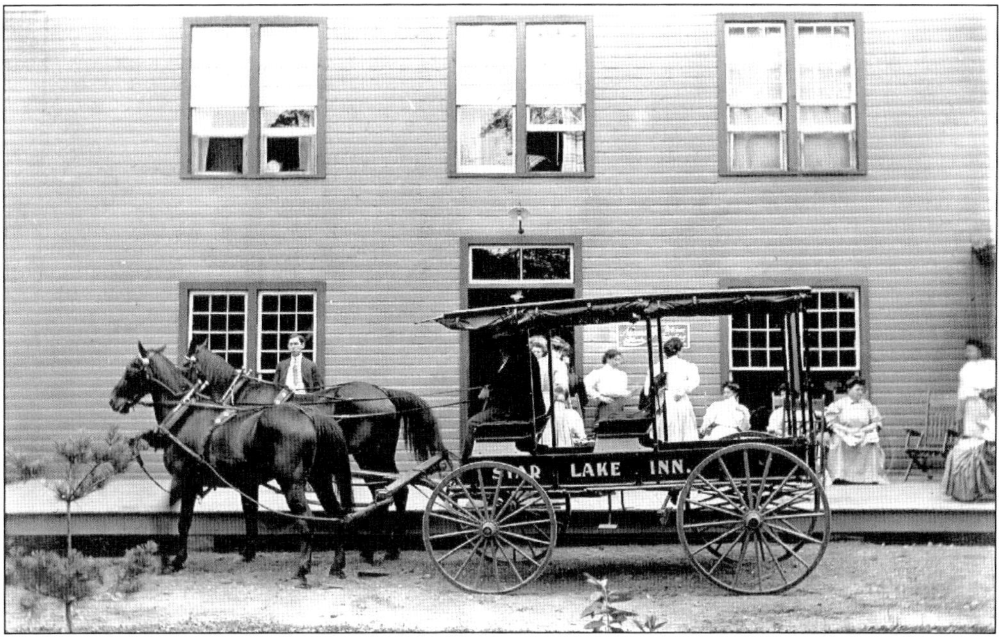

The Star Lake Inn surrey is driven by Winfred Backus around 1912. Originally, the passengers were picked up and dropped off at the Oswegatchie train depot, but eventually much of the traffic flow switched over to the Benson Mines depot. It was a two-mile trip from Benson Mines to Star Lake. Winfred Backus charged 25¢ per passenger each way.

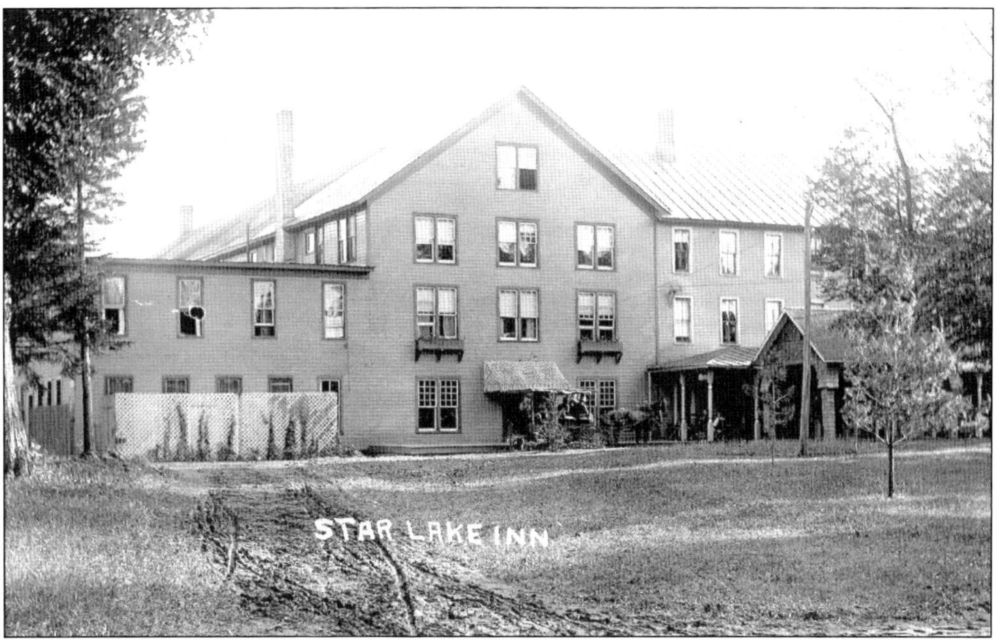

In 1905, rates for room and board at the inn were \$12.50 to \$17.50 per week and \$2.50 to \$3 per day. Guests desiring to stay through the entire season were given special discounted rates for the months of June and September.

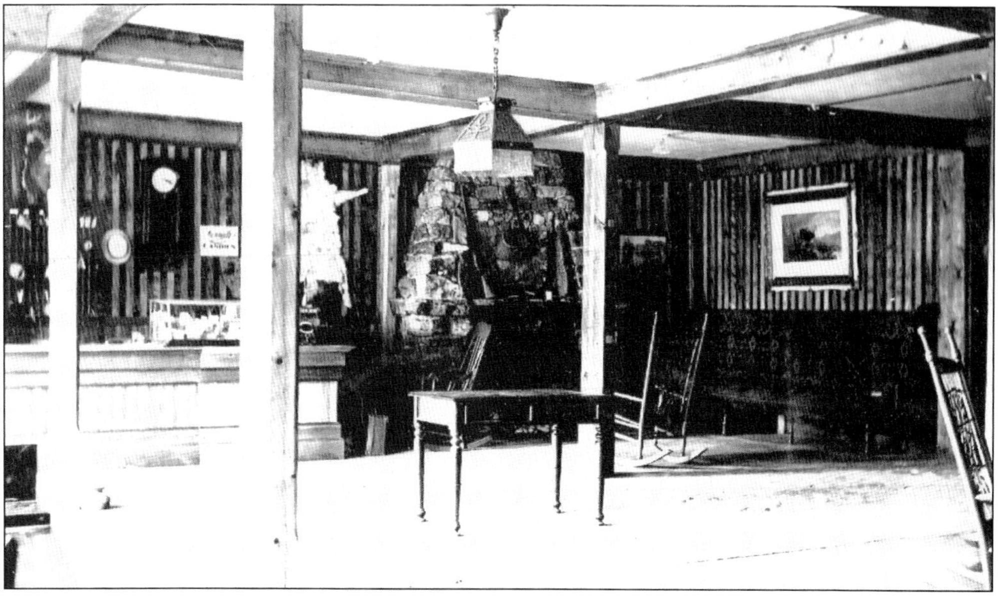

This *c.* 1915 photograph is of the lobby check-in area inside the Star Lake Inn. Guests would initially register here with the hotel clerk and receive their room keys. The glass showcase seen on the counter sold 10-cent cigars. A unique feature of the inn was that each of the 100 rooms had a bell to ring the office with. One ring signified the guests were in need of a chambermaid, and two rings meant they were in need of a bellhop. The rings would trigger an electromagnetic board in the manager's office, showing which room was requesting the service.

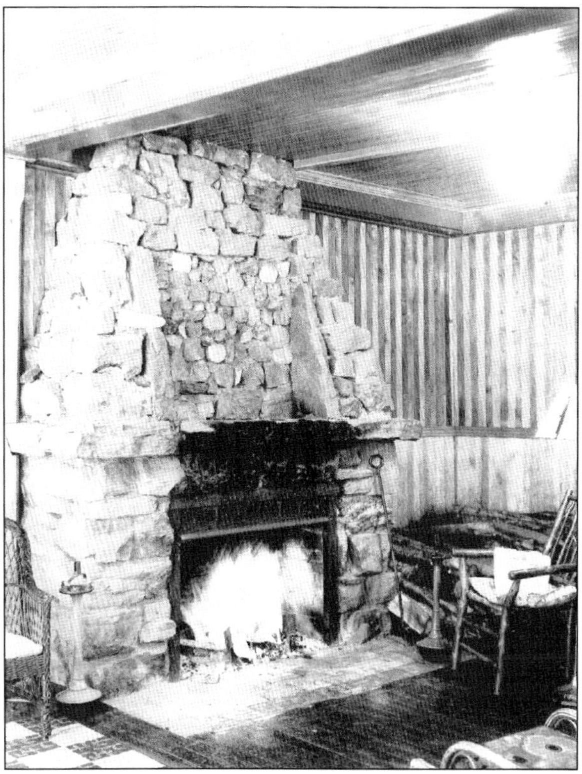

The focal point of the inn's lobby was the massive stone fireplace. In earlier views than this one from around 1920, the fireplace was decorated with a hanging fishing creel and double-barreled shotgun. The first floor of the inn had three other stone fireplaces.

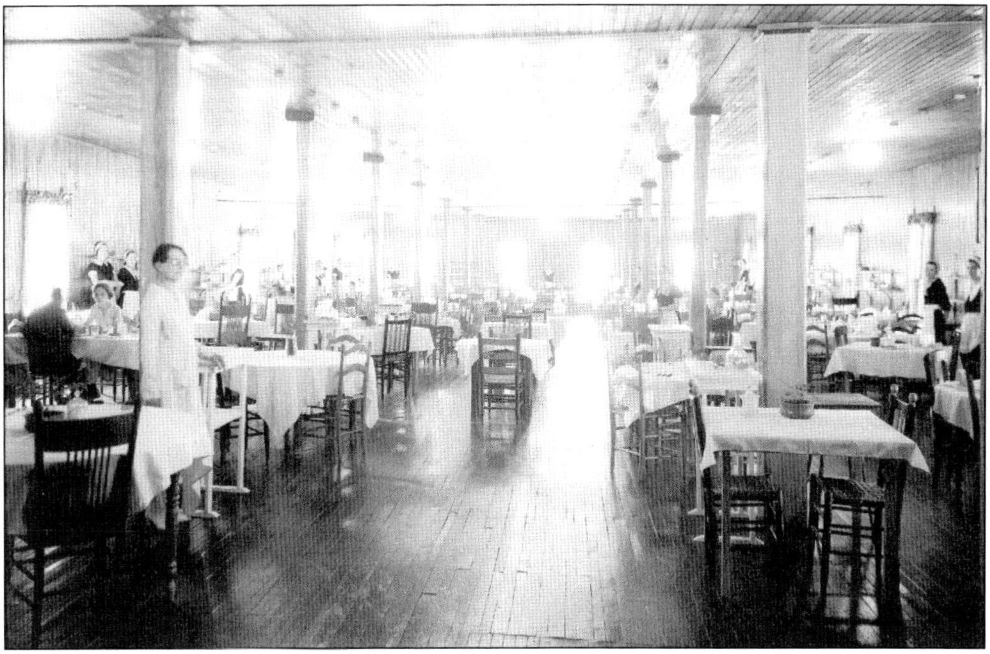

The dining room at the Star Lake Inn, pictured around 1915, could accommodate up to 250 guests. Two meals a day were served. Special effort was made to provide fresh trout and wild game at all times. Also advertised on the menu were fresh fruits, vegetables, milk, cream, butter, and eggs.

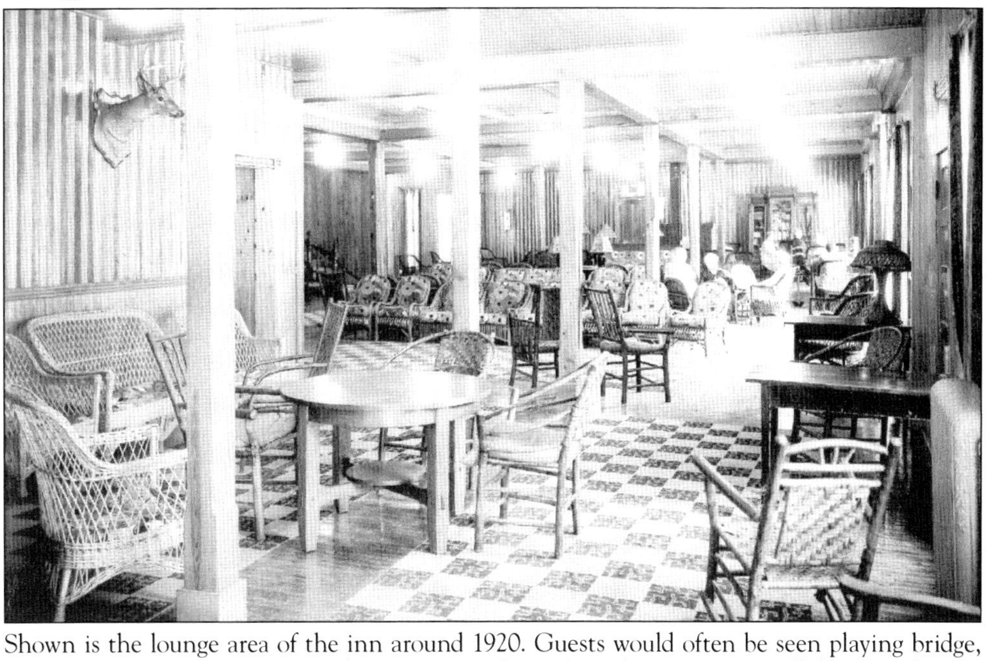

Shown is the lounge area of the inn around 1920. Guests would often be seen playing bridge, reading a book, or enjoying an afternoon cup of tea. A reading room just off the main lounge provided a quiet retreat in front of the open fireplace. Down one flight of stairs from the lounge was the Terrace Room. The dance floor was located on this lower level, along with Ping-Pong tables and a radio.

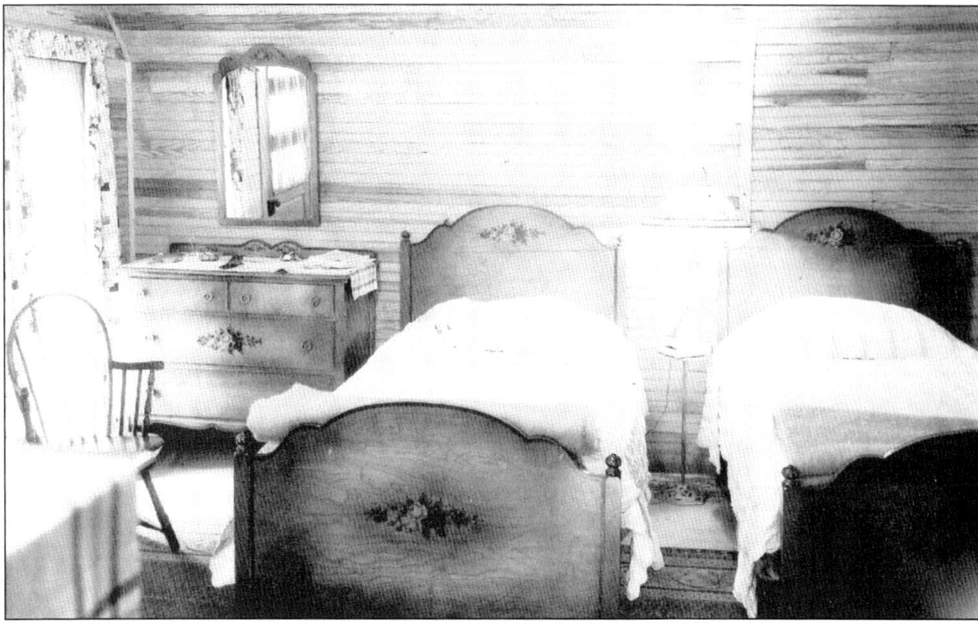

This interior view shows a single room at the Star Lake Inn around 1920. The bedroom walls and ceilings were all tongue-and-groove pine wainscot stained with an orange-tinted shellac. All rooms had with twin beds with Beautyrest mattresses and, except for a very few, private or connecting bathrooms. When the inn was sold at auction in 1962, the contents of each room were auctioned off separately.

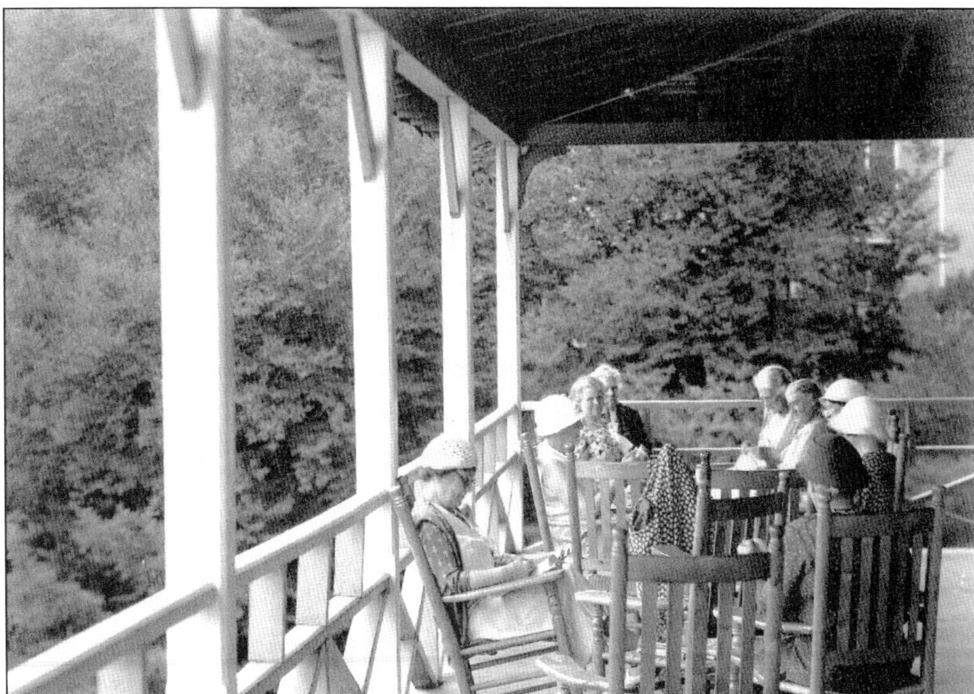

Several women relax on one of the many front porches of the inn on a hot summer day around 1920. Some of them are reading, one is knitting, and others are just "shooting the breeze."

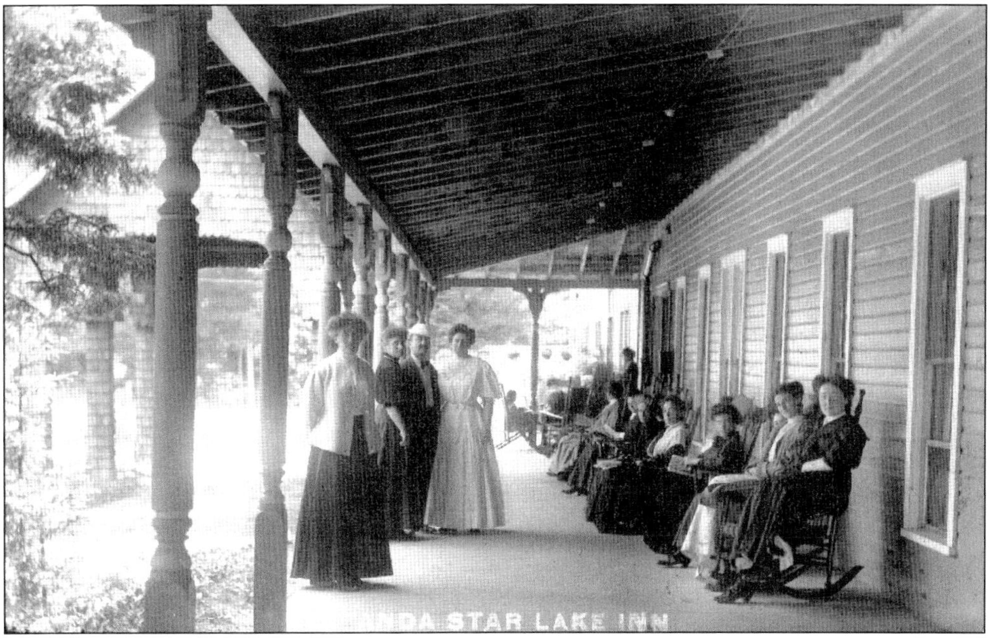

This view of the front veranda of the Star lake Inn dates from around 1908. Competition among the guests to secure their favorite rocking chair was a daily occurrence. Some guests attempted a solution by tying a name tag to their favorite chair, only to find it replaced the next day with a different name tag.

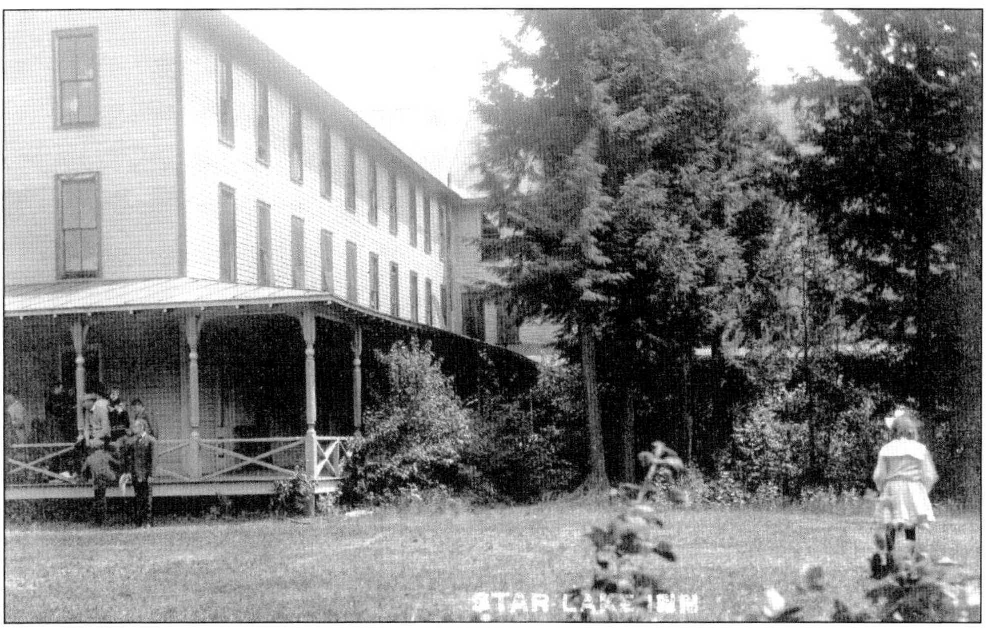

This west-end view of the inn is postmarked June 28, 1908. The postcard was sent by a chambermaid working at the inn. She writes, "We cleaned all of the rooms on the 2nd and 3rd floors seen in this picture, more than fifty rooms in all. We are over to Twin lakes this A.M."

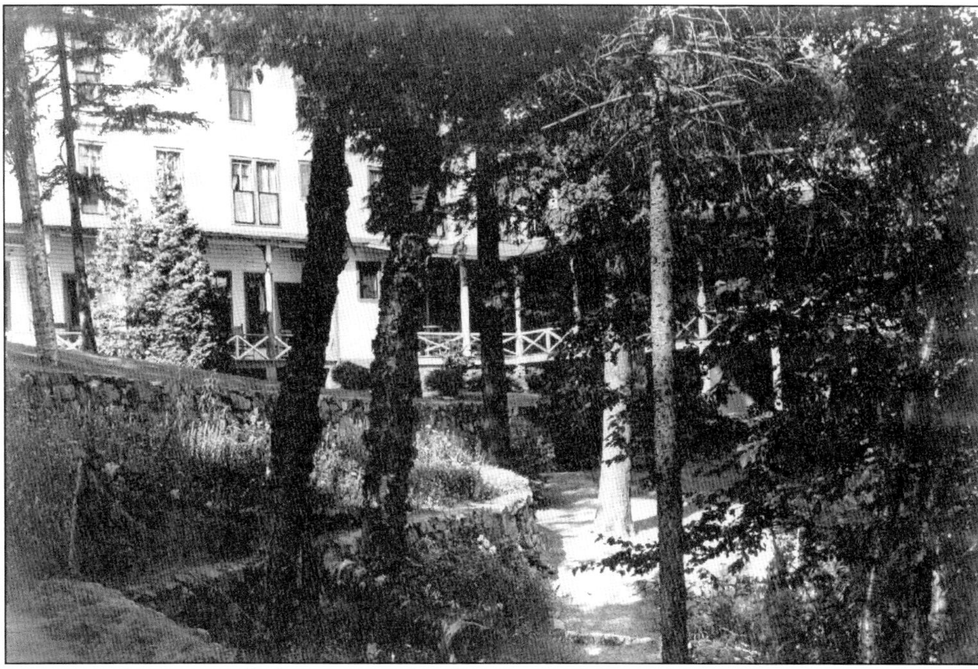

These are the stone-walled terraces and walkway near the Star lake Inn around 1920. The inn guests, along with the occupants of the 18 satellite cottages, used this walkway to access the beach and dock areas on the inn property.

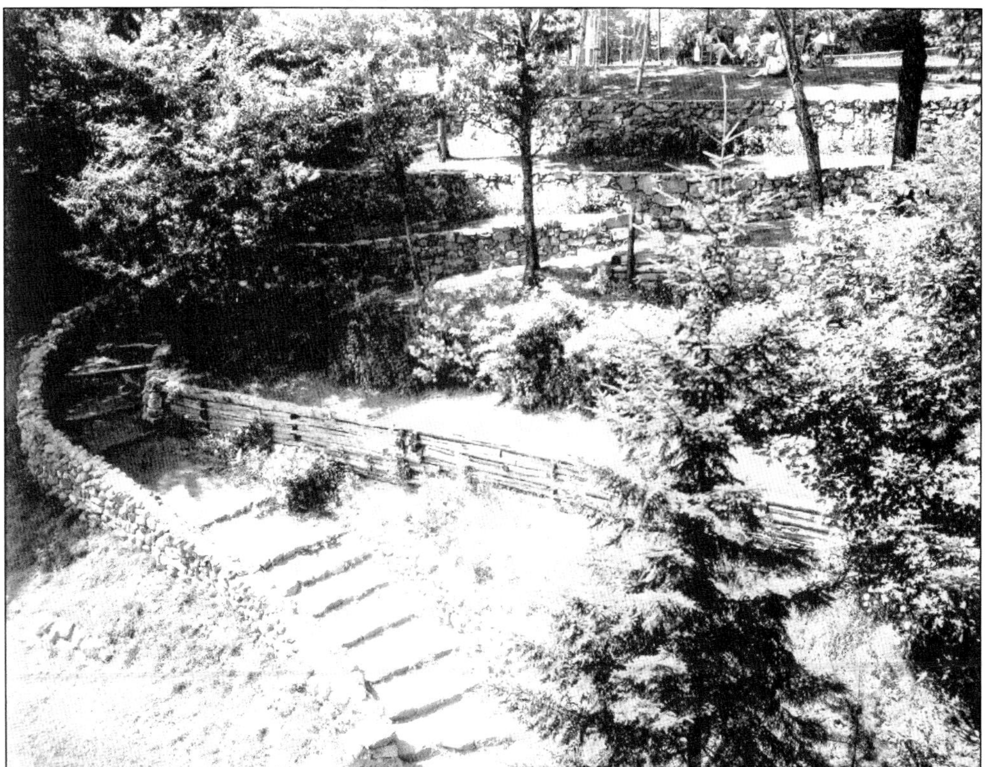

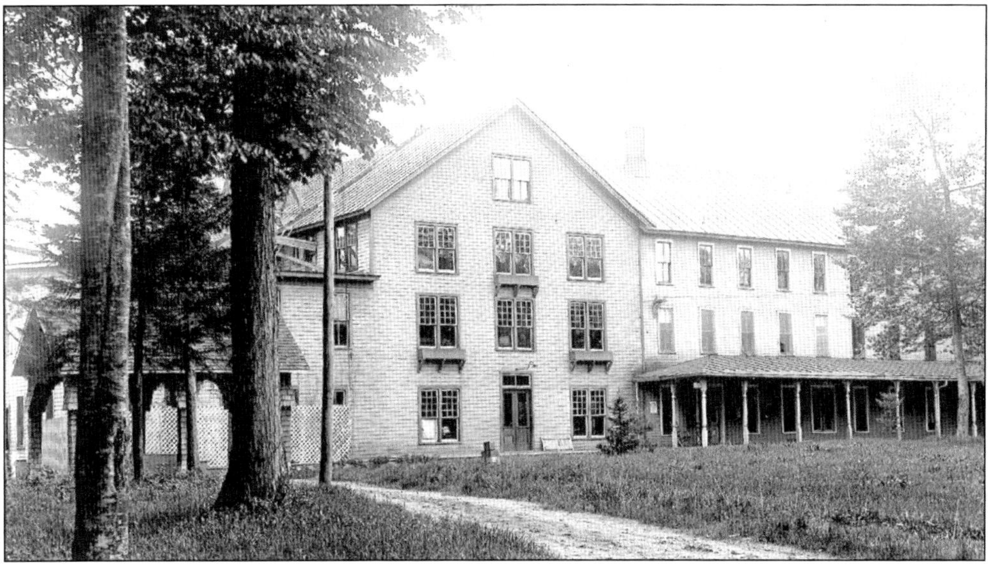

The Star Lake Inn was a seasonal operation, open from June to October. These two views of the inn around 1910 show a spring scene with the grass uncut and a fall scene with the front door boarded up and locked and the curtains in the windows drawn.

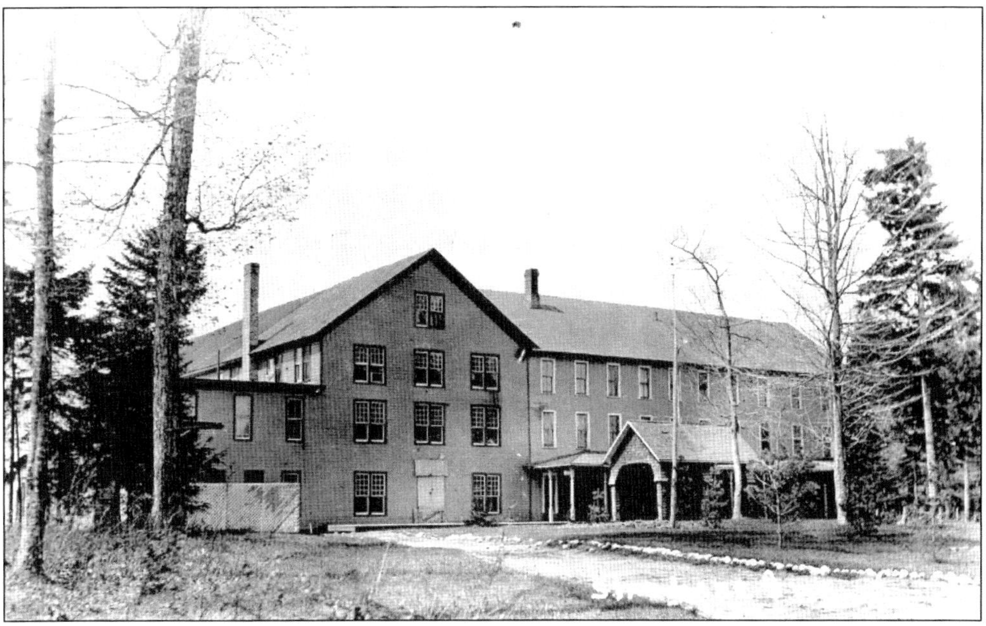

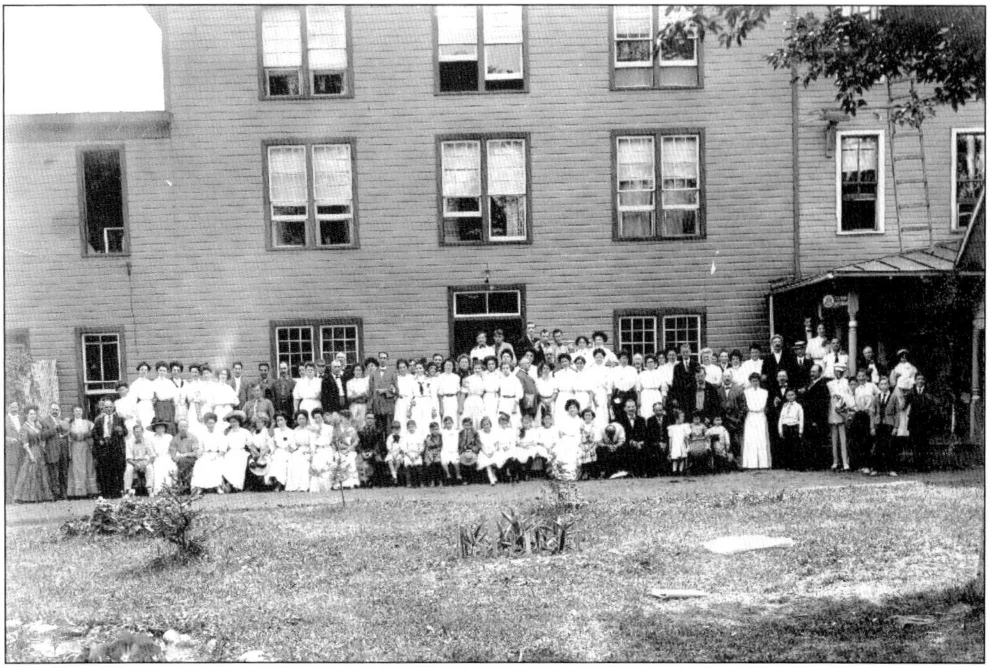

In 1905, rates for room and board at the inn were $12.50 to $17.50 per week and $2.50 to $3 per day. Guests desiring to stay through the entire season were given special discounted rates for the months of June and September.

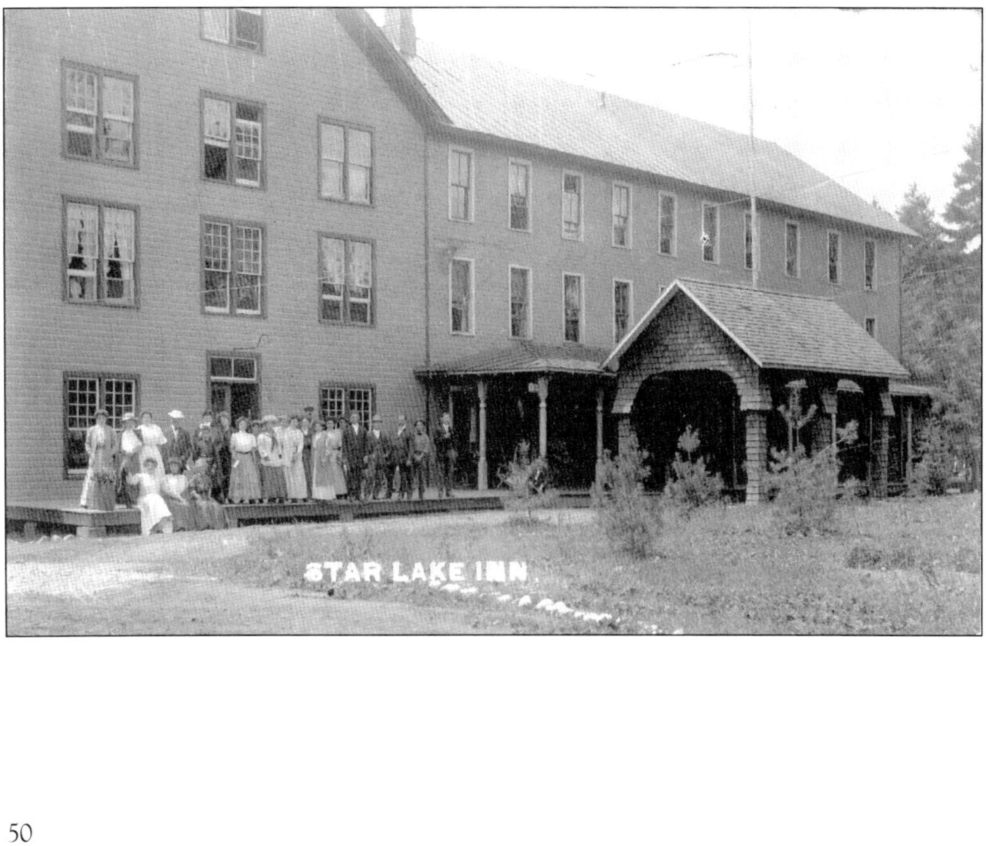

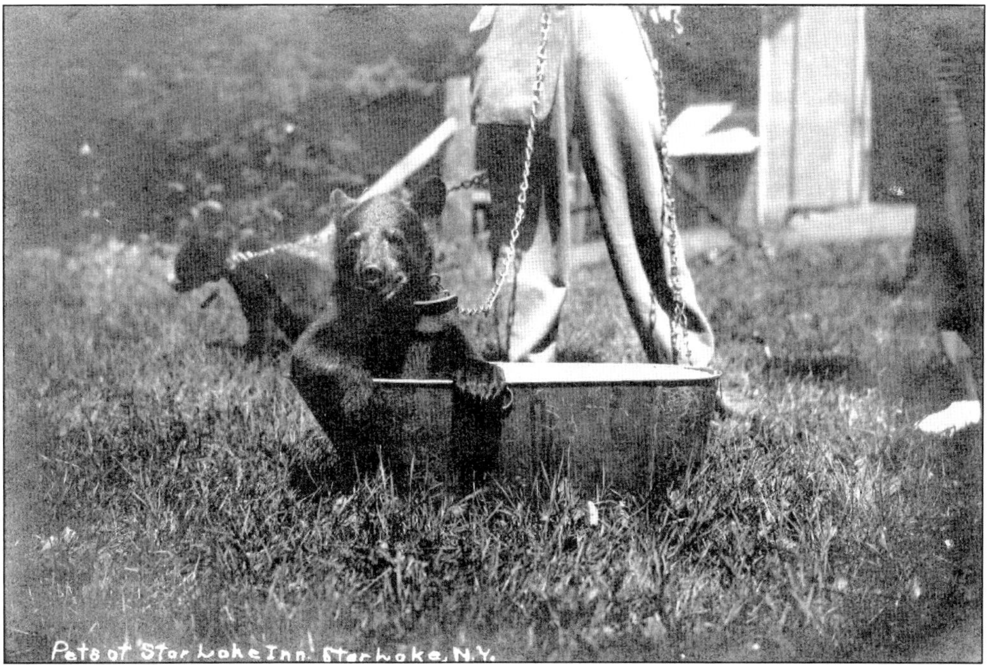

There was always plenty of entertainment at the Star Lake Inn. This pair of black bear cubs and the goat, used for wagon or cart rides, were pets owned by young Charles Sayles. At this time, around 1910, his father, John M. Sayles, was the proprietor of the inn. The Sayles family lived in the Aerie cottage, which was located directly across from the front yard of the inn.

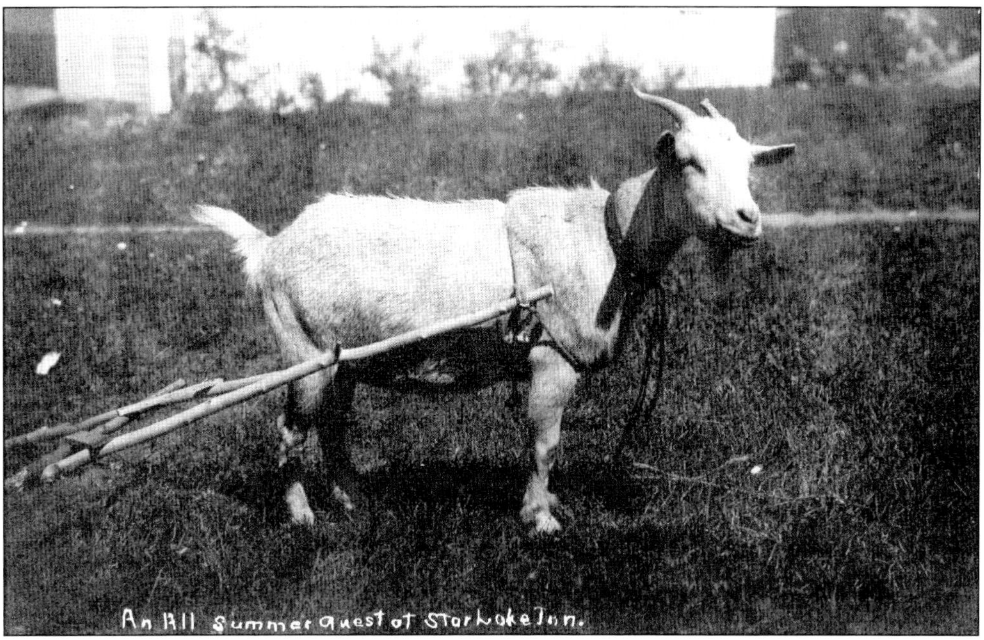

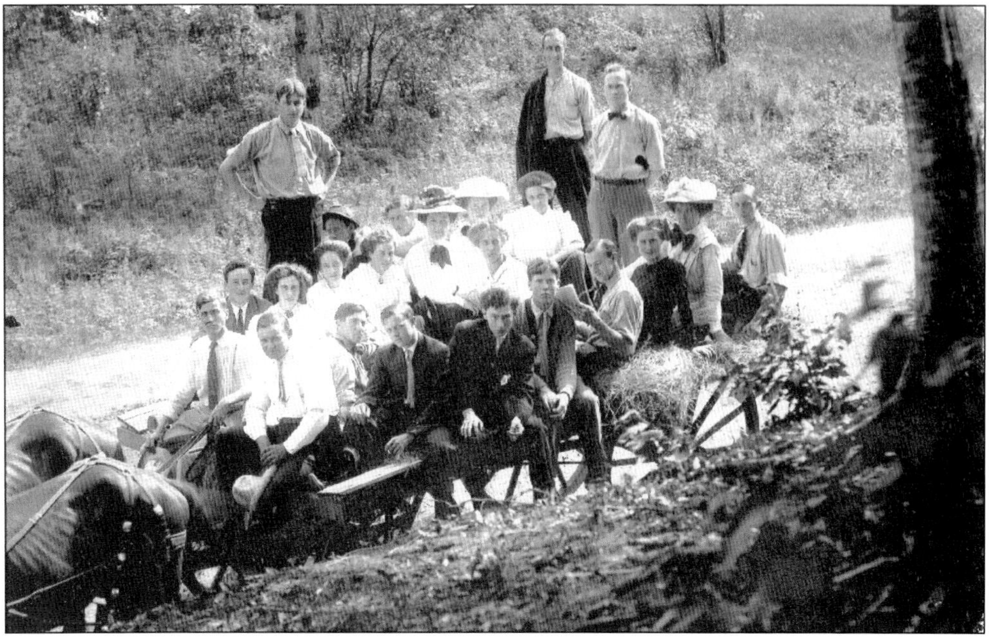

This was just one of the many summer activities guests at the Star Lake Inn could participate in around 1910: an afternoon horse-drawn hayride to Wanakena. The primitive dirt road leading to Wanakena must have made for quite an uncomfortable ride.

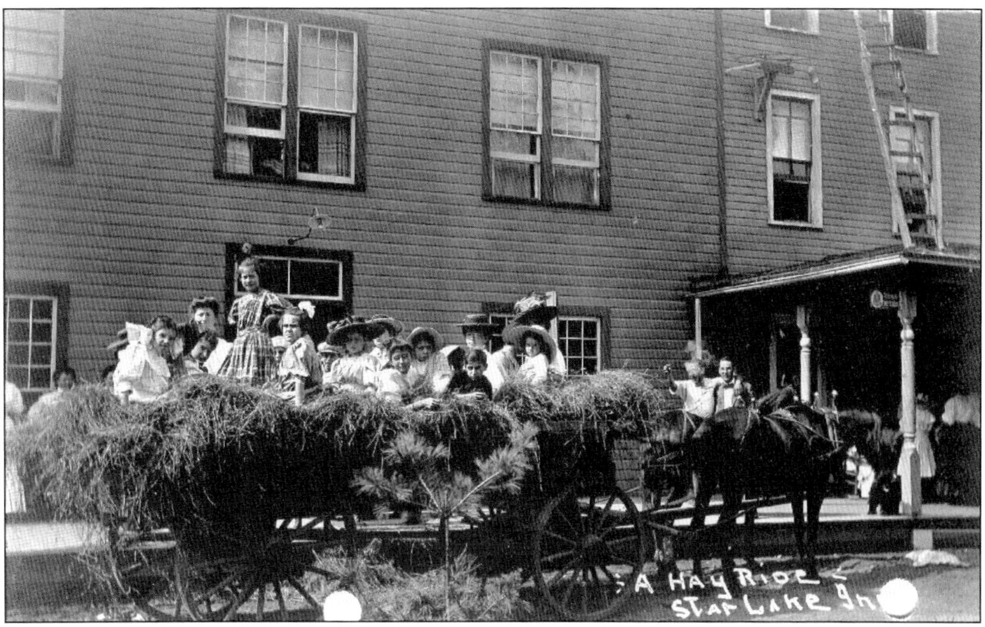

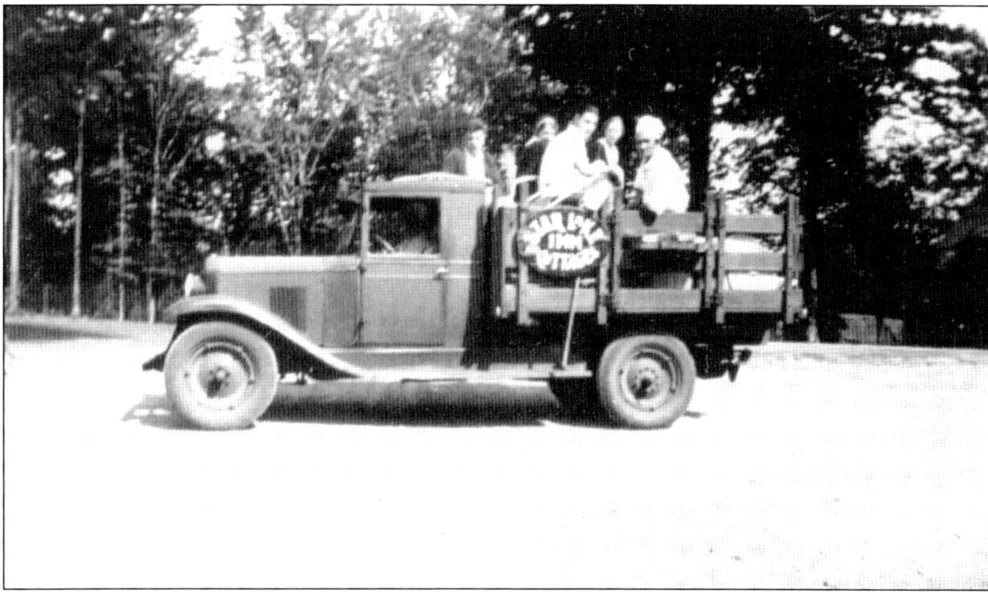

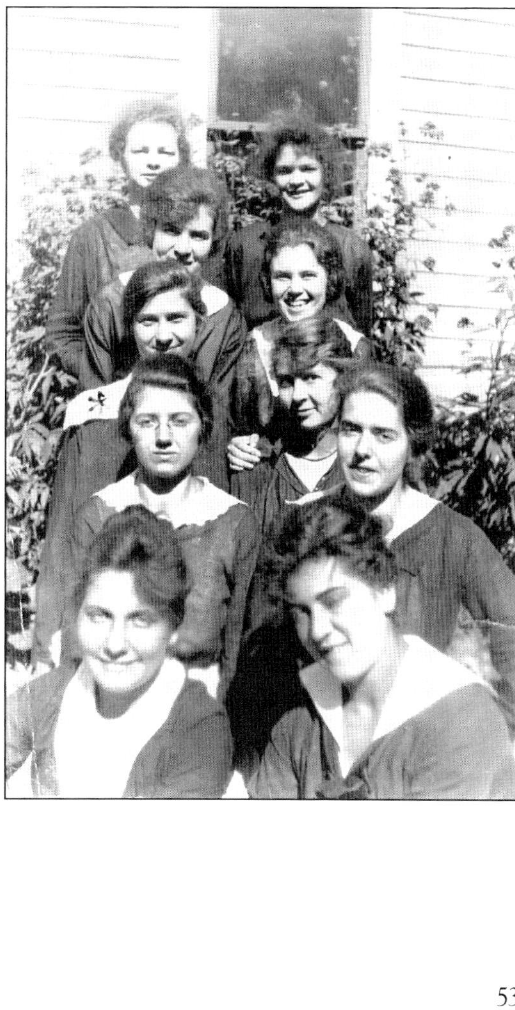

These were the waitresses at the Star Lake Inn around 1915. All of them wore black dresses and white aprons and had to wear their hair pulled back at all times. The female employees all slept in a dorm located above the kitchen, segregated from the male employees, who slept in a bunkhouse behind the Sudside satellite cottage. A prerequisite for the young men and women who were working as waitresses and bellhops during the summer season was that they had to be a college graduate or undergraduate. Laundry workers and chambermaids tended to be locals.

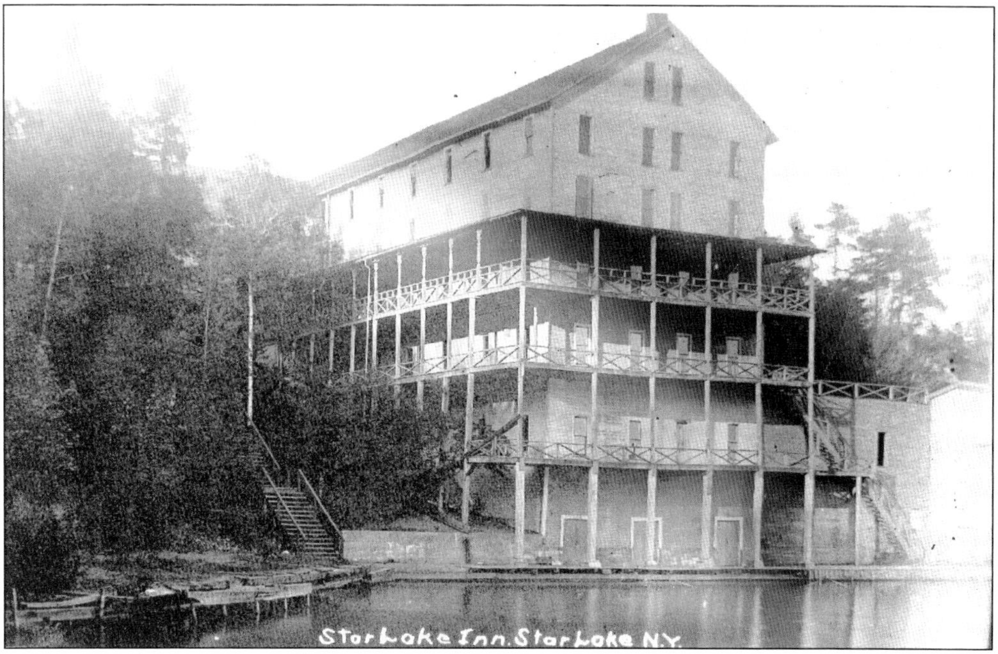

The Star Lake Inn, originally named the Edgewood House, was built in 1887 by George H. Freeman. In 1895, he sold it to J. C. Lee of Gouverneur. Lee then sold the inn in 1897 to Hiram F. Inglehart and Charles E. Brown of Watertown for a total of $9,700, which included the inn property and all of the contents associated with it. Inglehart was a famous hotel man who also owned the Normandie of New York City, the Columbian of Thousand Islands Park, and Hotel Westminster of Alexandria Bay. Brown was the president of the Watertown Carriage Company. John M. Sayles married Inglehart's daughter Grace, and Inglehart later sold his share of the inn to the groom. The inn remained in the Sayles family until it was sold at auction in 1962.

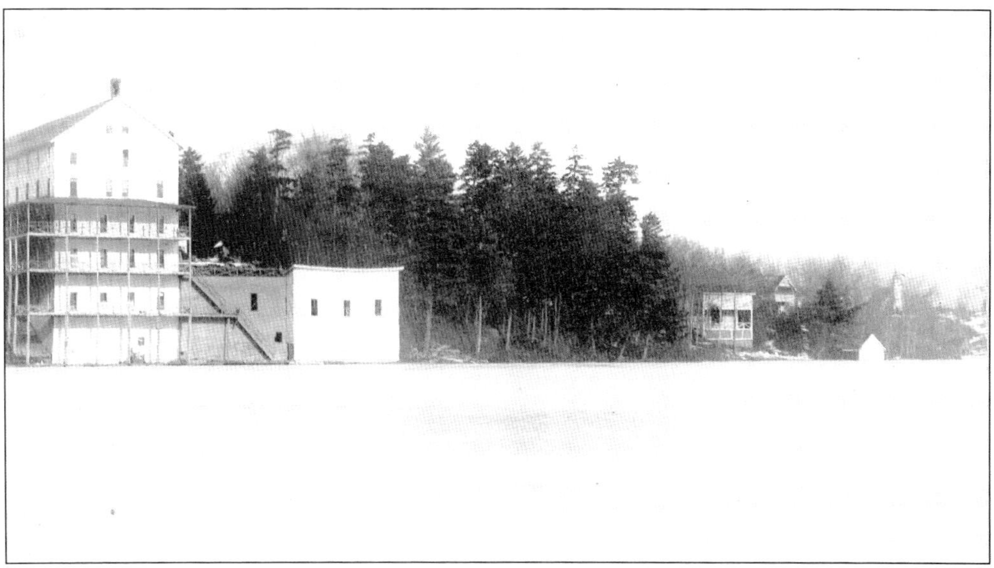

The view of the inn was taken on the ice in the dead of winter around 1907. Just In Villa cottage can be seen along the shoreline, as well as the church steeple along what is now Youngs Road.

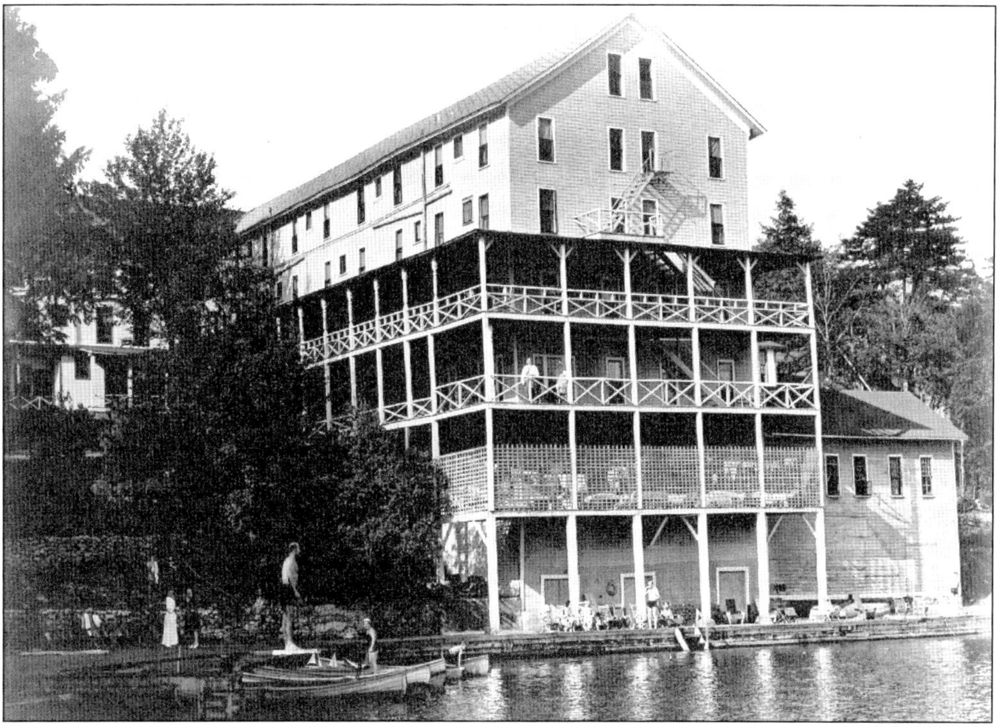

Pictured around 1920 is the floating dock with its diving board that was located in front of the Star Lake Inn. Employees were restricted from using the bathing area in front of the inn and would go to the public beach area, which was located behind Foley's Star Lake Hotel.

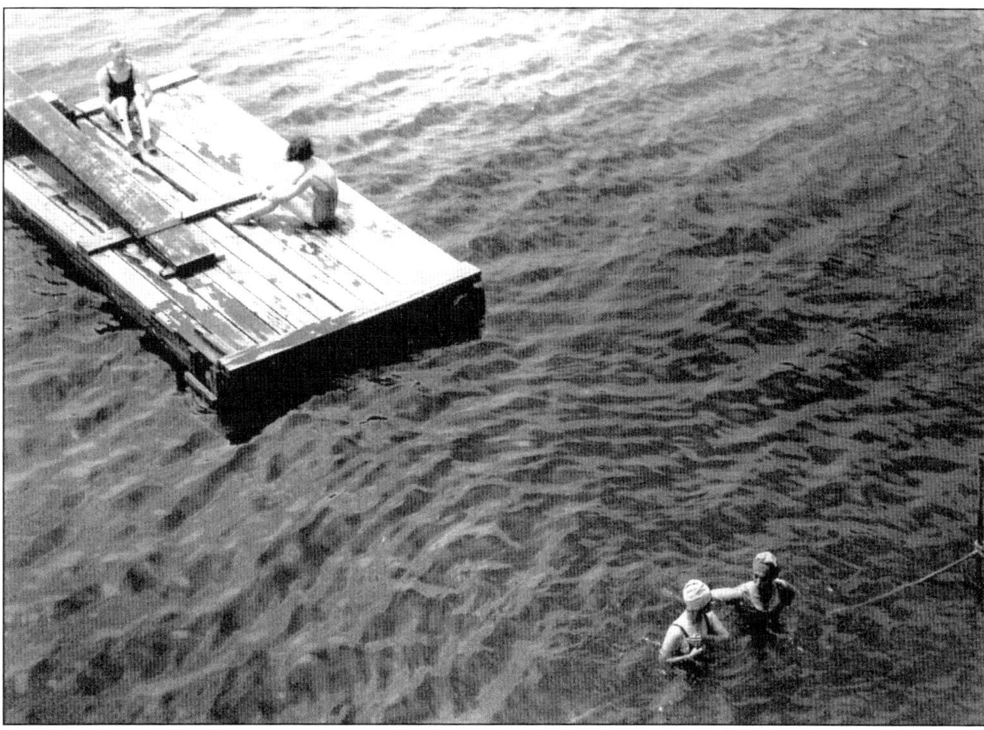

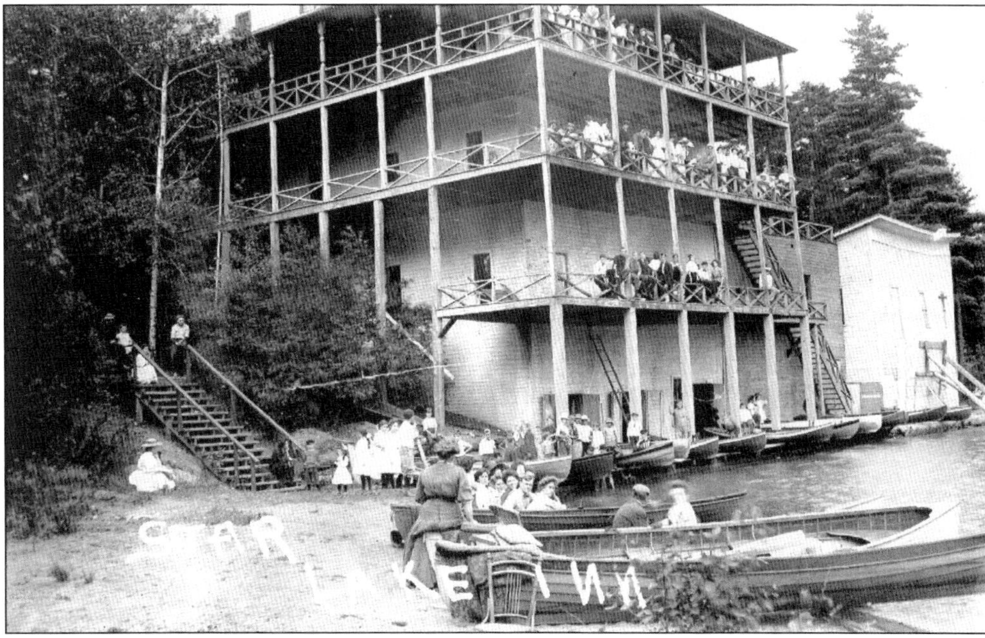

The Star Lake Inn also ran a small boat livery service for its patrons. Boats included St. Lawrence skiffs, rowboats, and canoes that could be rented by the day for 50¢ or by the week for $3. There were at least 10 skiffs, plus a few canoes, available for rent by guests at all times.

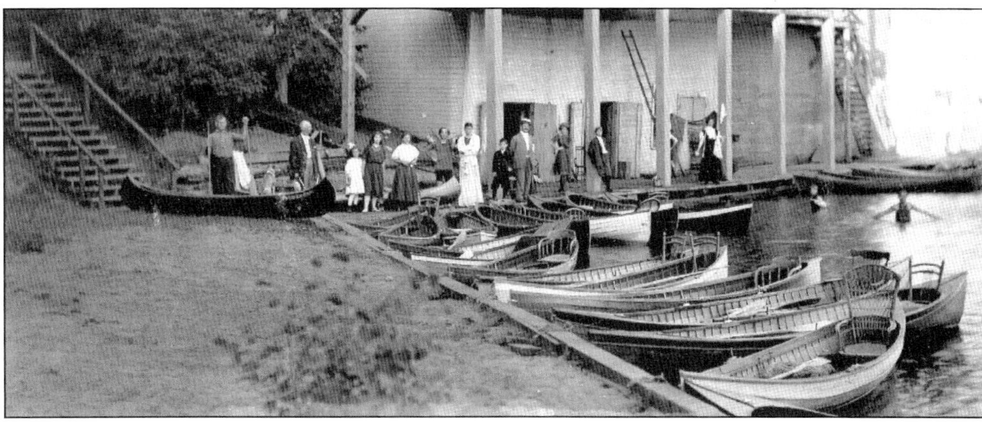

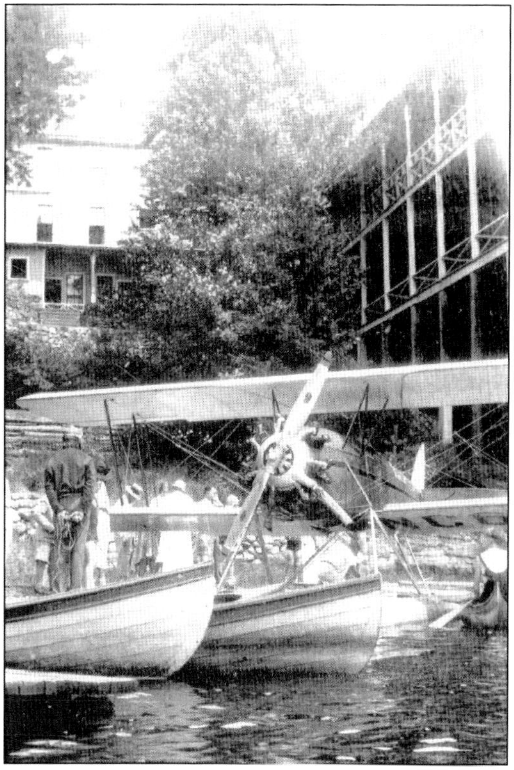

It was always an event when a seaplane landed at Star Lake. This *c.* 1930 photograph shows the pilot and plane docked in front of the Star Lake Inn. In the early days, seaplanes were sometimes seen docked at the Scott-Brace estate. Until recently, Feets Shelton could be seen landing his seaplane on the west side of the lake and docking it in front of his Shelton's Point cottage.

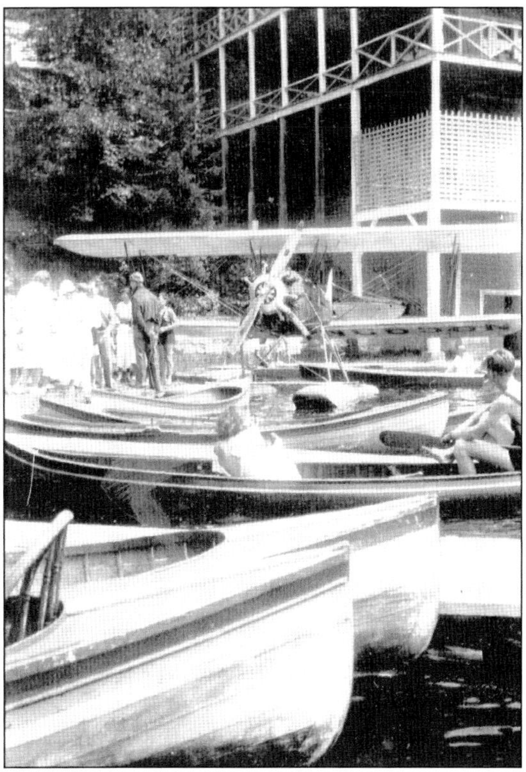

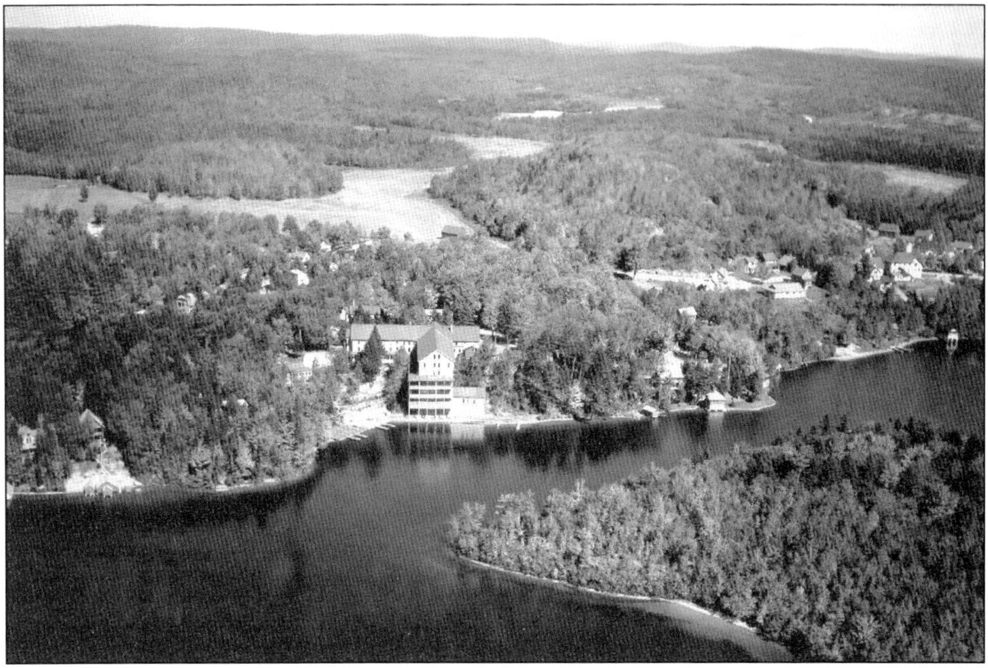

The Star Lake Inn was an enormous all-wooden structure standing seven stories tall. The second-floor balcony was later enclosed with lattice and used as a summer sleeping porch for the female employees.

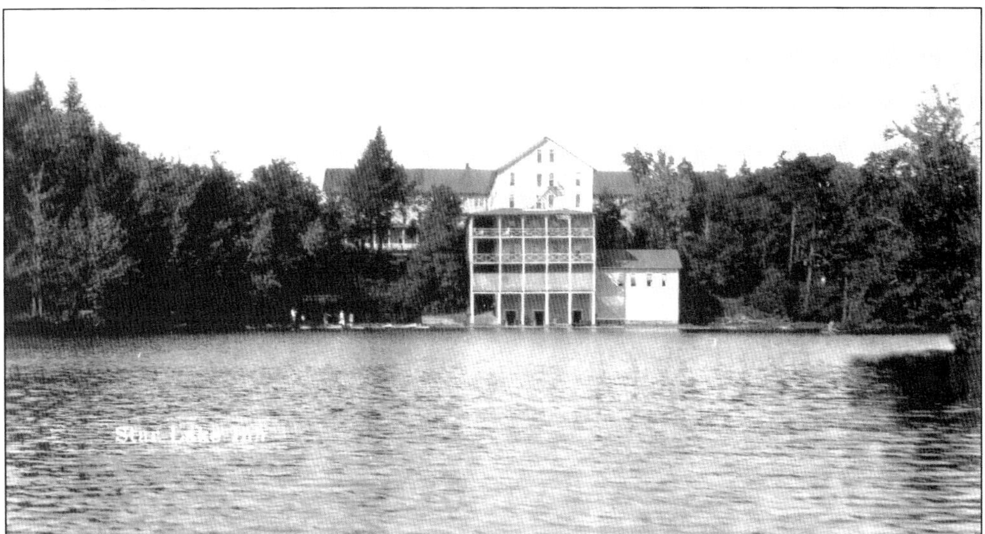

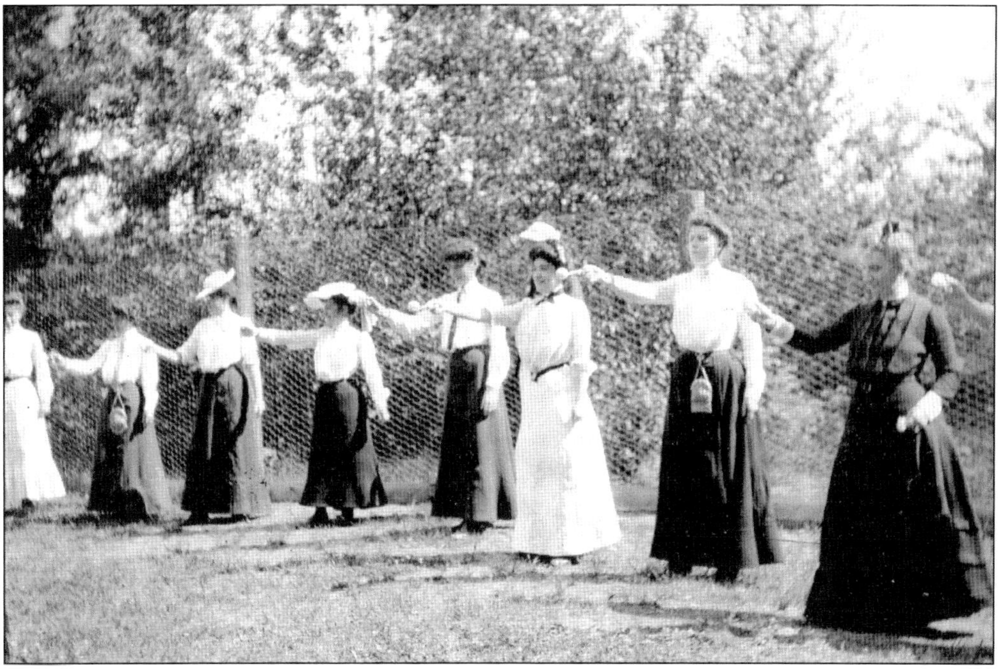

The annual Field Day events are under way at the Star Lake Inn around 1905. Women can be seen in the tennis court area, participating in an egg-on-a-spoon race. Canoe races, potato sack relays, log rolling, diving contests, and canoe tilting were just some of the participation events held at the inn and around town during this annual August weekend celebration.

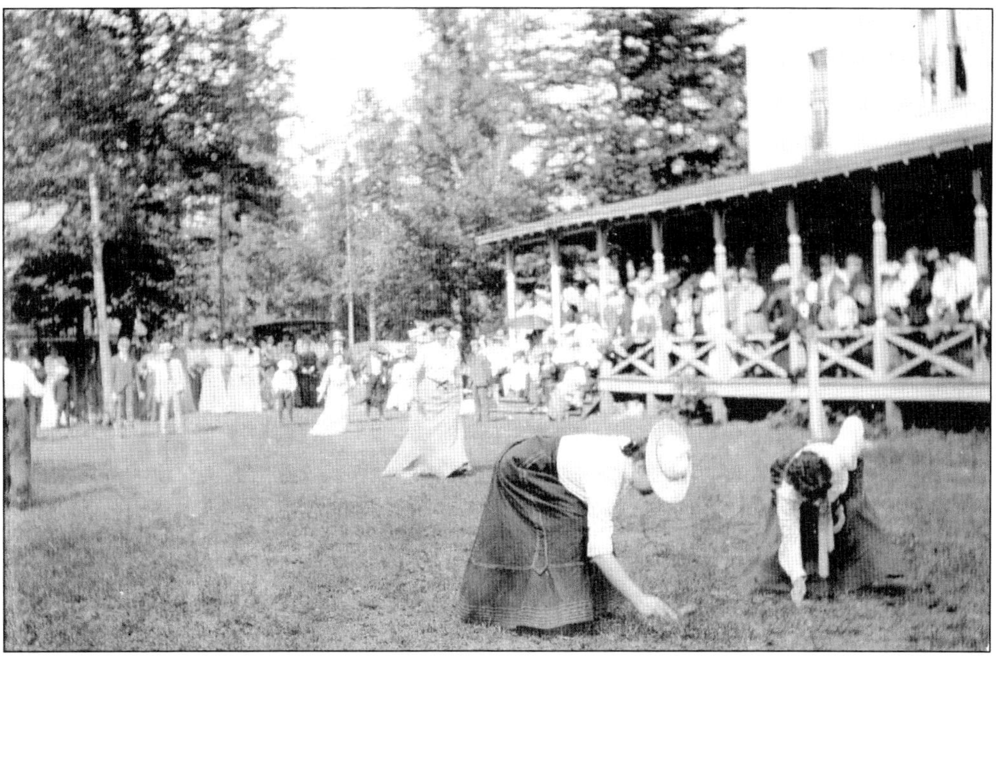

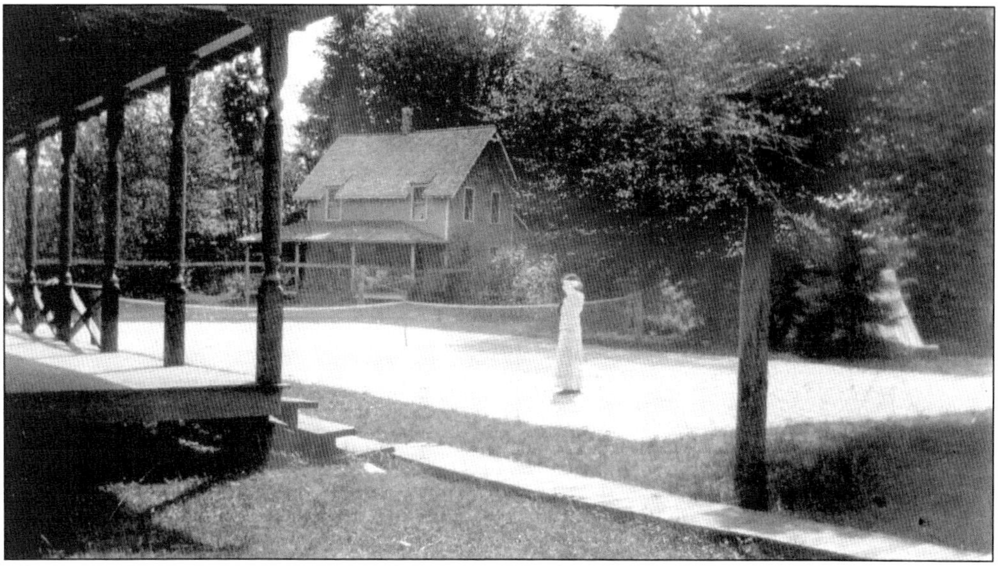

The Star Lake Inn's tennis court was located just to the west of the inn. It started out as a grass court and then was upgraded to a clay court. It is now an asphalt parking lot for the Homestead, Courtside, and Lakeview satellite cottages.

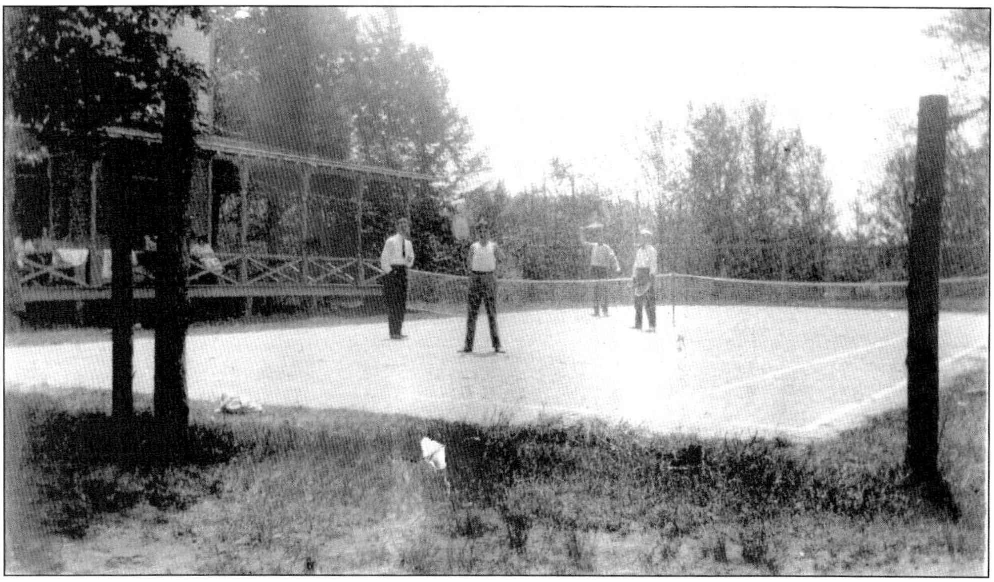

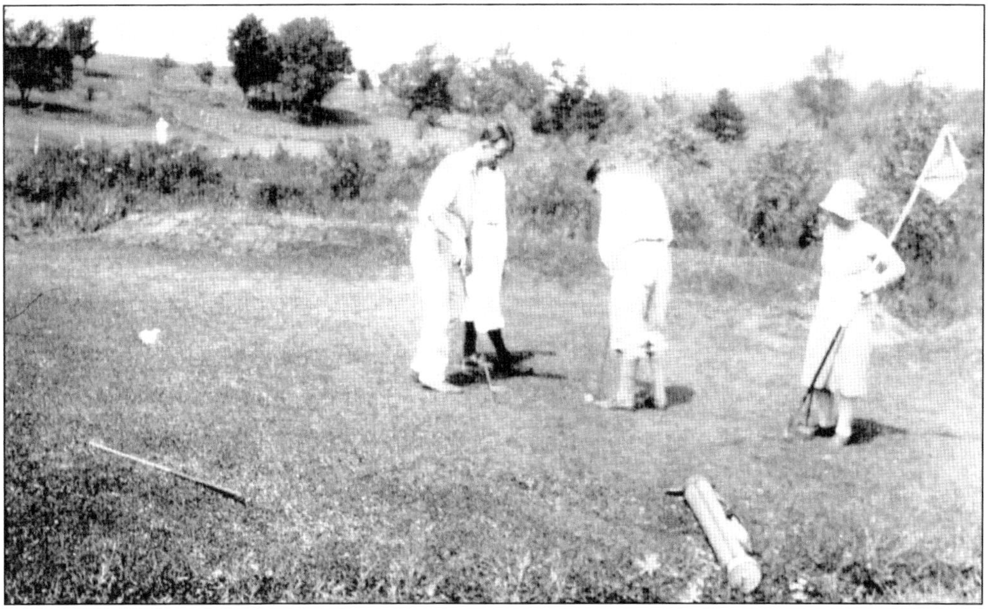

As the popularity of lawn croquet declined as a summer activity at the Star Lake Inn, interest in golf began to explode. Around 1920, inn proprietor Charles Sayles began construction of the Star Lake Inn golf course. Originally constructed as a five-hole course, it was eventually expanded to the present-day nine-hole course, and a pro shop was built. Caddies were paid 25¢ for a round of nine holes.

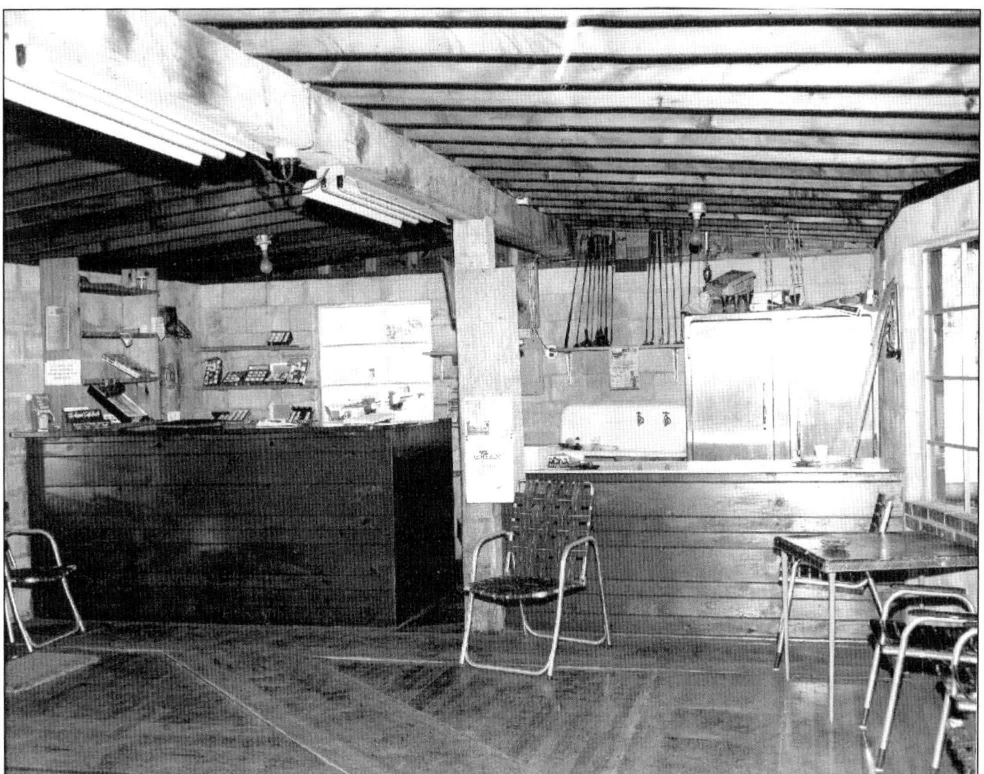

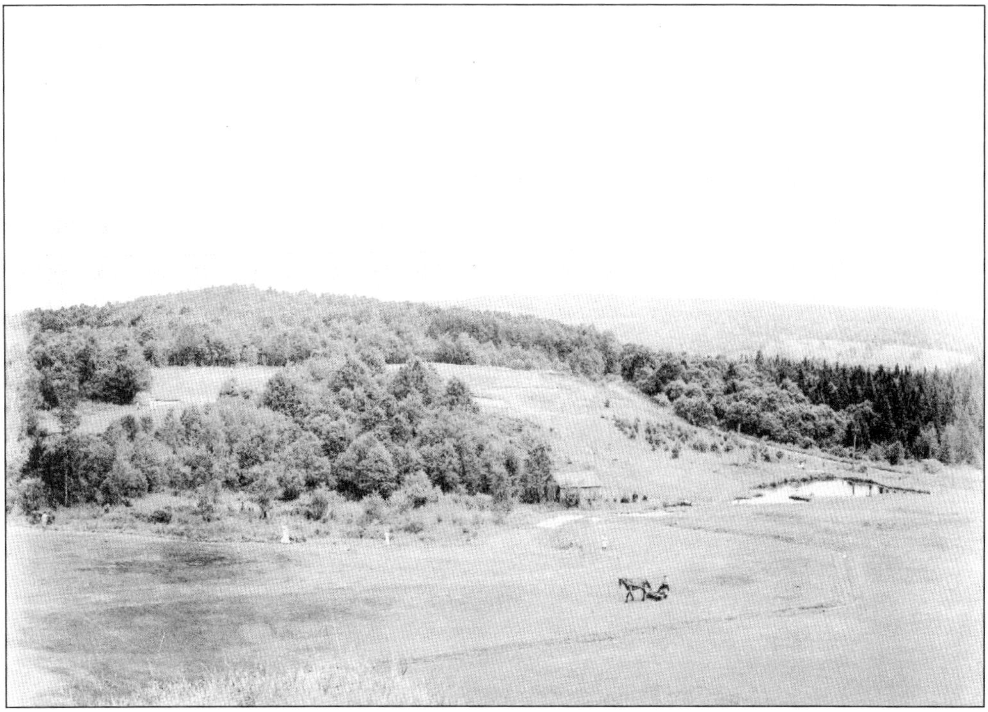

This *c.* 1920 photograph shows Dan Dellapent mowing the Star Lake Inn golf course with a horse and a tow-behind grass cutter.

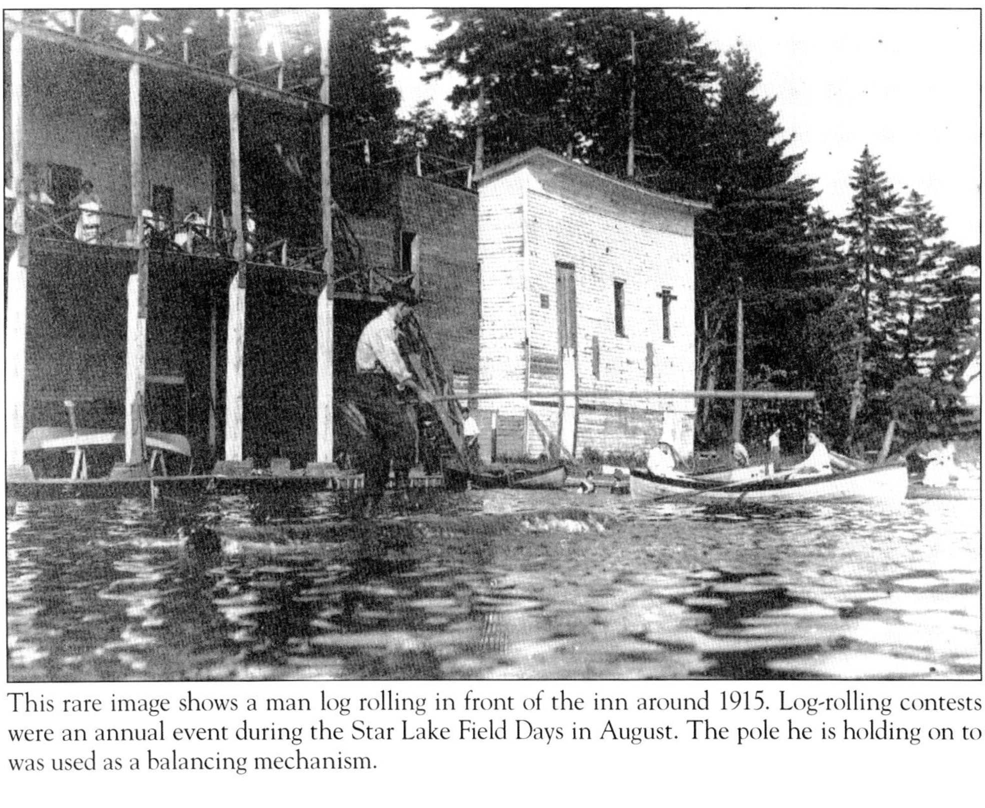

This rare image shows a man log rolling in front of the inn around 1915. Log-rolling contests were an annual event during the Star Lake Field Days in August. The pole he is holding on to was used as a balancing mechanism.

Four

Star Lake Cottages

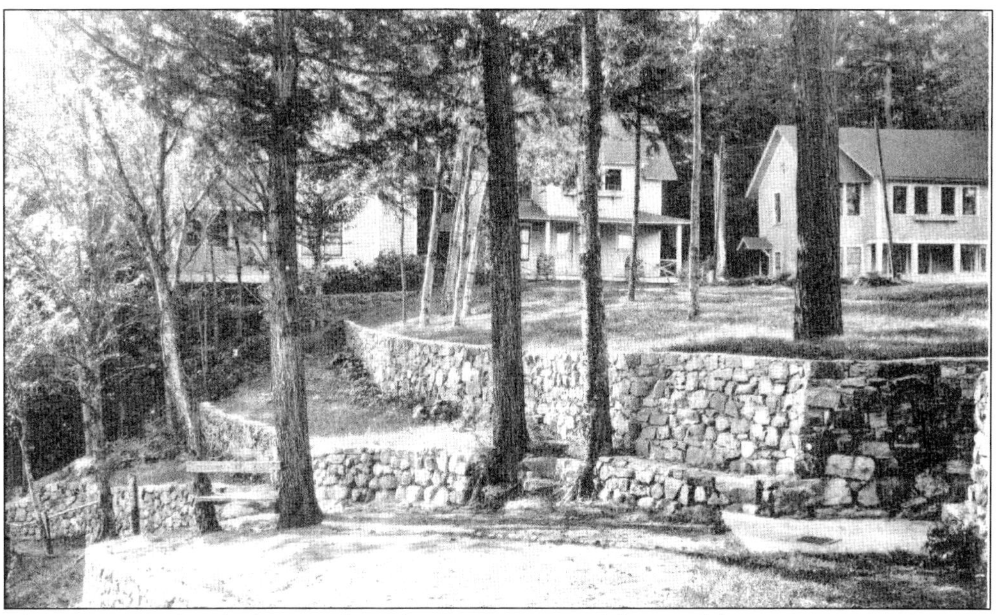

This view was taken looking up from the stone terraces of the Star lake Inn property. The Lake View, Homestead, and Courtside cottages can be seen.

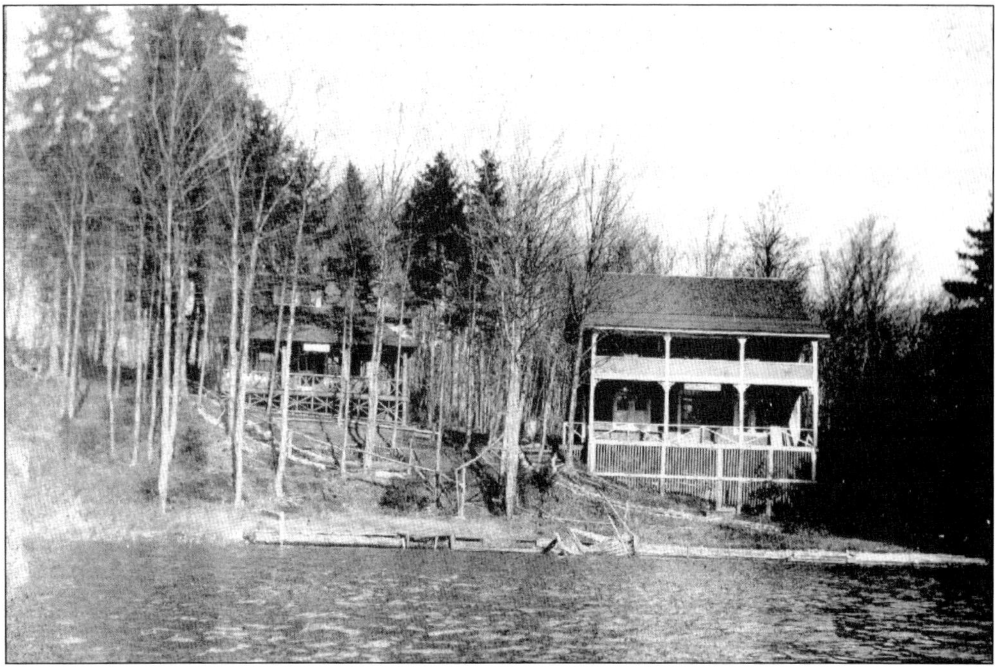

This *c.* 1907 view shows the Bally Bec cottage and the Just In Villa. Bally Bec was later purchased by the Star Lake Inn and renamed Lake Breeze. The Just In Villa cottage was later purchased by the Sayles family and renamed Lakeside

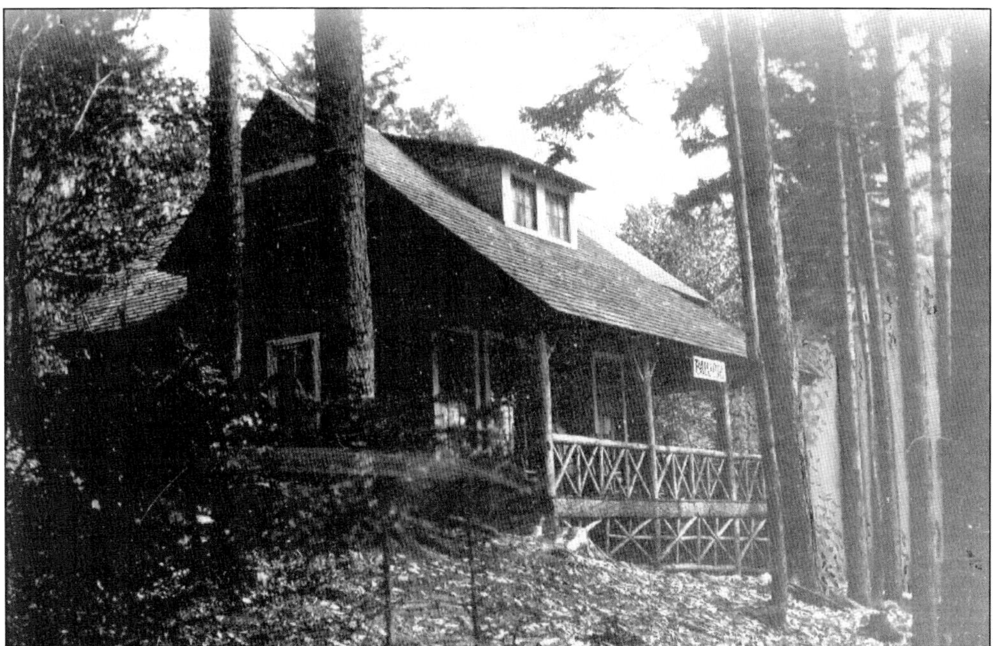

The Bally Bec cottage was one of the earlier cottages built on Star Lake. It is located along the north shore on the way toward Post Office Bay. It was later purchased by the Star Lake Inn, remodeled, renamed Lake Breeze, and rented for many years as a housekeeping cottage.

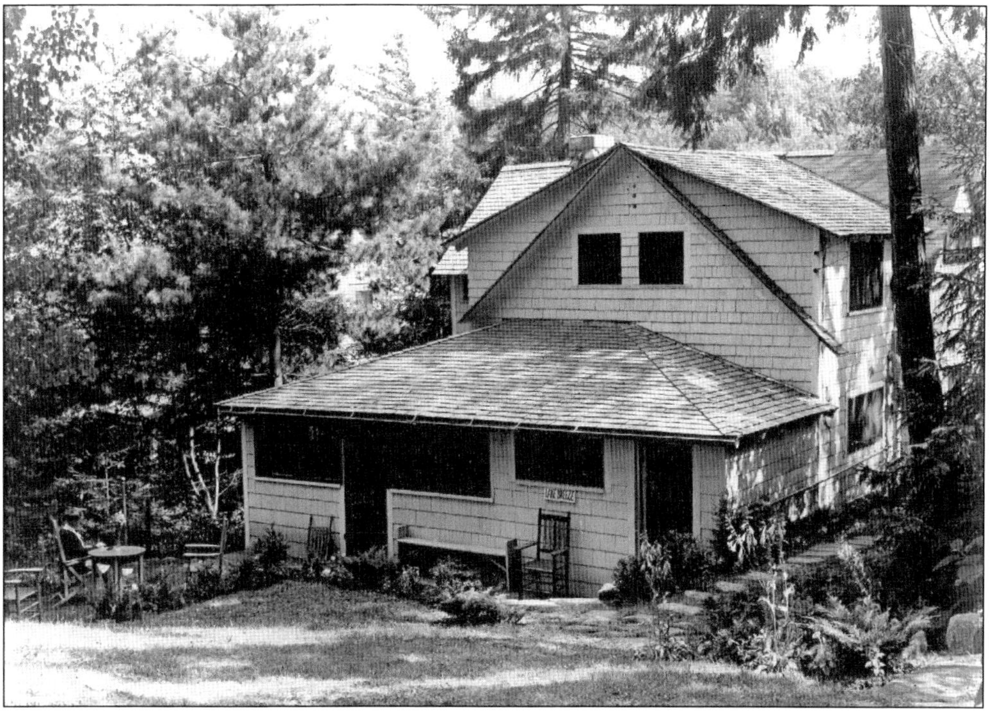

The Lake Breeze cottage, formerly Bally Bec, is located directly east of the Hillside cottage. Originally owned by Joe Burns, it was later purchased by the inn and used as a rental cottage.

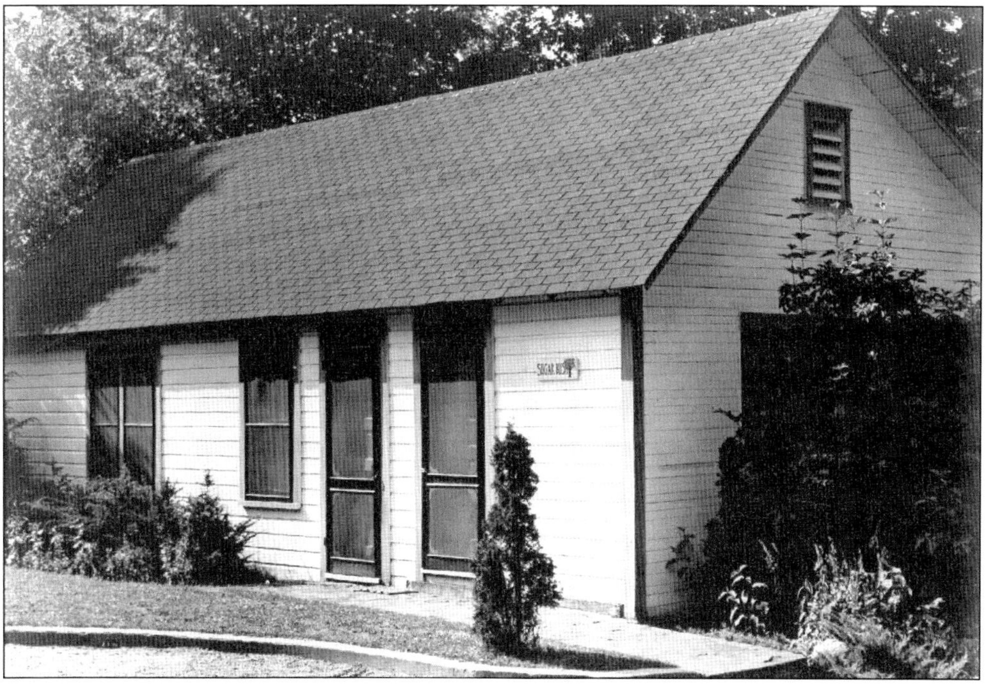

The three-room cottage named Sugar Bush was located directly behind the Loft cottage. It was built by the inn as a satellite rental cottage. It has recently been remodeled into a much larger two-story summer home.

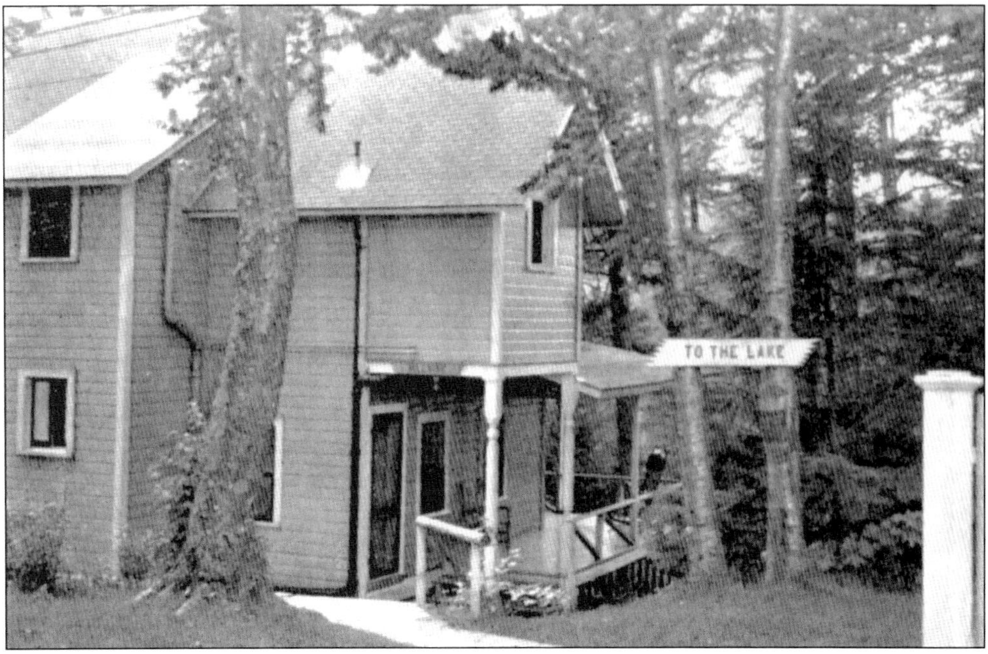

The Hillside cottage was located directly to the east of the inn. Tracing back old deeds to this property, the famous boat maker J. H. Rushton once had his summer camp located here.

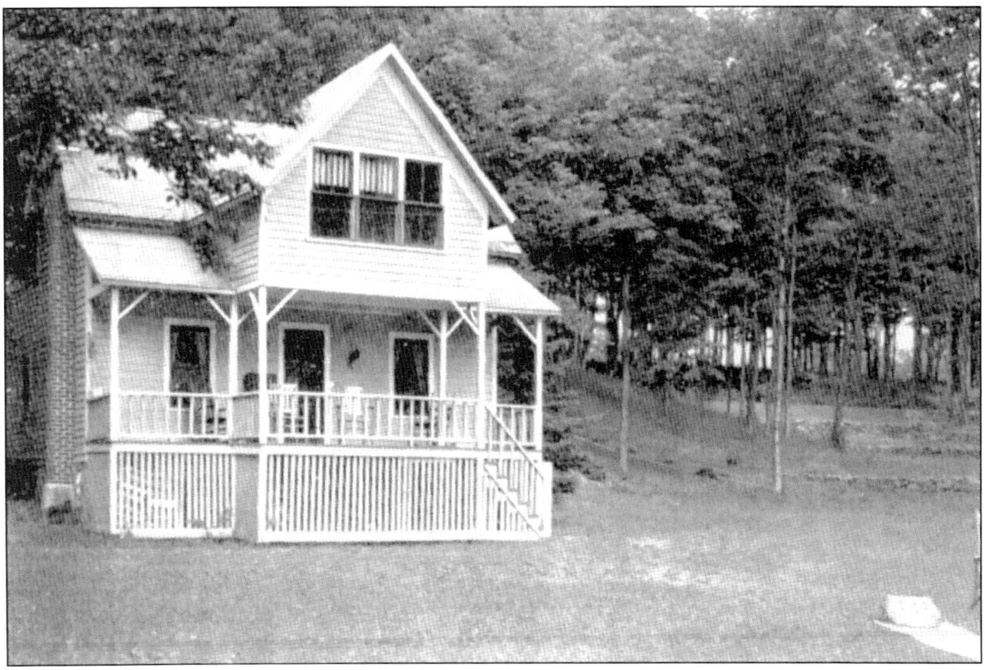

The Sunset cottage looks out onto Snug Harbor and the sandbar area. It was a full-housekeeping cottage for the inn, complete with a maid's room. At one time there was a boathouse, which was shared with the Tree Top cottage.

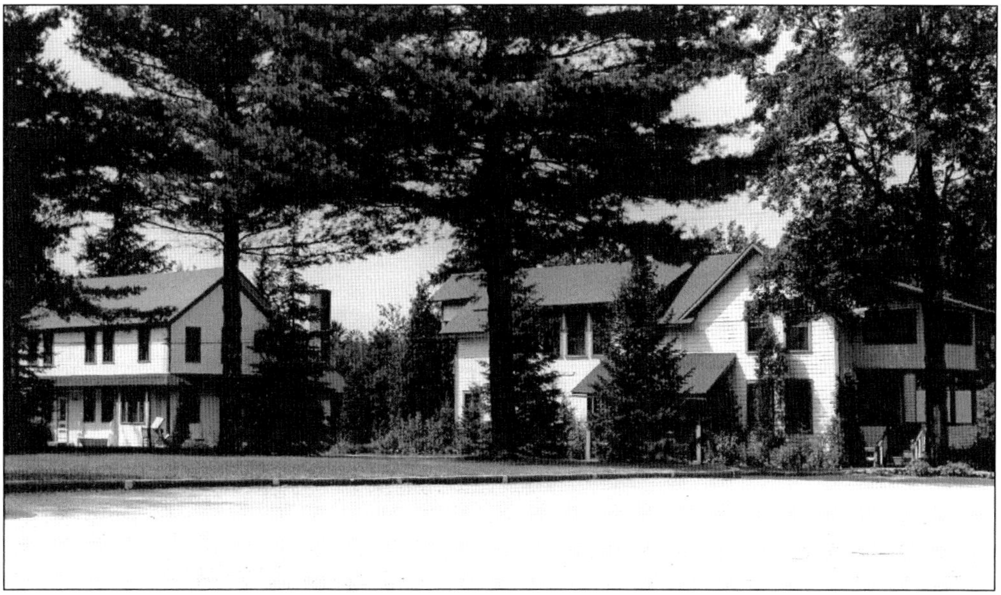

The Sudside cottage was the middle satellite cottage, located between the Aerie and the Loft. In back of this cottage was located the men's bunkhouse and the inn's laundry building. The inn supplied its own steam heat to not only the main inn but also the individual satellite cottages.

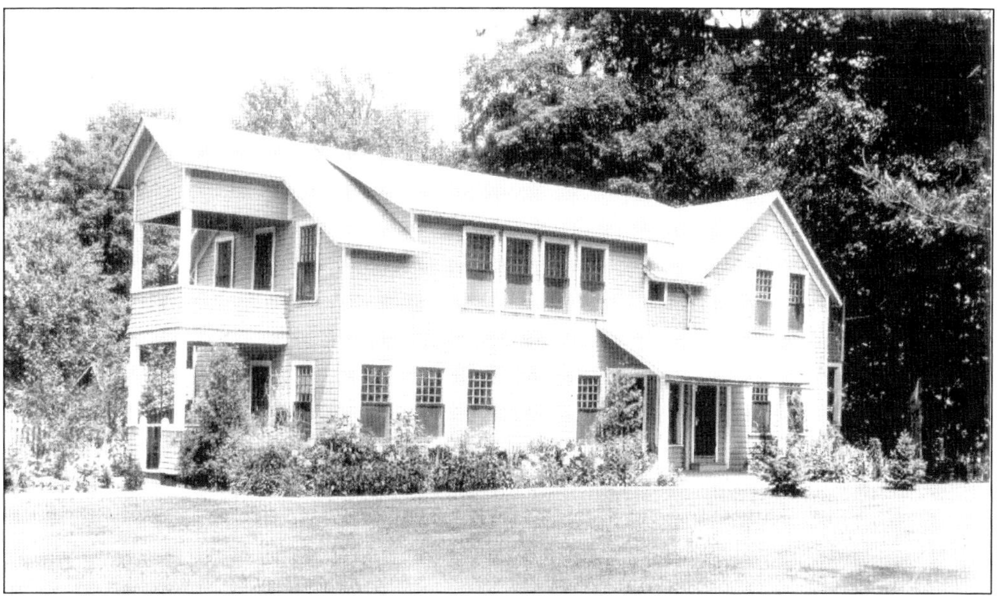

The Loft, pictured around 1920, was the largest of the inn's satellite cottages, with eight rental rooms. The well-maintained gardens and goldfish pond were located just to the left of the cottage. Before the Loft was built, the inn's barn and horse stables were located here. After the Loft was built, the stables for the inn's carriage horses were located in the basement.

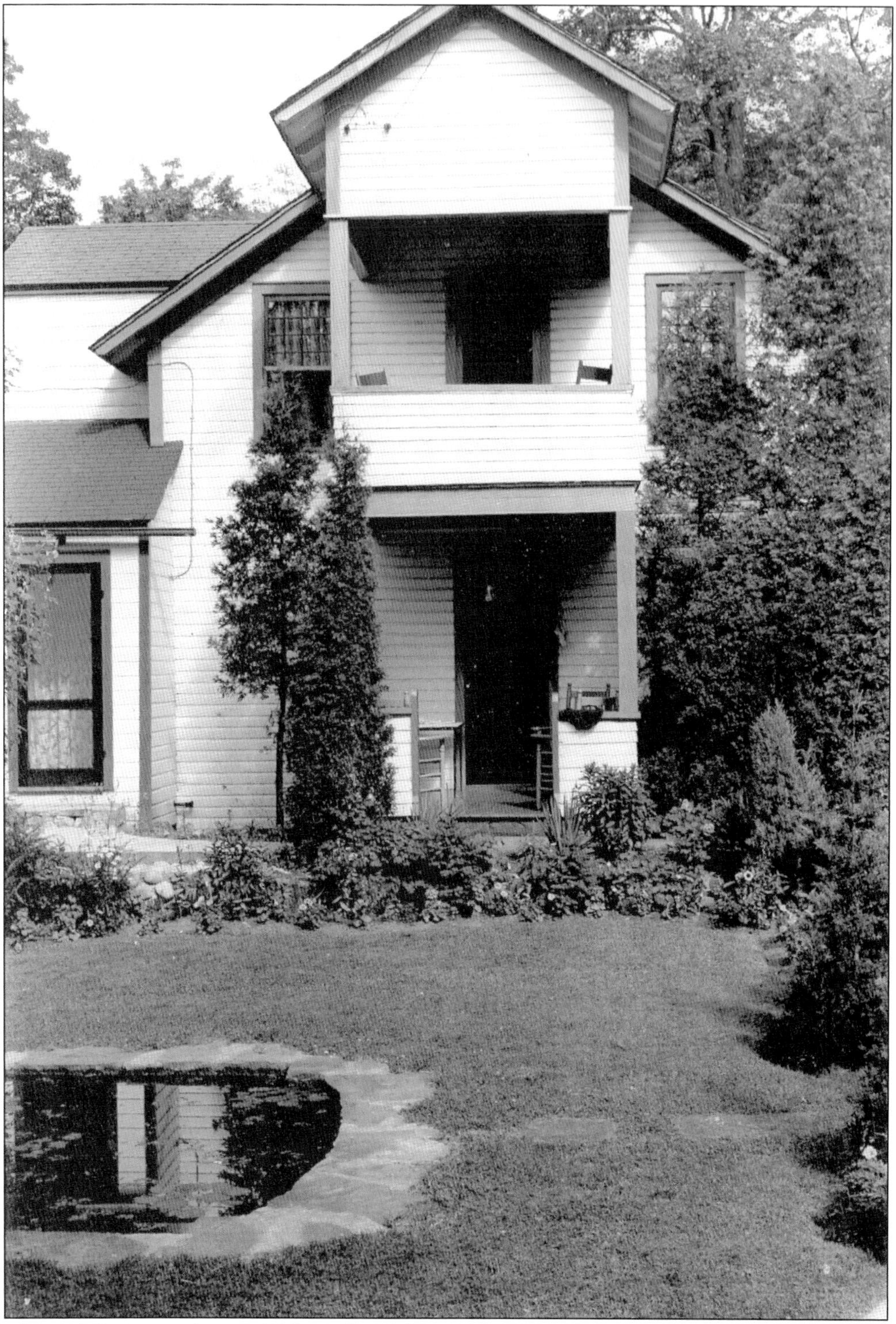

The inn's flower gardens and fishpond were located between the Loft and Sudside cottages.

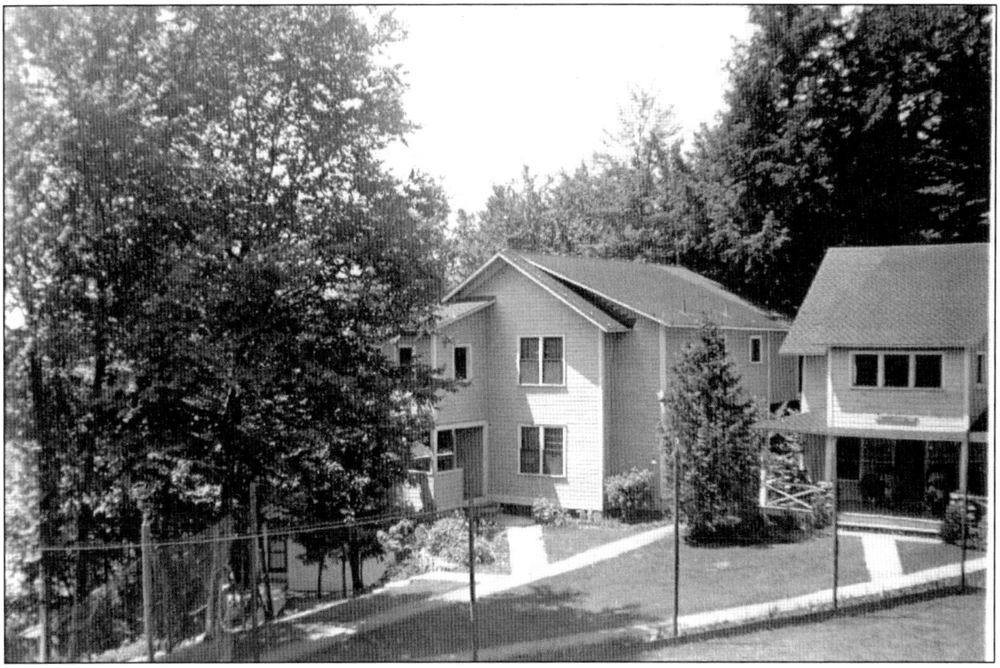

The Lakeview, seen on the left, was a four-bedroom satellite cottage built by the inn for rental purposes. It also had two sleeping porches and was located between the Homestead and Bay View cottages. Lakeview was later destroyed by a windstorm.

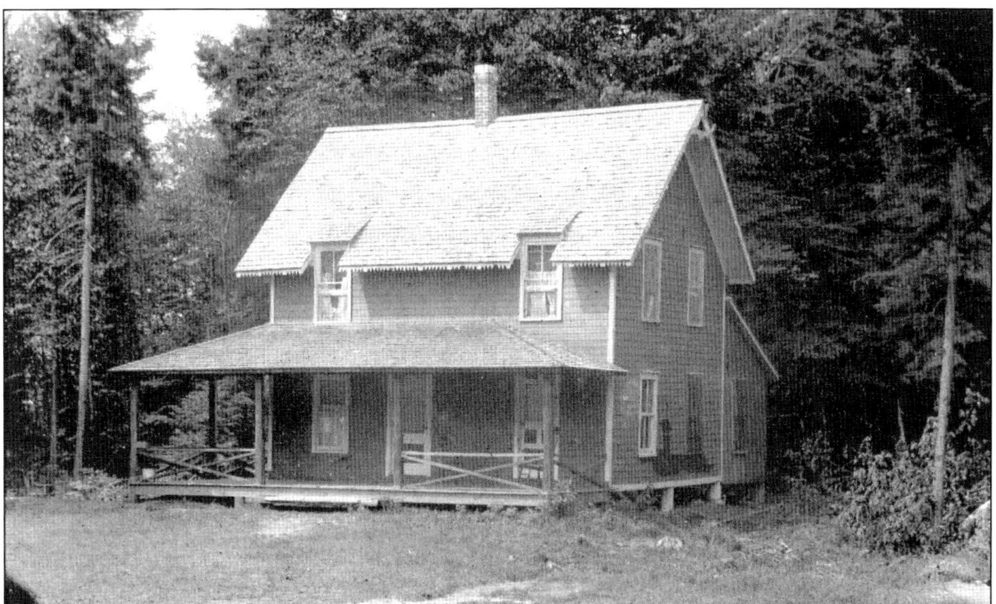

Shown here is the four-bedroom satellite cottage known as Homestead, before it was remodeled. Homestead was one of the early cottages built by the inn. It was located between the Courtside and Lakeview cottages. The chalk outline of the grass tennis court can be seen in this photograph.

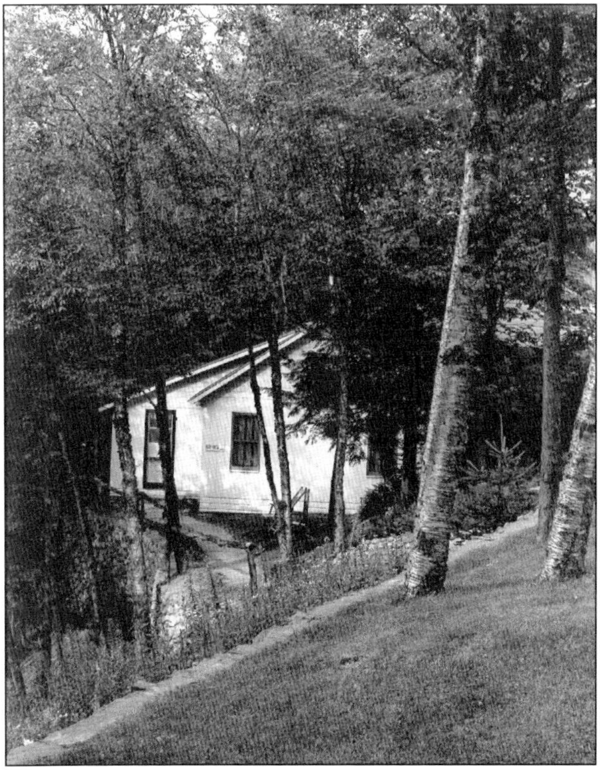

The Bay View cottage was a small two-bedroom rental cottage built by the Star Lake Inn. It was located below the Lakeview cottage, to the west of the inn.

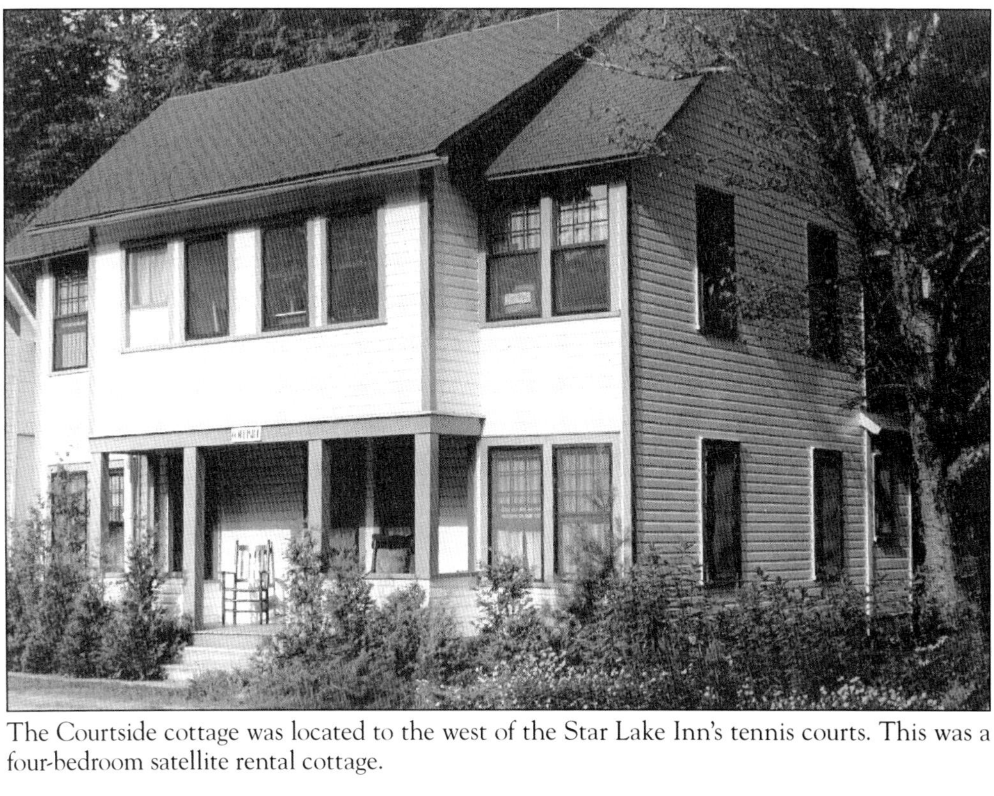

The Courtside cottage was located to the west of the Star Lake Inn's tennis courts. This was a four-bedroom satellite rental cottage.

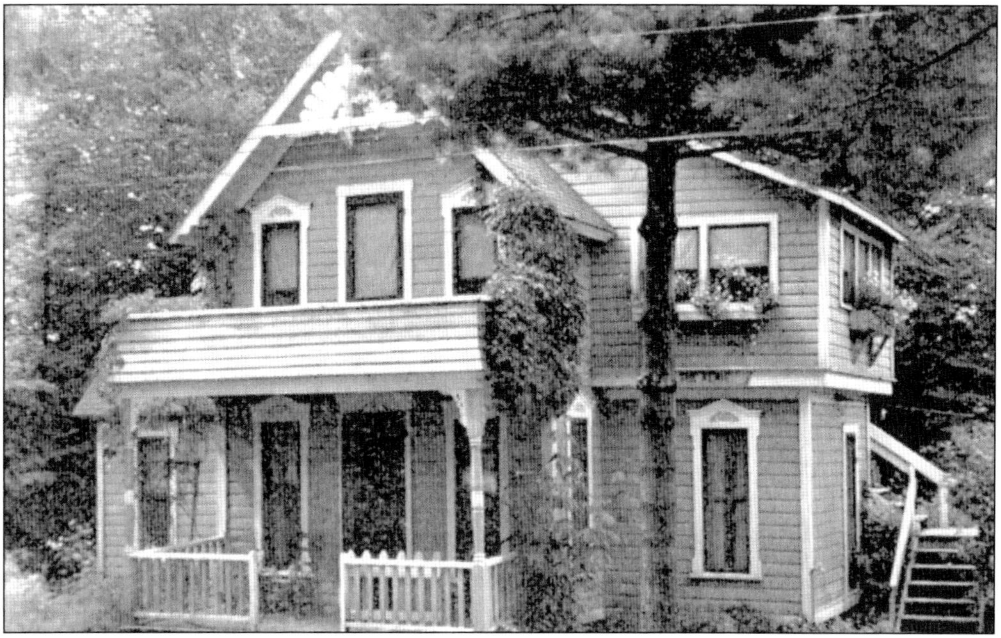

The Victorian four-bedroom cottage named Aerie, built by the Sisson family, was later purchased by the inn and used for rentals. The cottage was later enlarged and converted to a year-round residence.

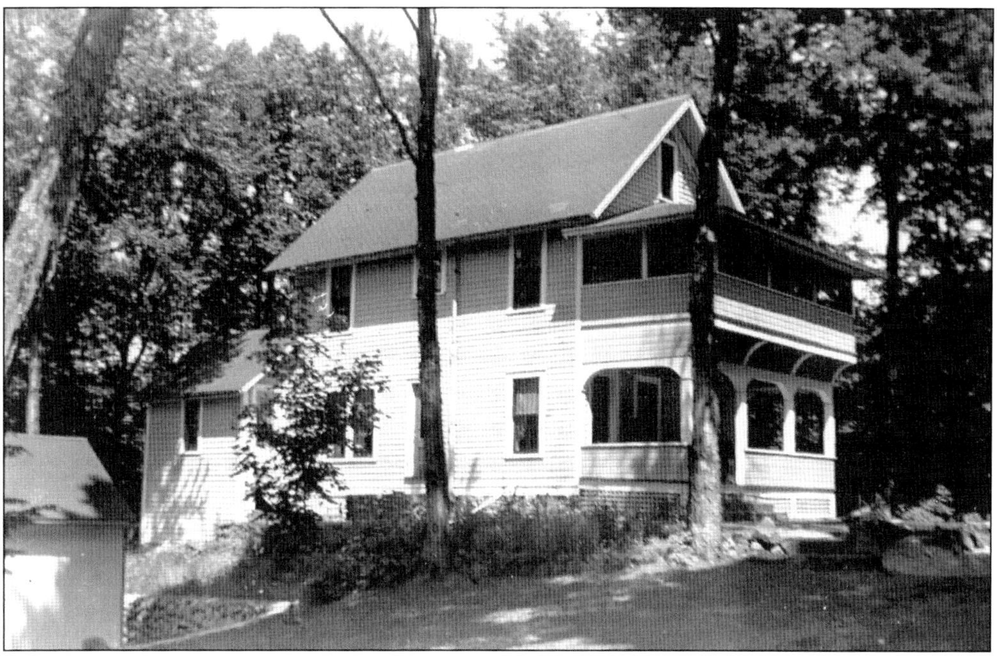

The Tree Top cottage was the largest of the housekeeping satellite cottages available for rent at the inn. It was built by the Star Lake Inn in the 1920s. The first floor had a living room, dining room, kitchen, pantry, and maid's bedroom. The upstairs had a sleeping porch, three large sleeping rooms, and a bathroom.

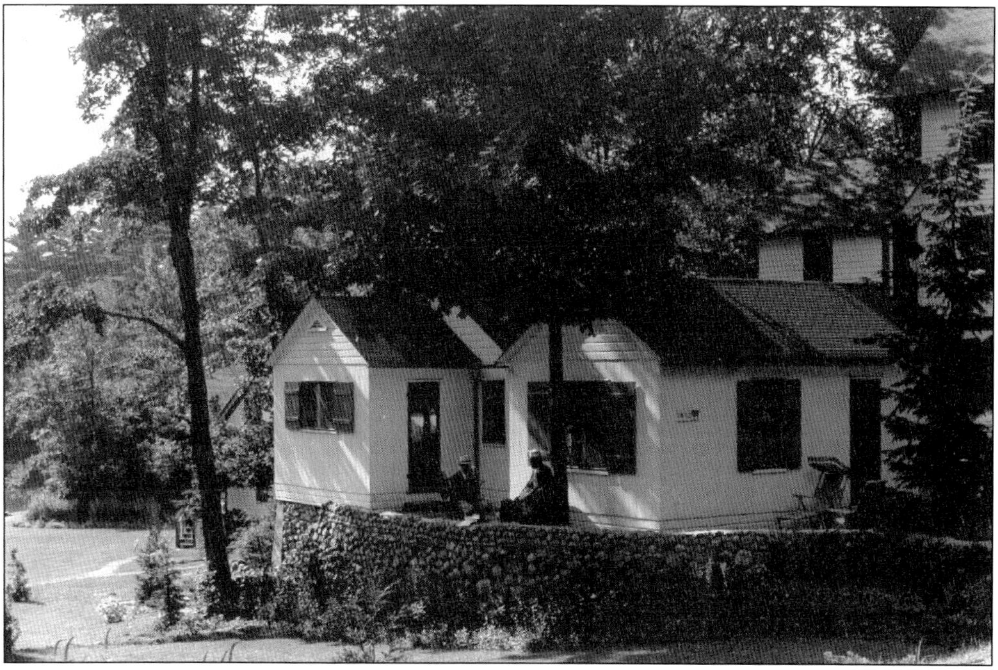

The Twin Trees cottage was built by the Star Lake Inn and was rented as three separate rental units, each with a bedroom and bathroom. A front porch and a kitchen were later added to the cottage. Inn proprietor Charles Sayles named the large terraced rock waterfall and pond in front of Twin Trees "Chipmunk Falls."

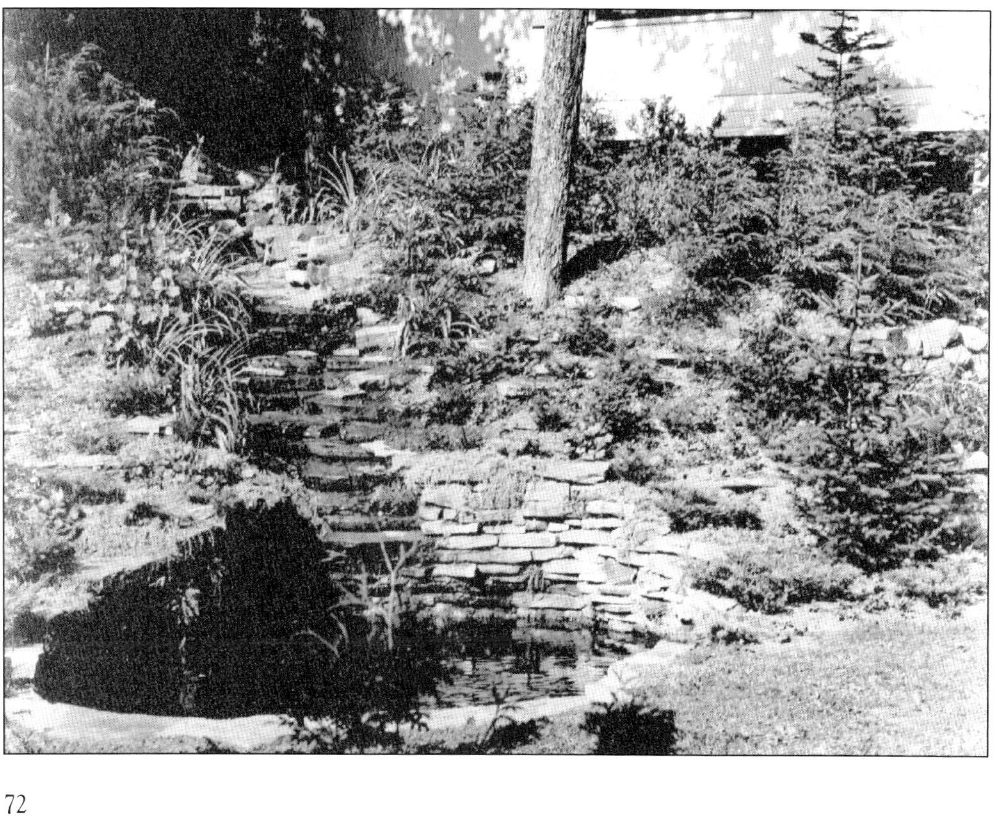

Five

CAMPS AND OTHER COTTAGES

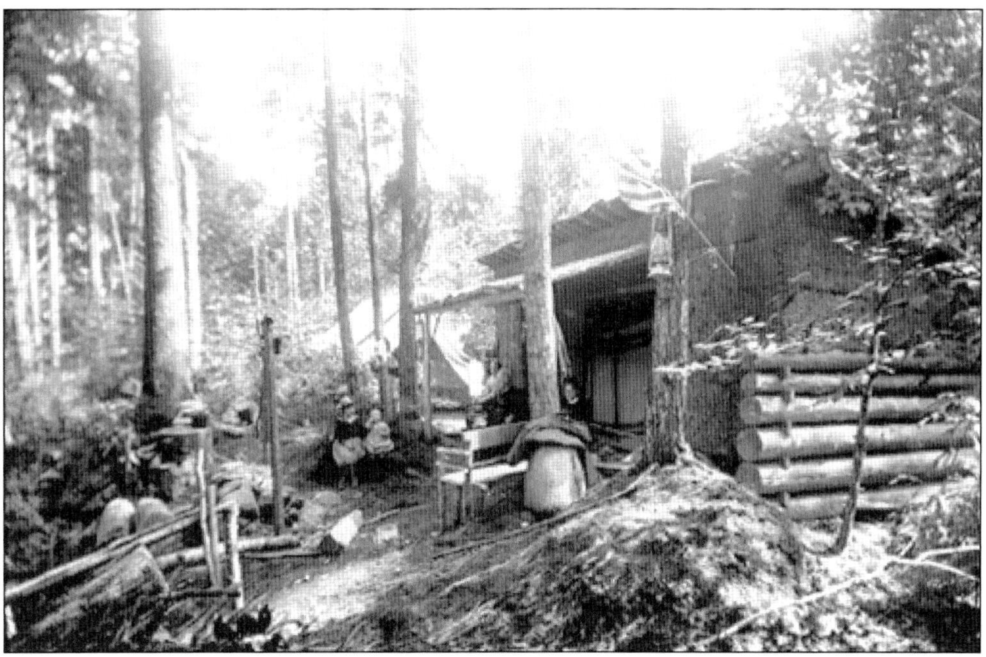

This view of Camp Pauline in Star Lake is dated 1899. Camp Pauline was owned by Mrs. W. L. Proctor of Ogdensburg. This Adirondack camp, as this type of structure was popularly called, was nothing more than an open-faced log lean-to, covered on the sides and roof with tree bark. The Proctor family originally owned much of the land around Swiss Point.

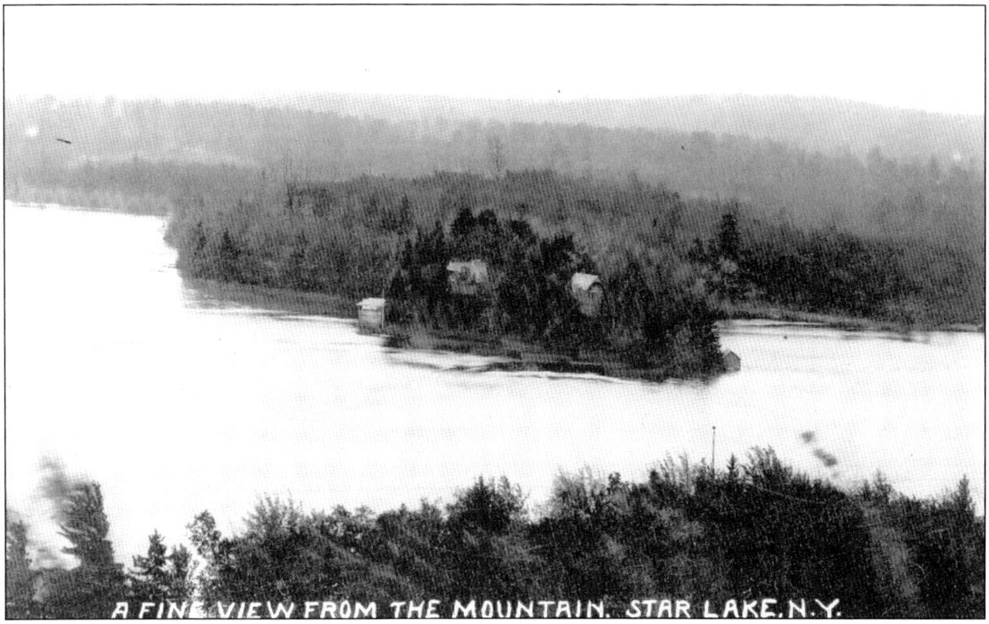

This c. 1910 photograph shows an unnamed point on Third Lake. The Loftus cottage, Minnie-Belle, and the Leiterman camp were located on this point.

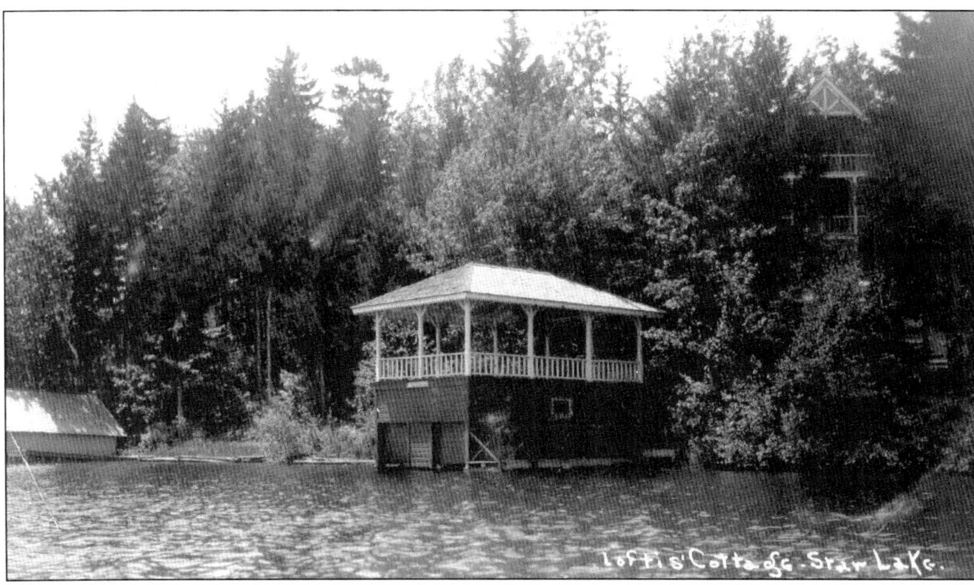

The original owner of this cottage and boathouse was Peter Loftus. The cottage is located on Third Lake.

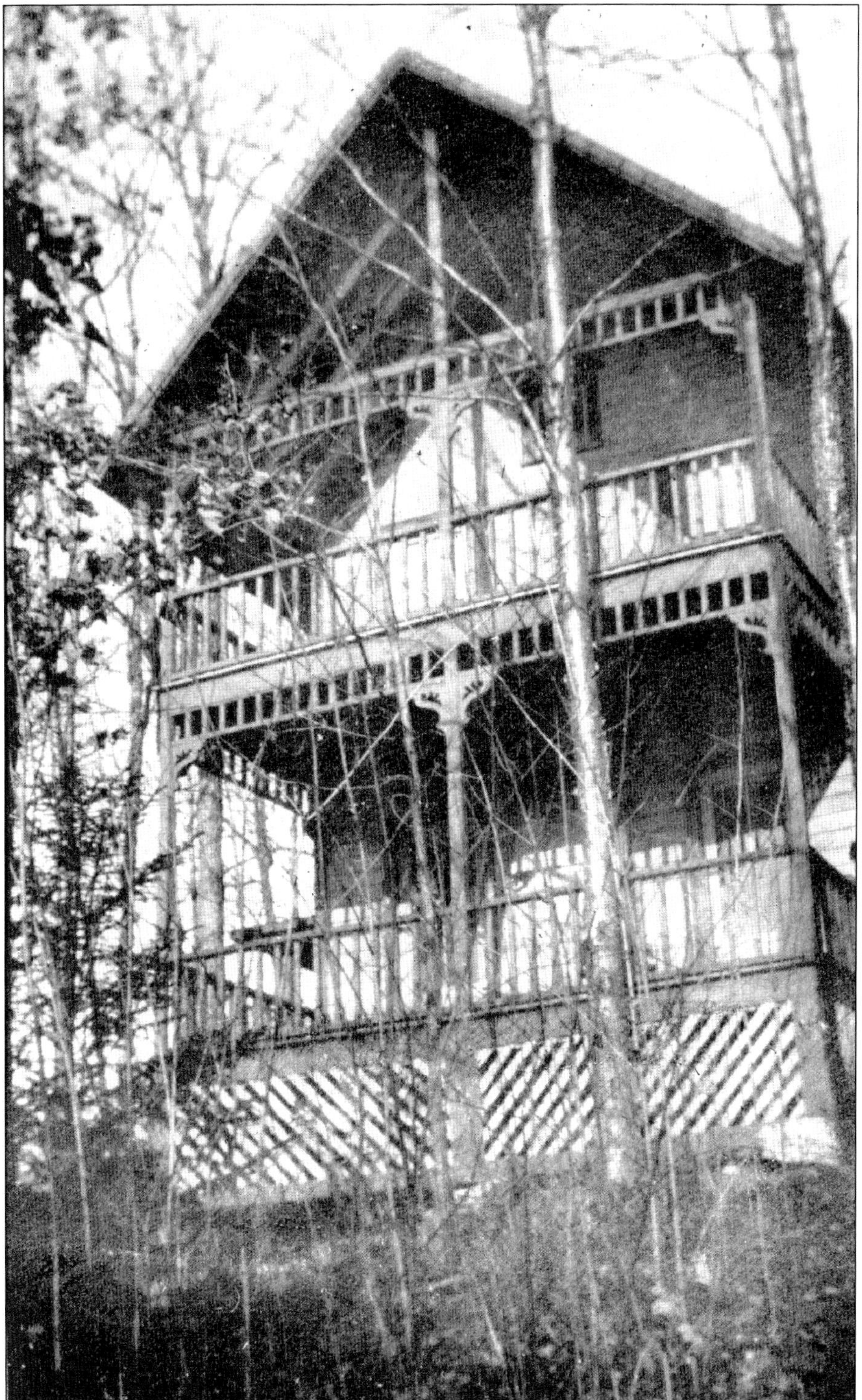

This photograph shows the Leonard Leiterman cottage around 1920. It was located on an unnamed point on Third Lake. The Leiterman family was from Clayton, New York.

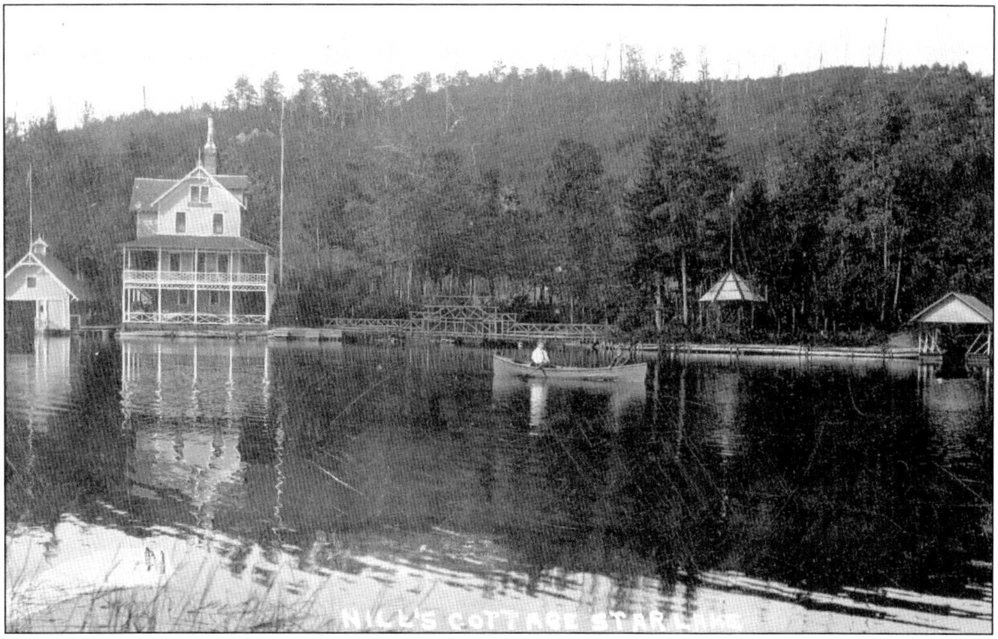

These *c.* 1908 views are of Germania Park and Cobblecrest, owned by John Nill of Watertown. In 1901, Nill founded the Star Lake Protective Association and was president of the organization for the first 15 years. Its primary goals were to protect and beautify the lake, as well as to regulate the lake's water level.

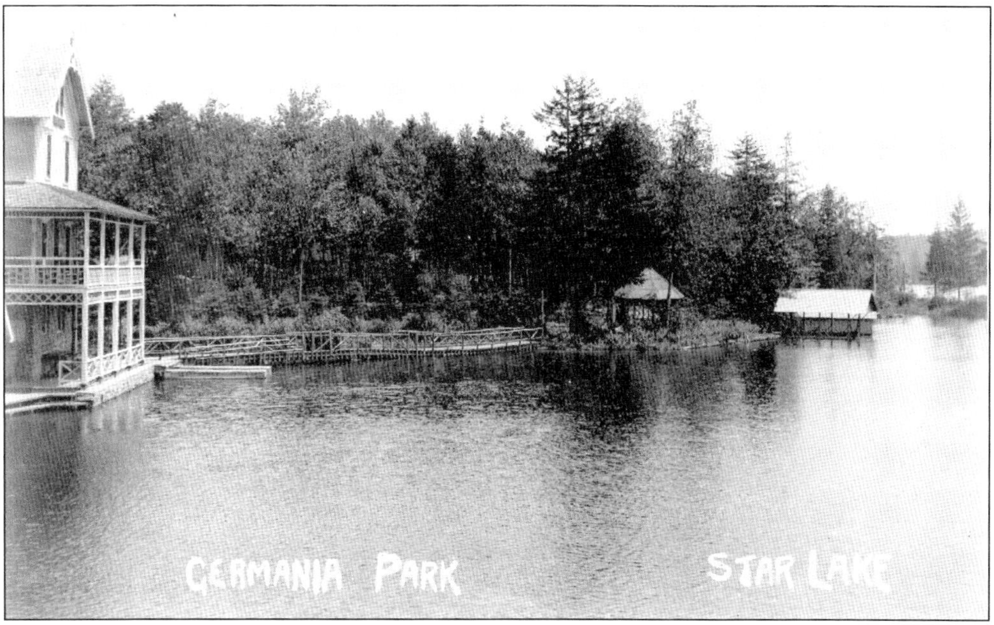

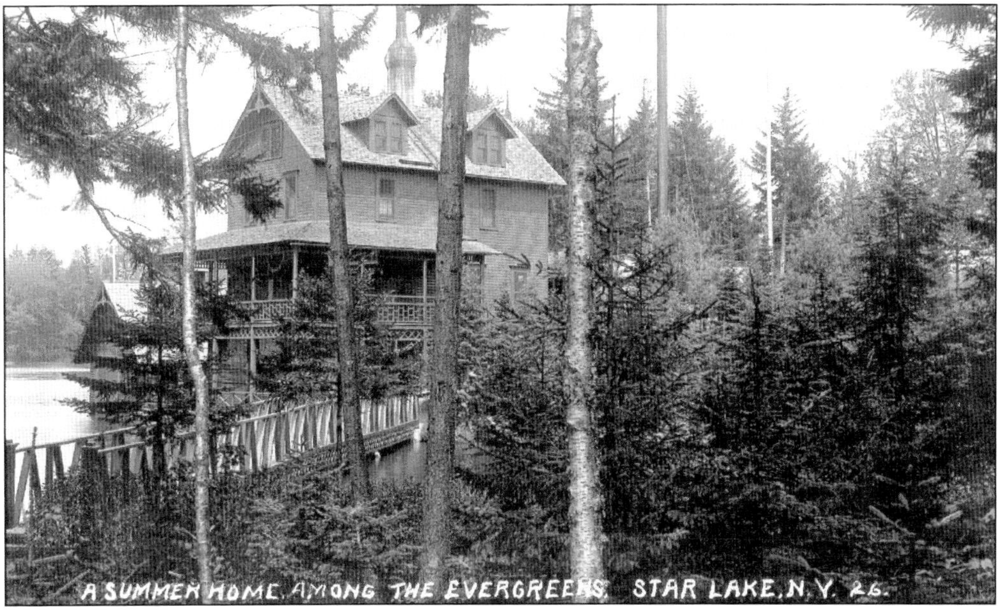

John Nill was co-owner of the Nill & Jess Company, which was a large wholesale baking and confectionery company located in Watertown. The unusually large chimney, seen in the early photographs of this cottage, was used to vent Nill's custom-made baking furnace located in the kitchen area.

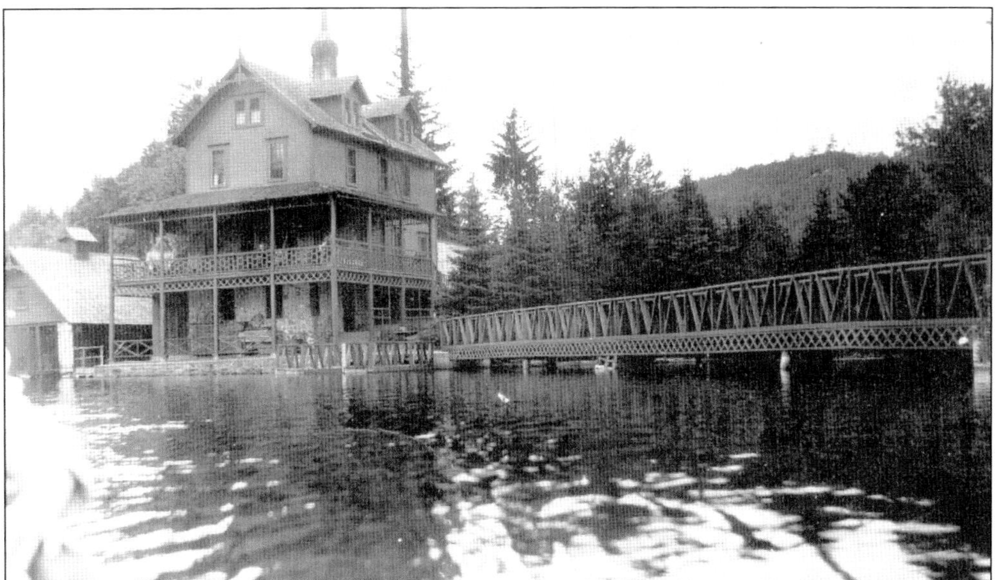

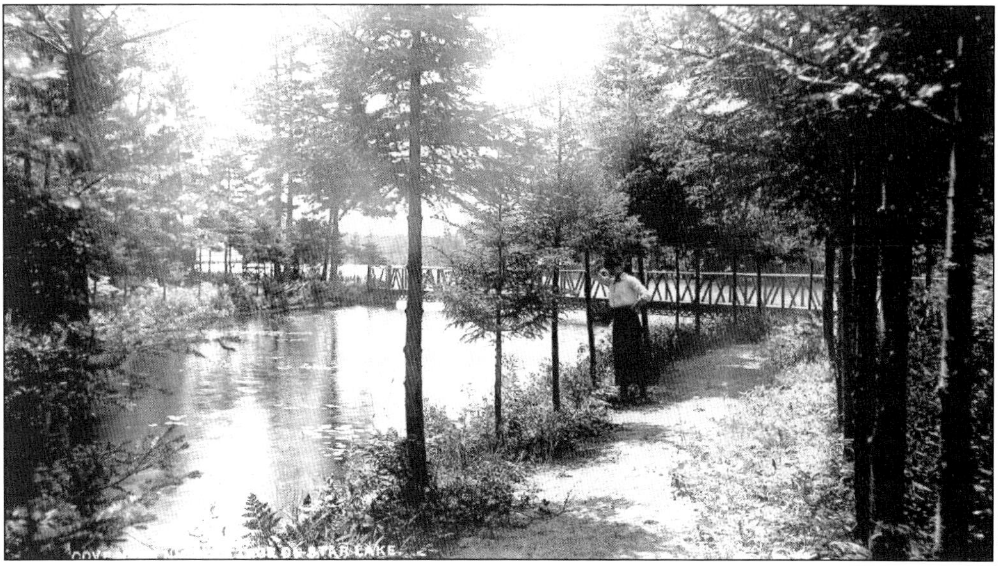

A woman poses for a photograph around 1912 near John Nill's summer cottage. The wood walkway bridge can be seen nearby.

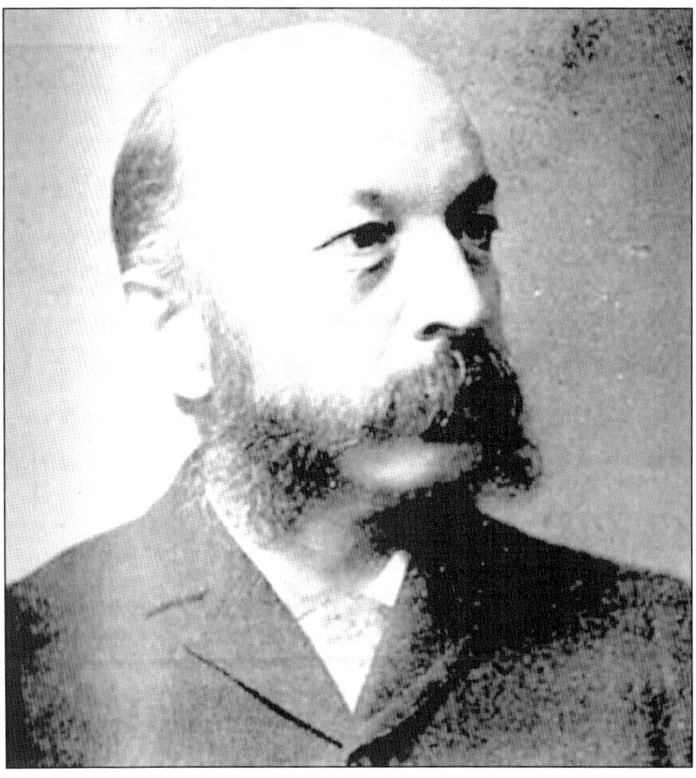

This c. 1905 portrait is of John Nill. Nill was widely known and highly respected as a summer resident of Star Lake. He built the Cobblecrest cottage and was the first president of the Star Lake Protective Association.

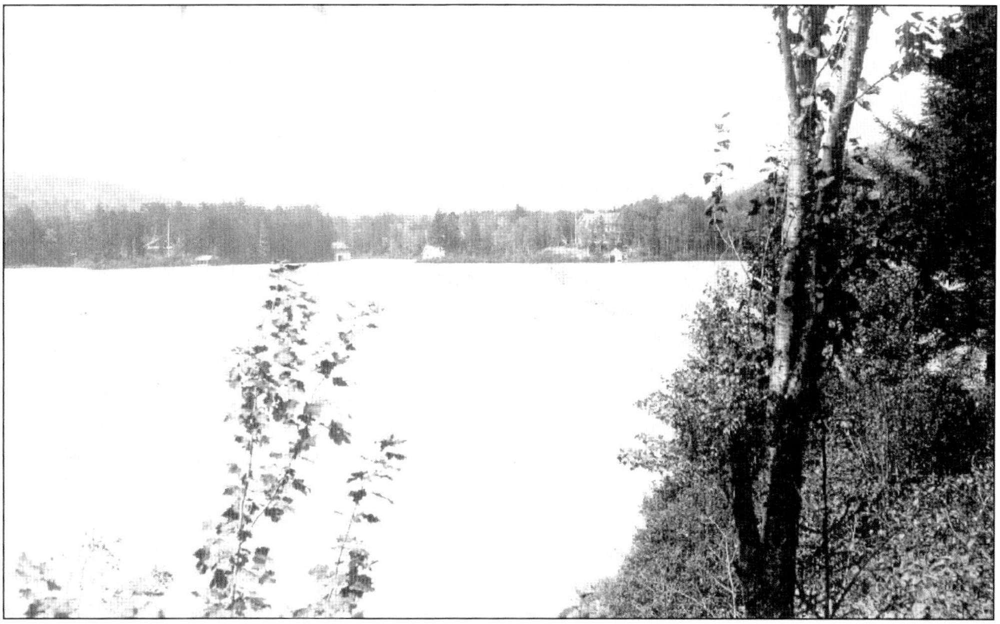

This *c.* 1907 view shows the westernmost area of the lake. From left to right are Swiss Point, Minnie-Belle, Nill's Cobblecrest, and Risley's Crystal Beach cottage.

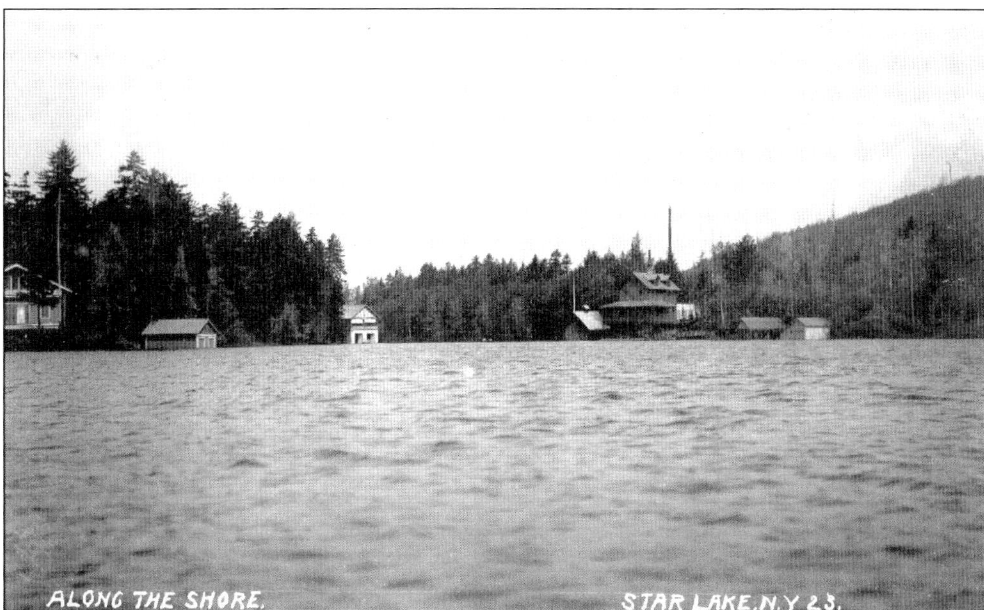

This *c.* 1910 view of the west bay of Star Lake shows the Swiss Point cottage, on the far left. John Nill's Cobblecrest cottage can be seen in the middle.

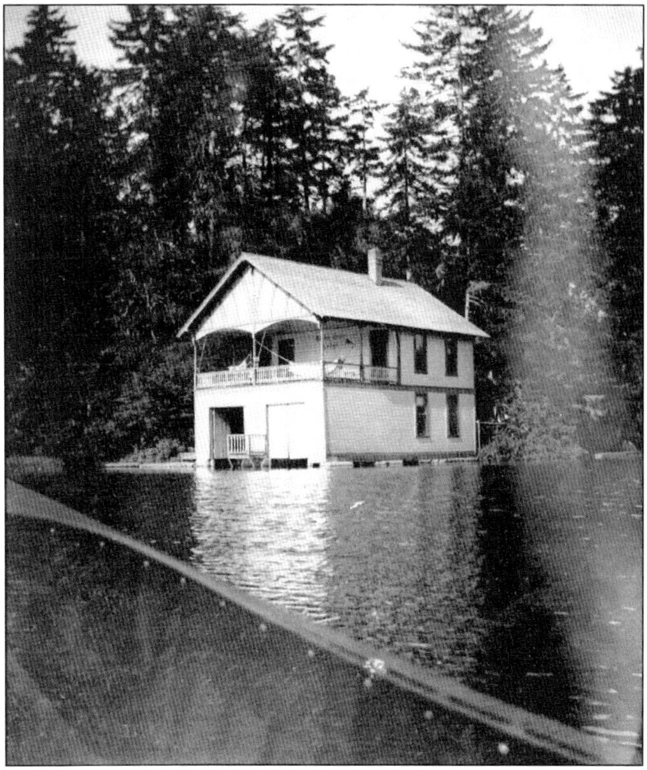

This photograph of the Minnie-Belle Lodge was taken in June 1921. Built by Minnie Olney and Leonard Leiterman, the Minnie-Belle Lodge is located across the bay from Cobblecrest cottage. It was built as a boathouse, with the living quarters located above.

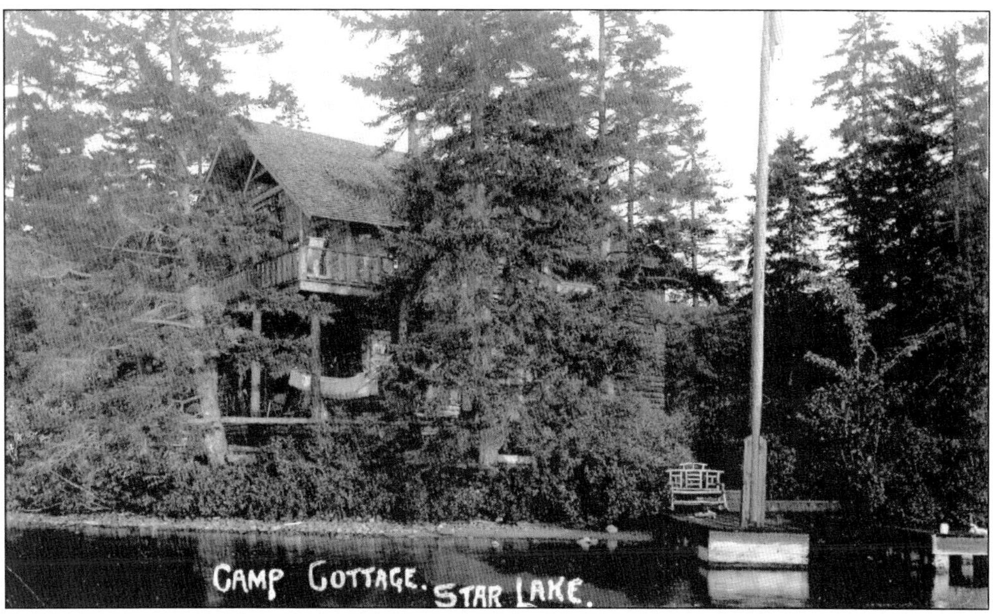

Walter H. Camp, a well-to-do banker from Watertown, contracted with Christopher Backus to build this island cottage in 1900. Known as Camp's Island, it was later destroyed by fire.

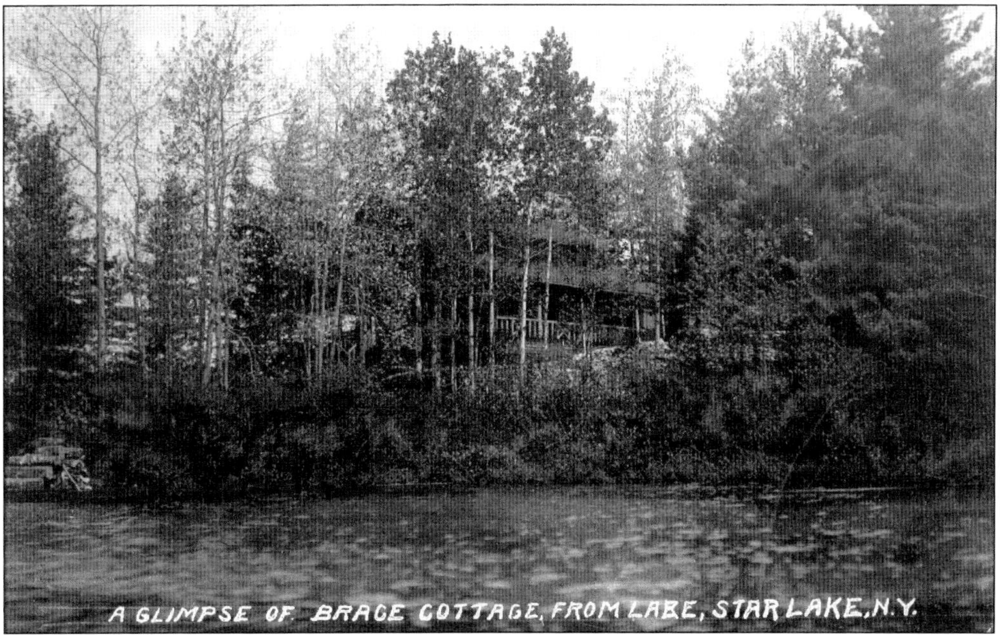

This was the first cottage built on the Scott-Brace property. Christopher Backus completed construction around 1909. It was originally named Camp Marion. Five other cottages were later built by the Scott and Brace families, along with a boathouse, a stone garage, and a tennis court.

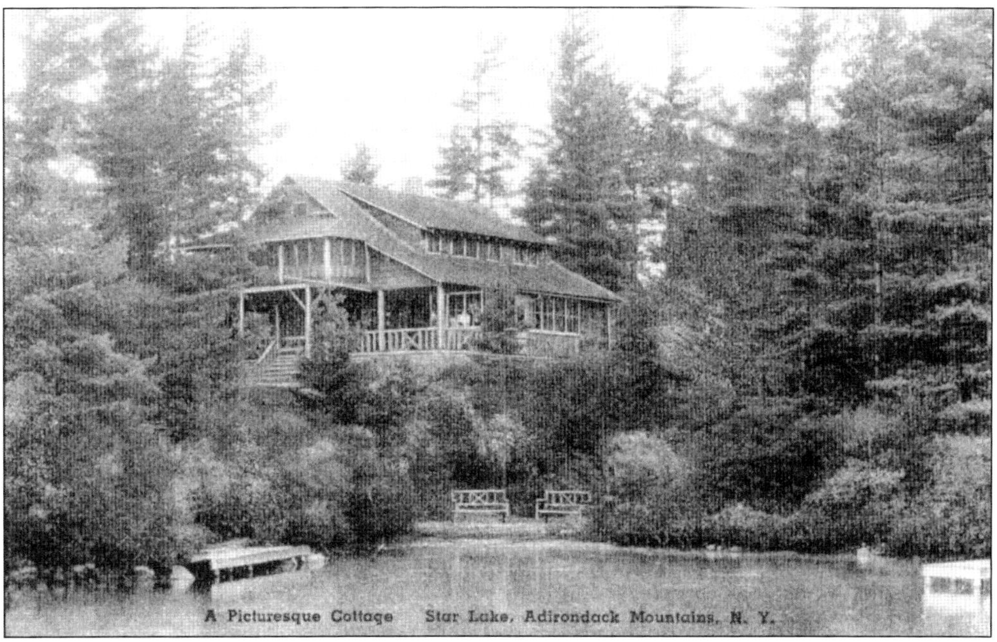

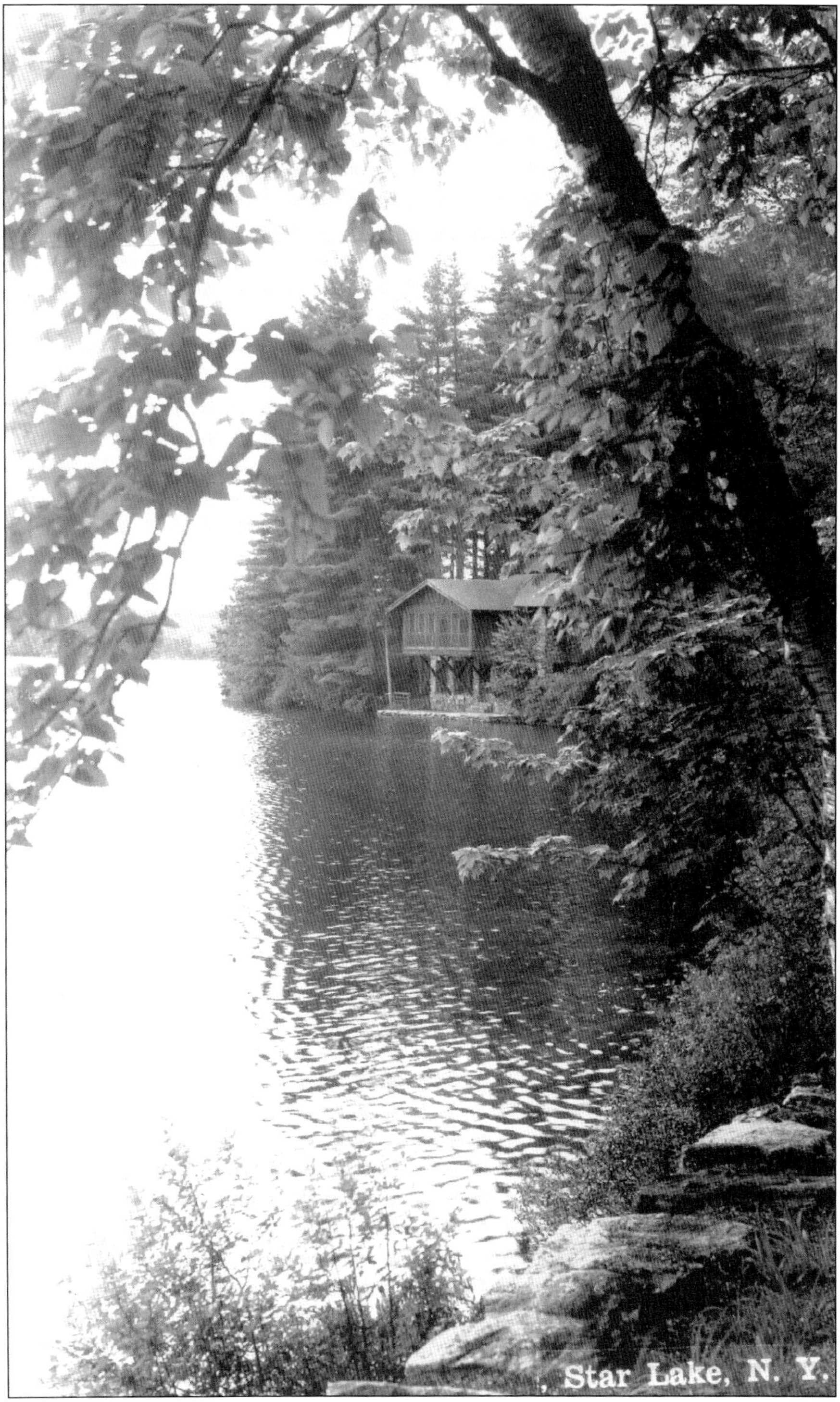

Located on the Scott-Brace Point, the Stone House cottage was built around 1940 by Maxwell and Marion Brace. The stone cottage was built into the side of the hill, with the cantilevered second story as the sleeping quarters.

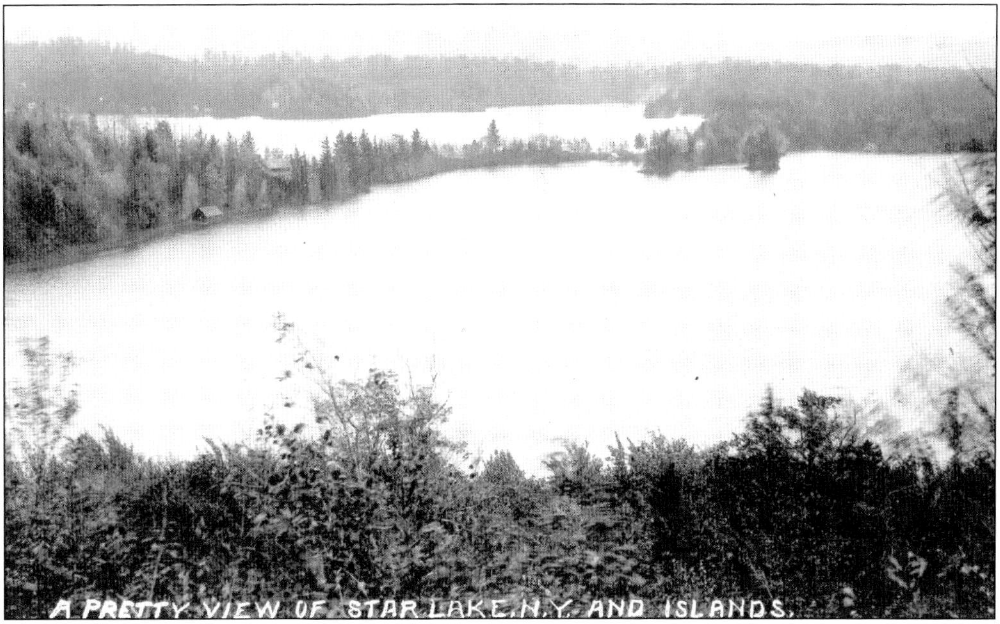

This early panoramic view was taken around 1910. The Scott-Brace estate can be seen on the far left. The long Shelton peninsula can also be seen. Frederick B. Scott purchased the 19-acre point and sold off three acres to Charles C. Brace. Brace was a physician from Boulder, Colorado, who later moved to Tarrytown. He first visited Star Lake after his daughter Mabel married Scott's son Harold.

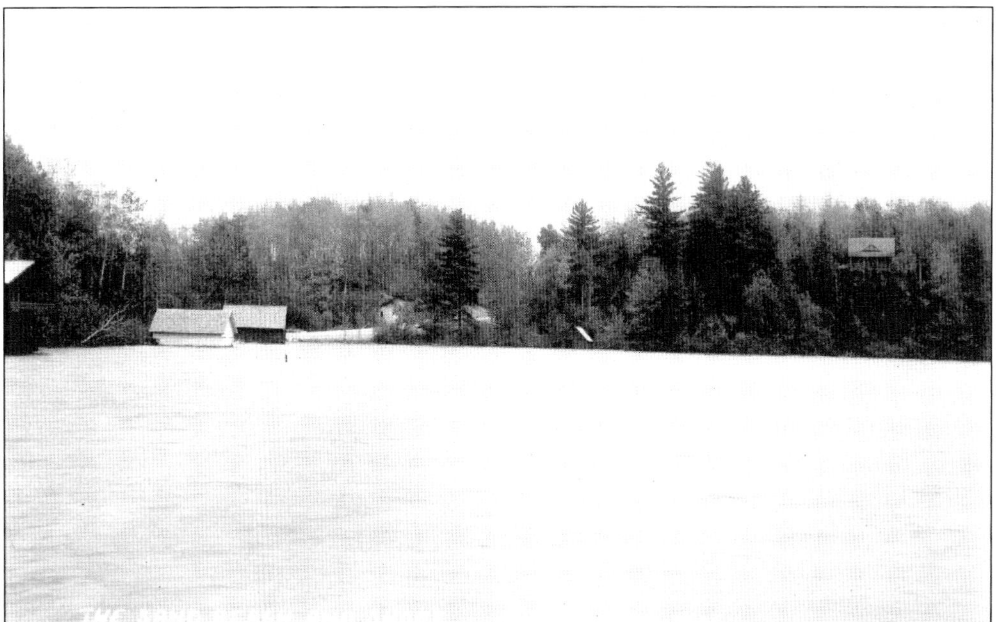

A view of a large camp near the Scott-Brace estate can be seen on the right. The small log cabin camp to the left of the cottage still stands, as does the small boathouse below it. The dirt road with boathouses at the far left is the old Oswegatchie Trail Road before it was widened.

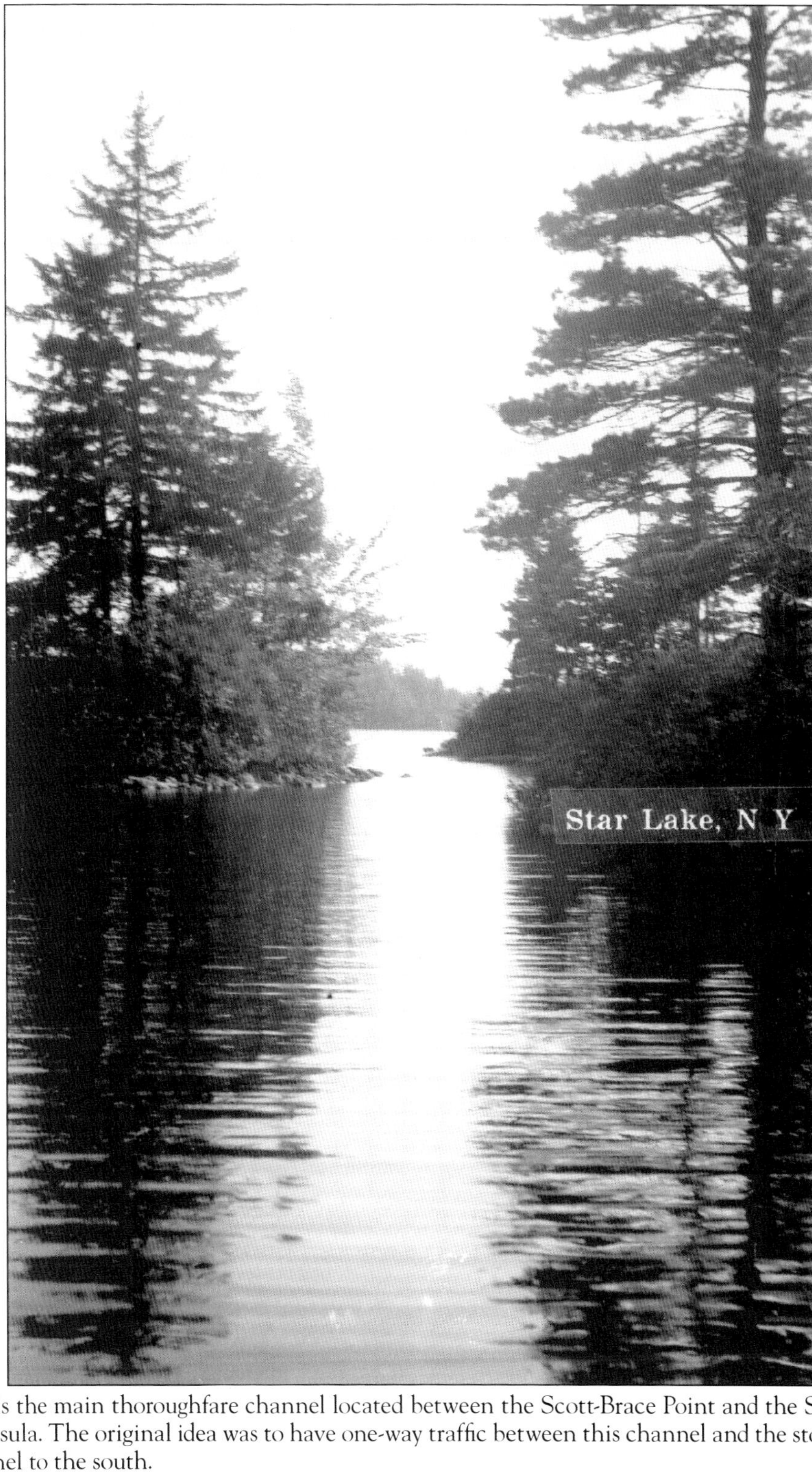

This is the main thoroughfare channel located between the Scott-Brace Point and the Shelton peninsula. The original idea was to have one-way traffic between this channel and the stone cut channel to the south.

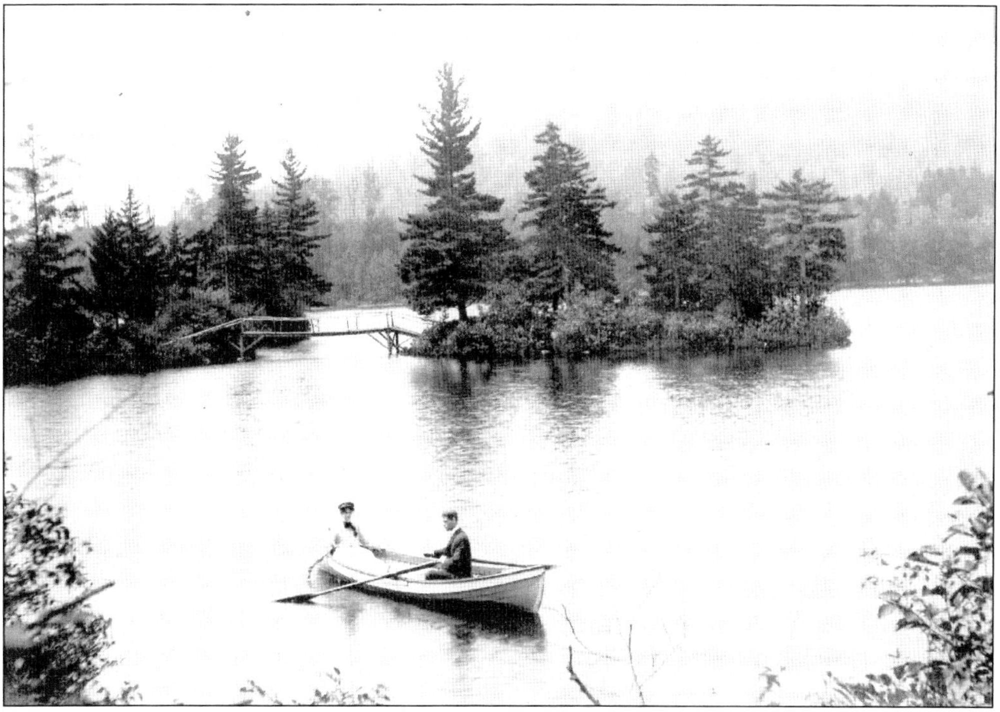

This c. 1905 view shows a couple enjoying a summer's day in an Adirondack guide boat in front of Shelton's islands. The rustic footbridge is no longer standing.

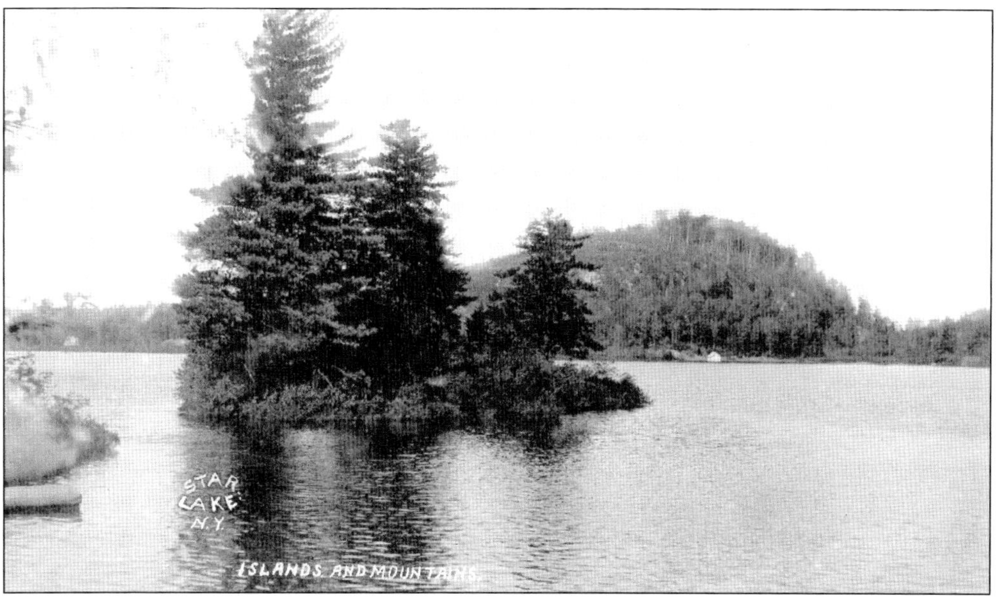

Shown is one of the small islands in Third Lake around 1908. It is most likely one of the two small Shelton Islands. Maple Mountain can be seen in the distance.

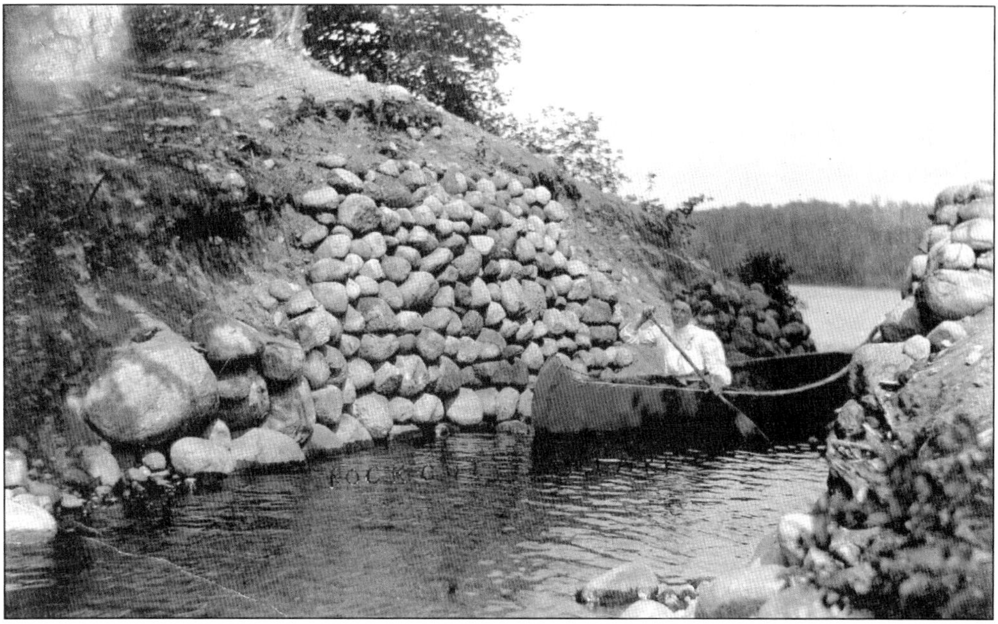

This *c.* 1905 view shows a woman canoeing through the rock cut in Star Lake. The cut was also known as Moody's Channel. This channel was later reinforced with steel and serves as a bridge to Interlochen and Shelton's Point.

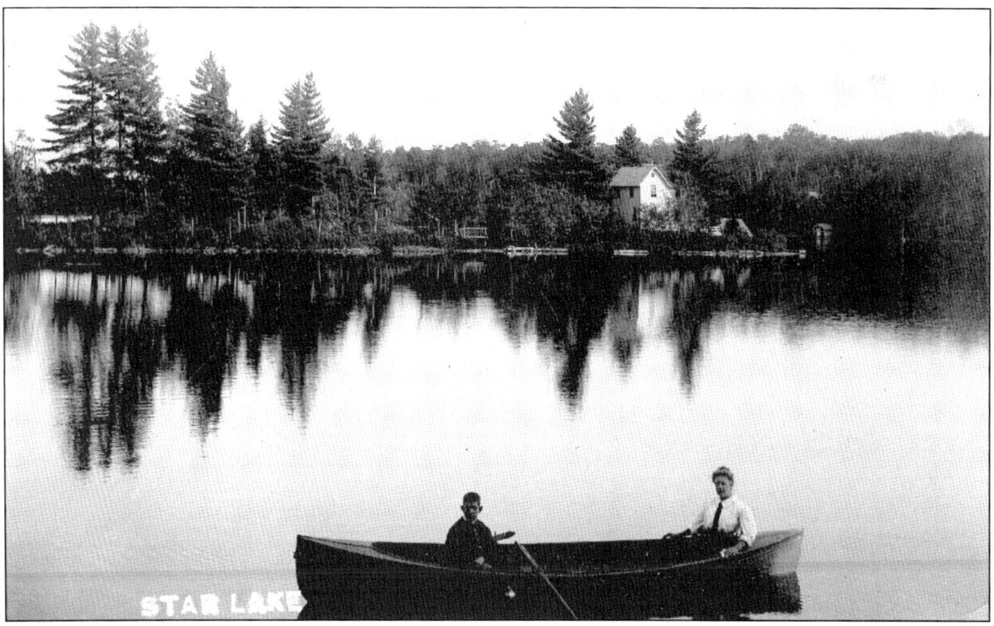

This *c.* 1908 view shows a woman and boy in a St. Lawrence skiff, with Hiawatha Island cottage in the background.

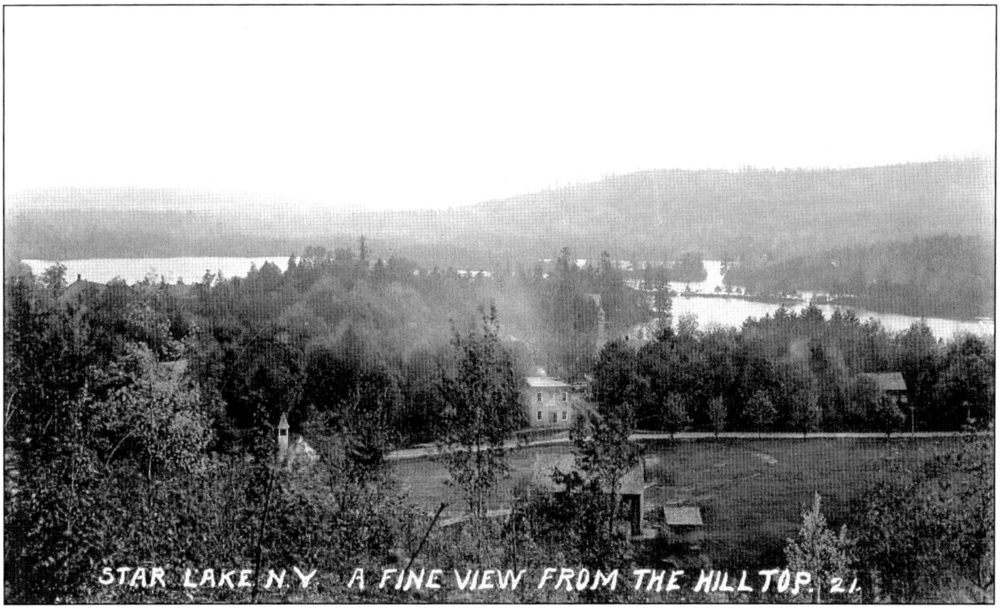

Looking down from Bald Mountain, this c. 1910 view shows Potter's Grocery Store. A close look reveals the Scott-Brace channel, two of the three islands, W. T. Clark's camp, Sam Spain's barn, the front porch of Frank Redway's Cottage Hotel (to the right of Potter's Grocery), and Maple Mountain in the distance.

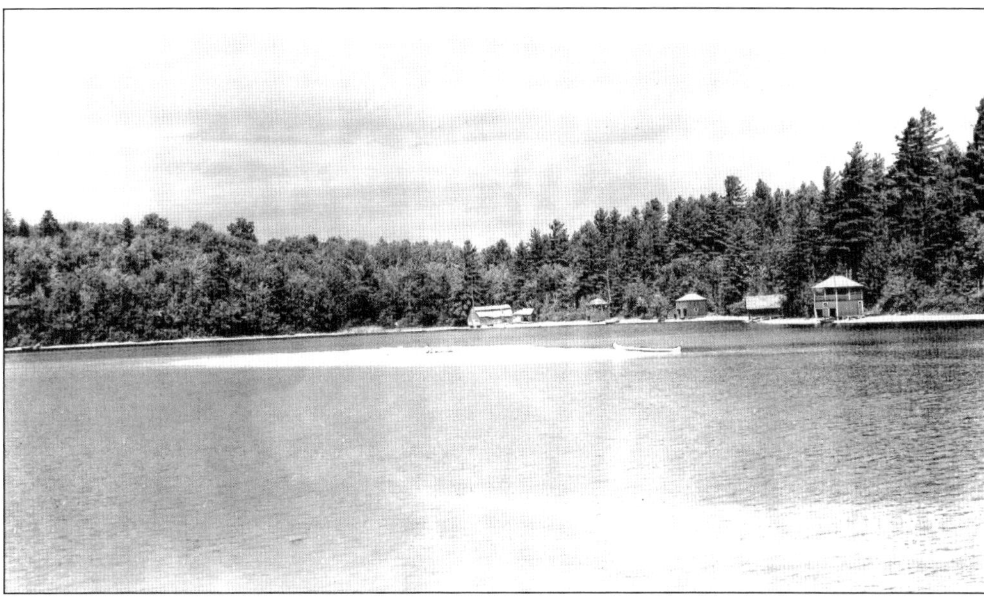

The sandbar is still a popular destination for summer residents and visitors of Star Lake. This view of the sandbar was taken in the 1930s and shows an actual strip of sand above water. The water levels in the lake have increased significantly since this time, and now the sandbar is submerged just below the surface.

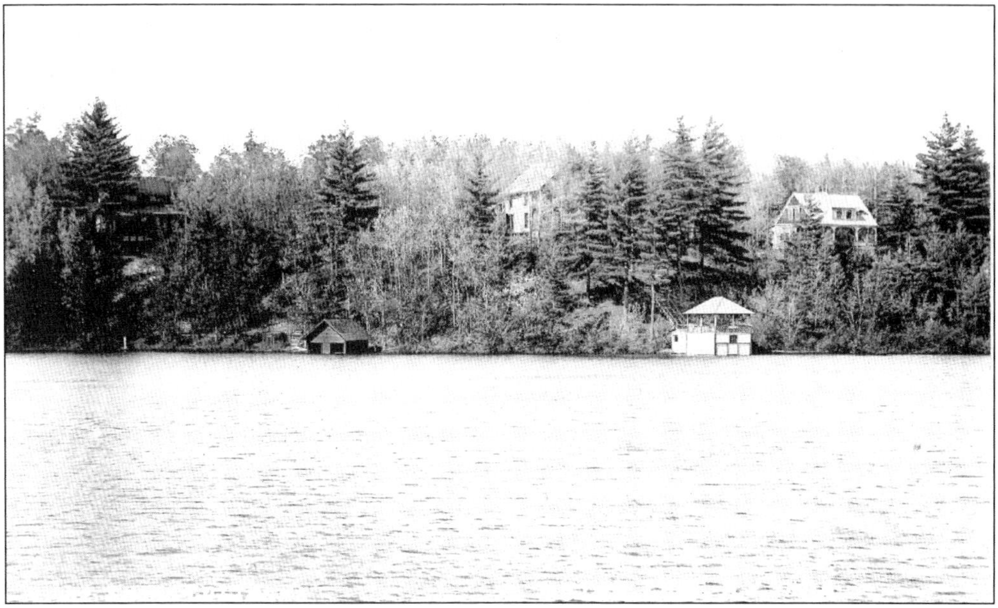

This *c.* 1910 view shows the cottages along the north shore of First Lake. These cottages were accessed from Main Street. Woodcroft cottage, built by Dr. Fowler Smith of Syracuse, can be seen on the far left. The middle cottage was originally owned by Dr. Burton and was built by Christopher Backus.

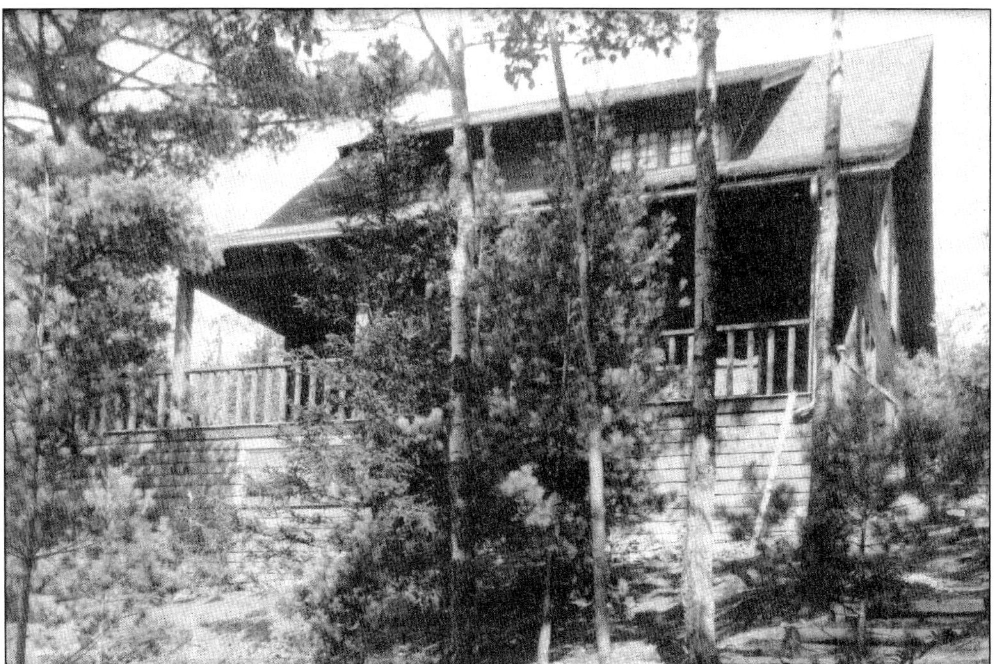

This *c.* 1910 view shows the Woodcroft cottage. It is one of the few early cottages that still retains much of its original look, inside and out. The cottage also had a built-in one-hole bathroom and a walk-in icebox room for cold storage.

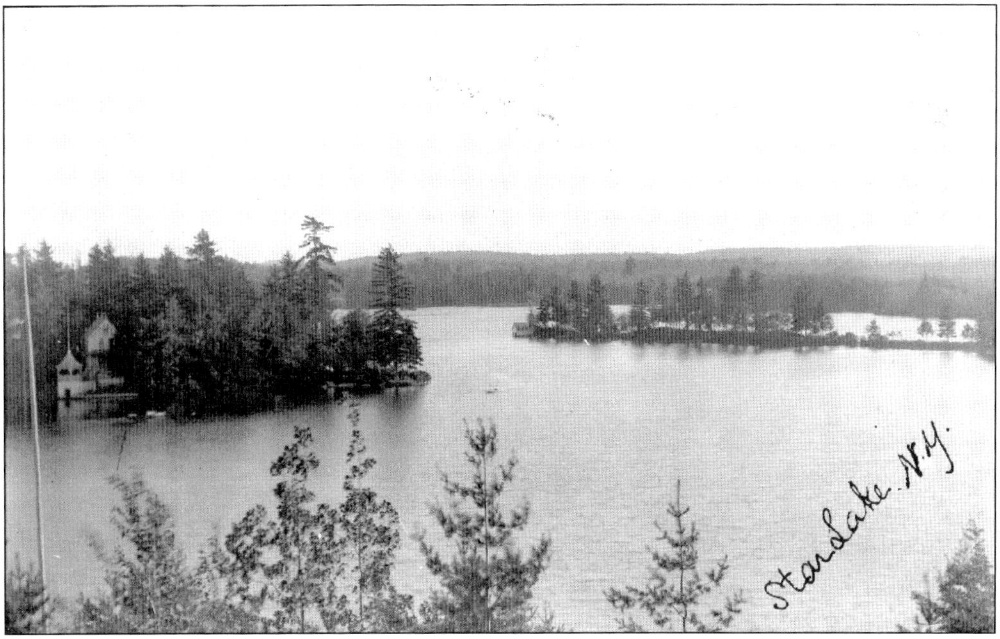

Shown are the William T. Clark camp and Scott's Point around 1910. The islands can be seen on the far right. William Clark was president of the Star Lake Protective Association in 1940.

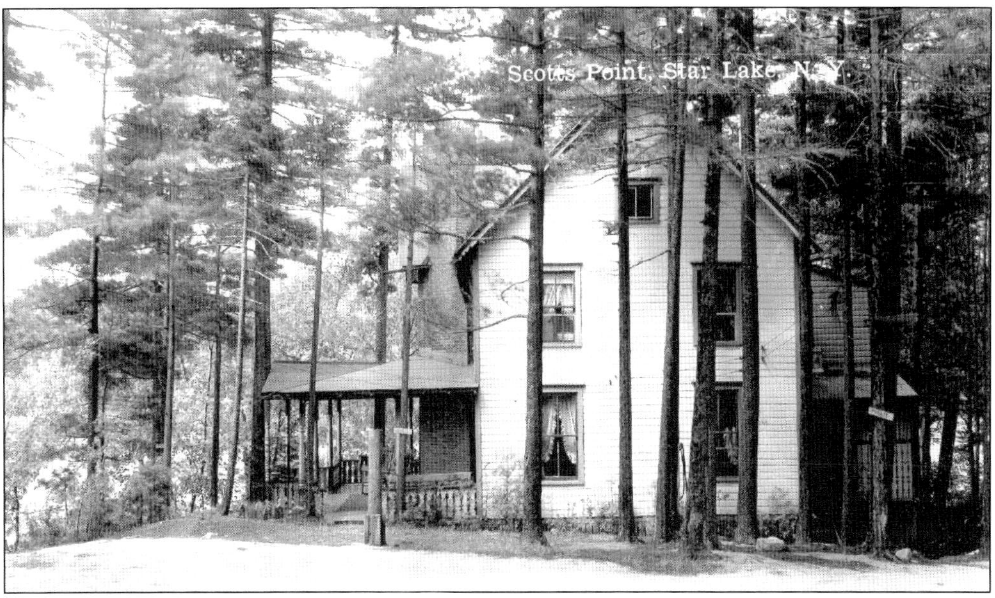

Scott's Point cottage, pictured around 1920, was built by John Scott and then sold to Ken Chapman, who owned it for many years. The camp is located on the point at the end of what is now known as Scott's Point Road.

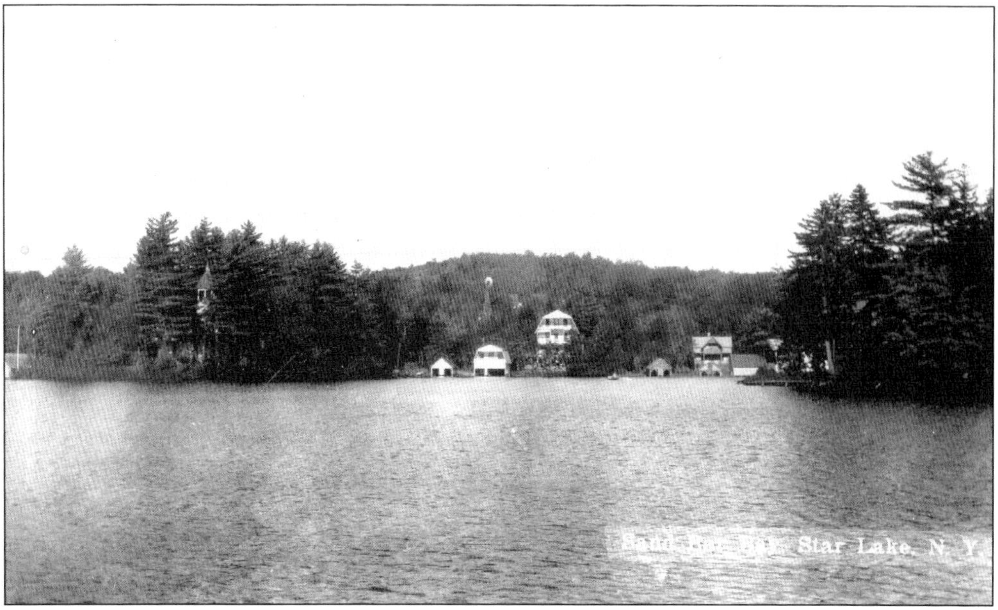

From left to right are Reeves-Gillette cottage (on the point that extends into the sand bar), the Peacock Lodge, Sunset cottage, and Scott's cottage (on Scott's Point Road). The small bay was referred to as Snug Harbor or Sunset Bay.

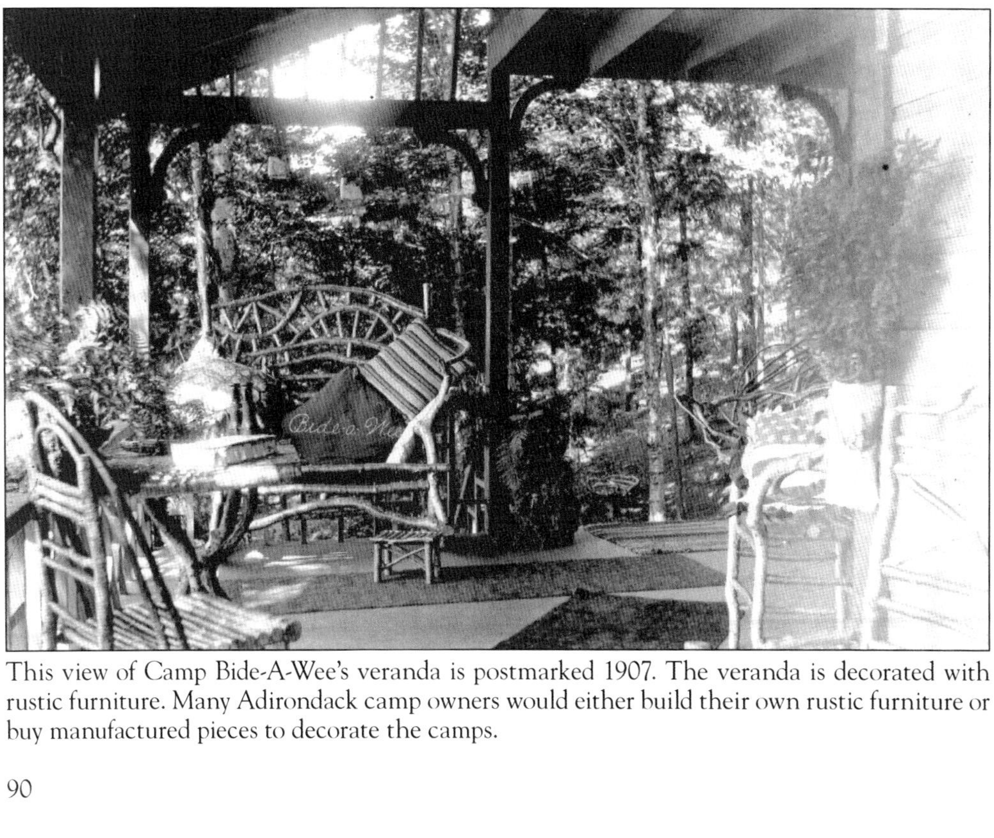

This view of Camp Bide-A-Wee's veranda is postmarked 1907. The veranda is decorated with rustic furniture. Many Adirondack camp owners would either build their own rustic furniture or buy manufactured pieces to decorate the camps.

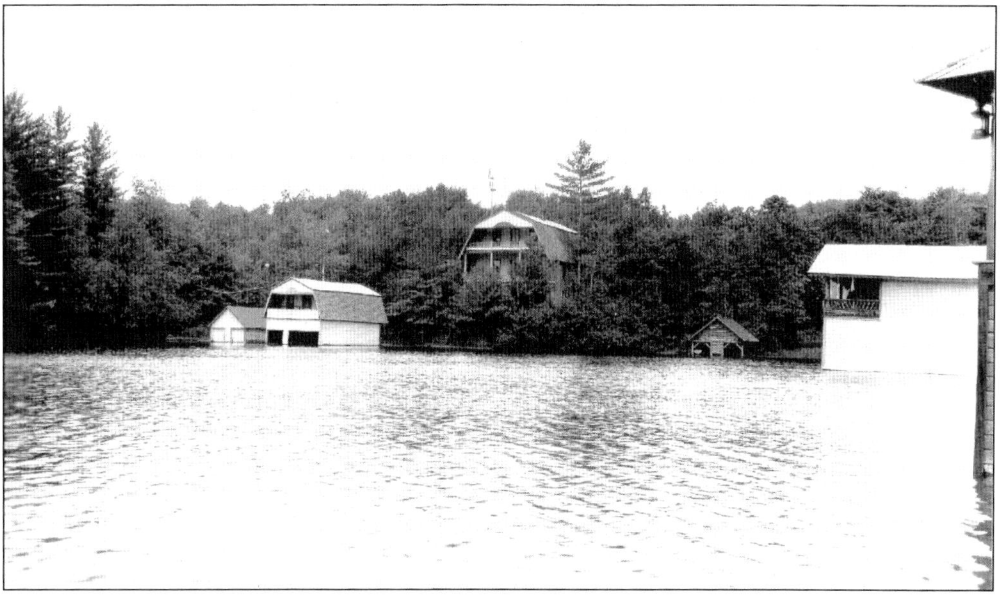

These two views are of Snug Harbor, or Sunset Bay, around 1915 and 1920. The large four-story Peacock Lodge and its matching two-story boathouse, named We-Ha-Ha, are still standing. An early Aermotor windmill can be seen behind the camp. This was used to pump drinking water from an underground well or from the lake into the camp. The Sunset cottage was built later, in the 1920s, by the Star Lake Inn to be used as a rental cottage.

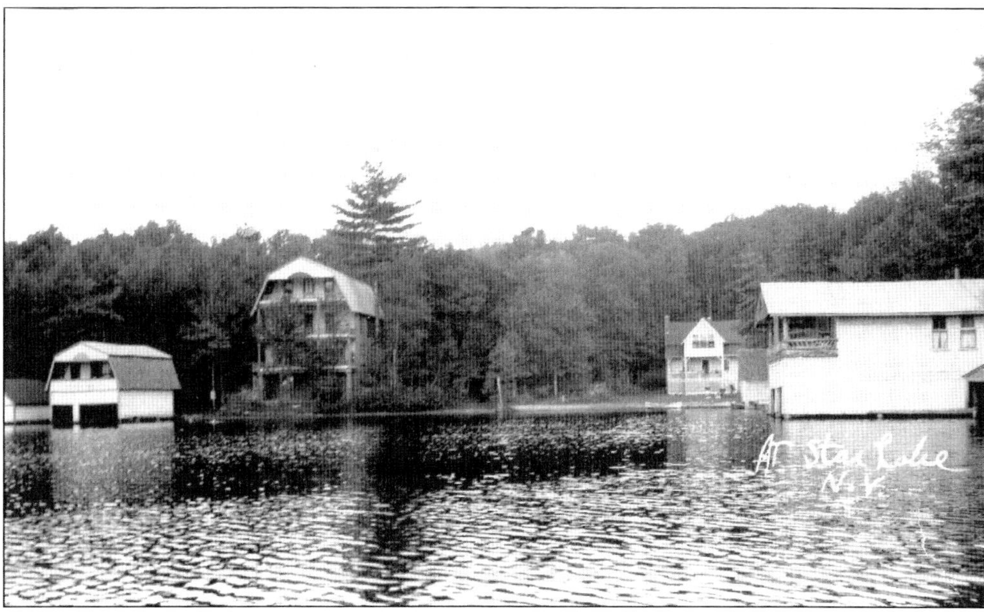

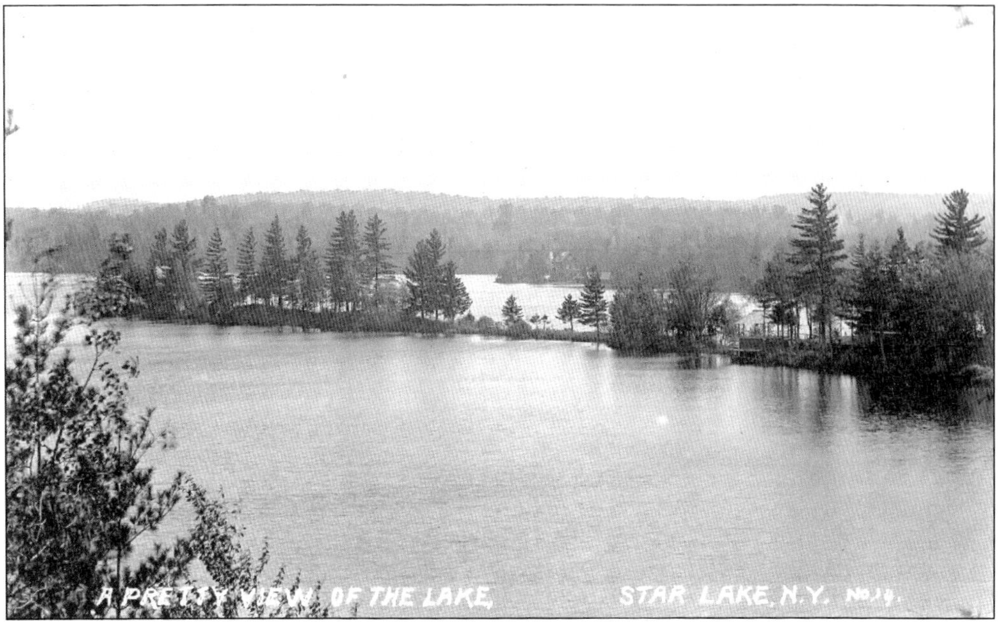

Three small islands can be seen in this *c.* 1910 view. Originally, the island was a single strip of land. It was later parceled into three islands by making two cuts. Each island was connected by a small rustic footbridge like the one seen below. Camp Hiawatha was the island farthest south, and Camp I Like It was located on the island farthest to the north. There was never electricity run to any of the island camps.

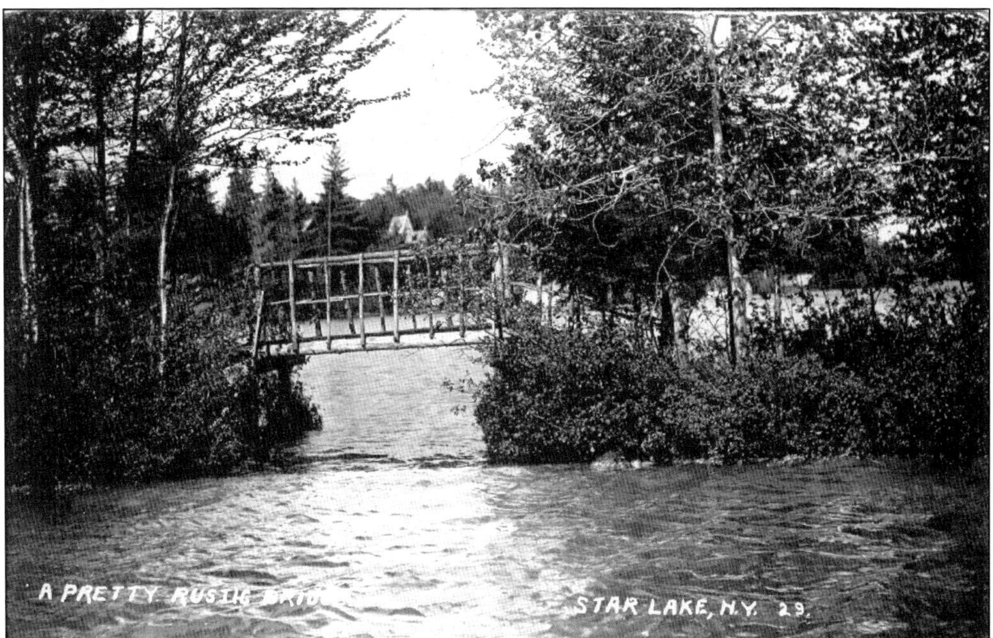

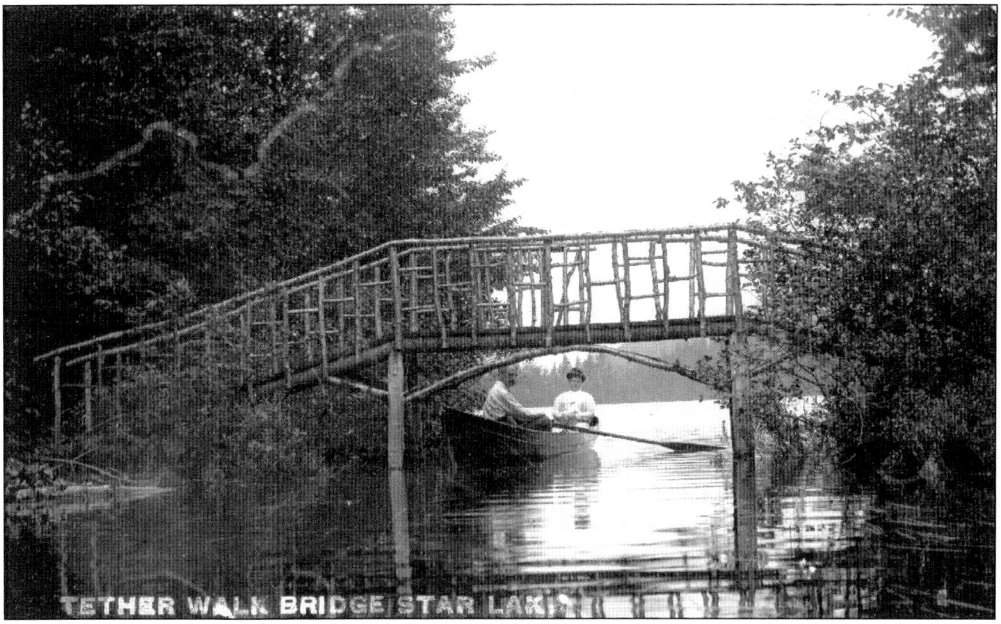

Pictured around 1910, the rustic tether footbridge was constructed of yellow birch logs and wooden planks. It was the crossing point for the northernmost island's Camp I Like It, which was owned at one point by Gerald Marshall.

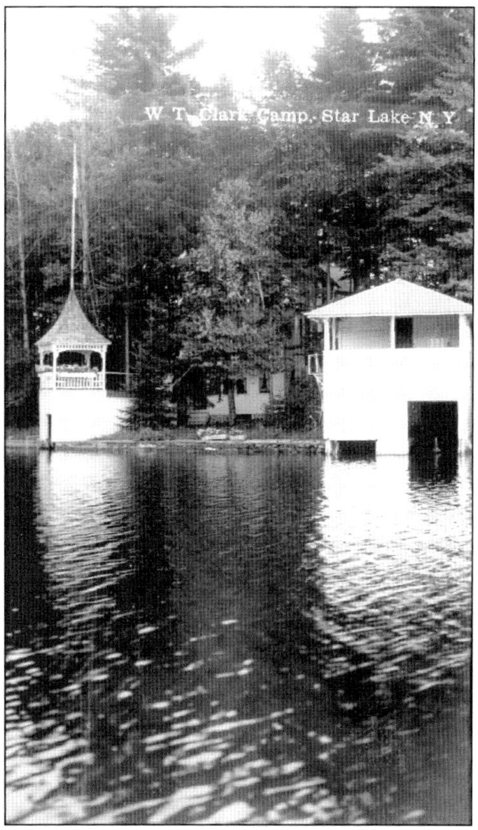

Shown around 1920, the William T. Clark camp was located on Sunset Bay, looking toward the sandbar. William T. Clark was the president of the Star Lake Protective Association for many years. The camp was later renamed Camp Budweiser, and the boathouse, on the right, was named Bud Light.

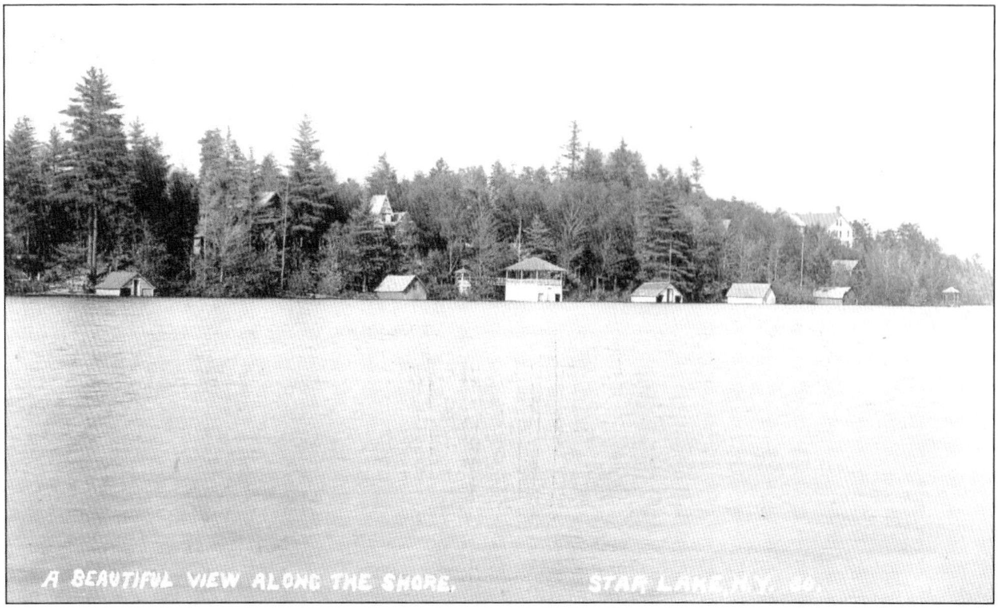

This beautiful view along the north shore was taken looking east toward Post Office Bay around 1910. The high pointed peak of the Grey Gables cottage can be seen in this photograph.

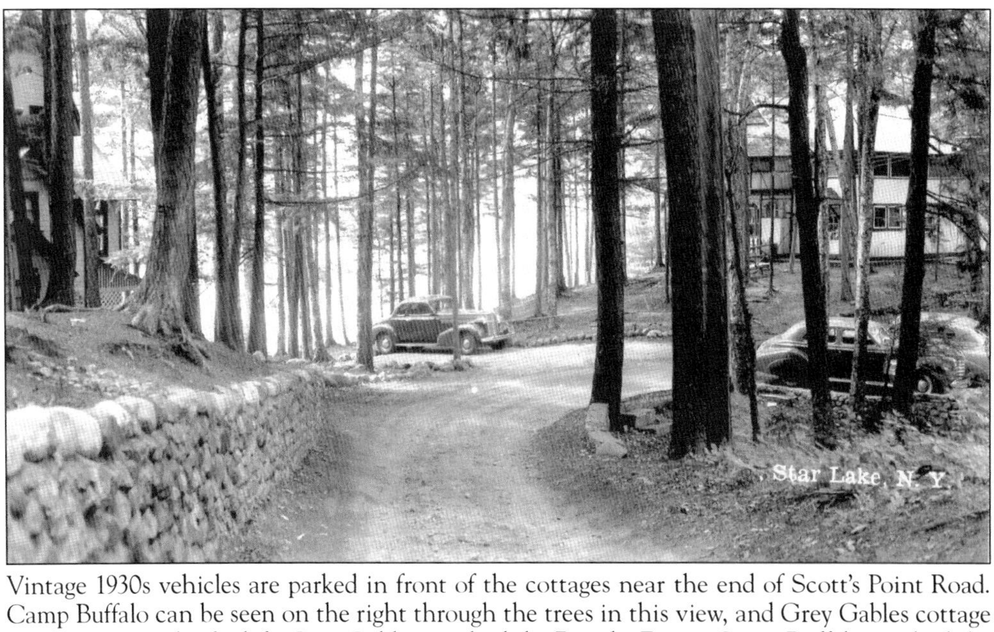

Vintage 1930s vehicles are parked in front of the cottages near the end of Scott's Point Road. Camp Buffalo can be seen on the right through the trees in this view, and Grey Gables cottage can be seen on the far left. Grey Gables was built by Dwight Foster. Camp Buffalo was built by Ed Anderson of Chicago, Illinois.

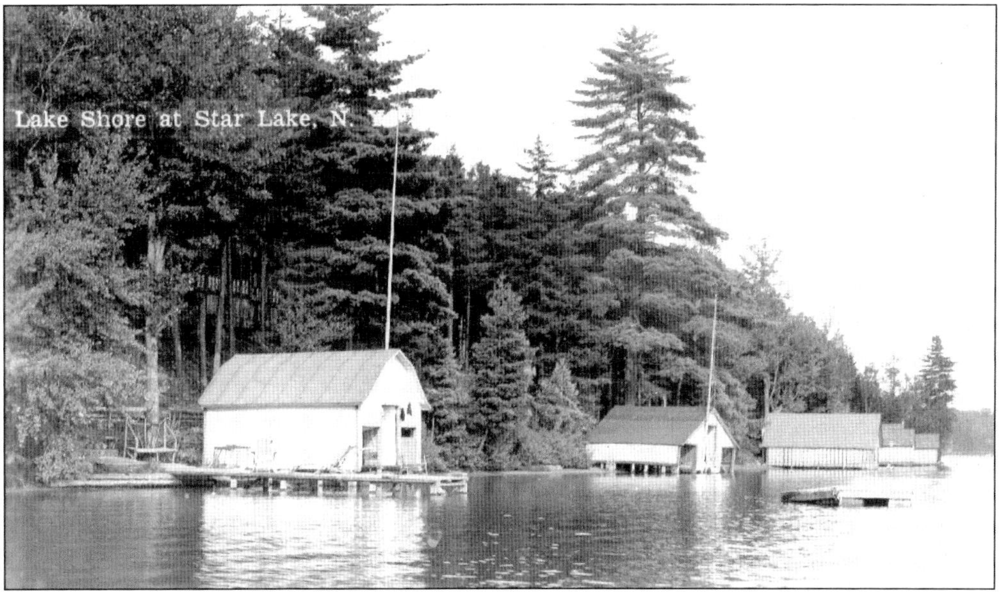

Looking east toward Post Office Bay, this c. 1920 view shows the many boathouses along the shoreline. From left to right are Scott's Point, Dr. Broad's, Camp Buffalo, Grey Gables, Golden's, Zimmerman's, and Bondy's.

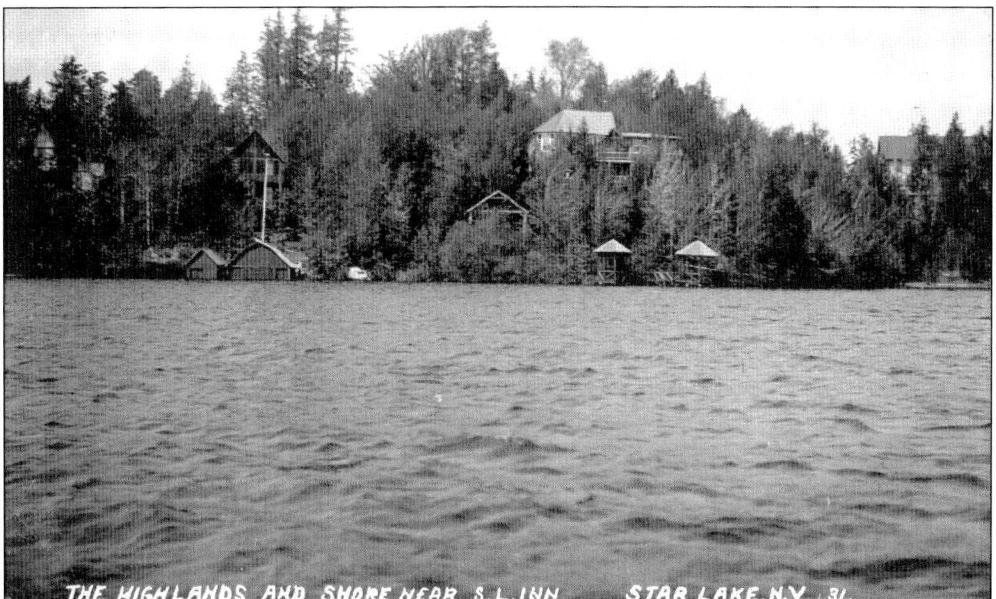

Shown are the highlands and shore near the Star Lake Inn. Joseph Bondy's cottage was located just to the west of the inn, which is on the far right. Nearly all of the cottages except Bondy's still stand. Zimmerman's cottage can be seen to the immediate left of Bondy's.

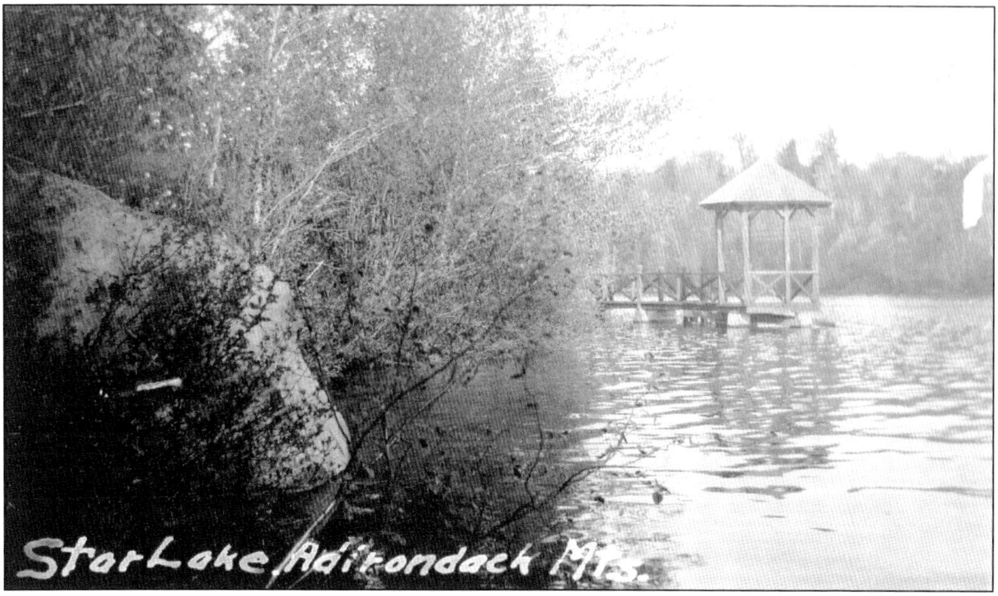

This view of Zimmerman's rock was taken around 1910. Joseph Bondy's dock and pavilion can be seen in the distance. This large rock can still be seen along the shore in front of Zimmerman's cottage.

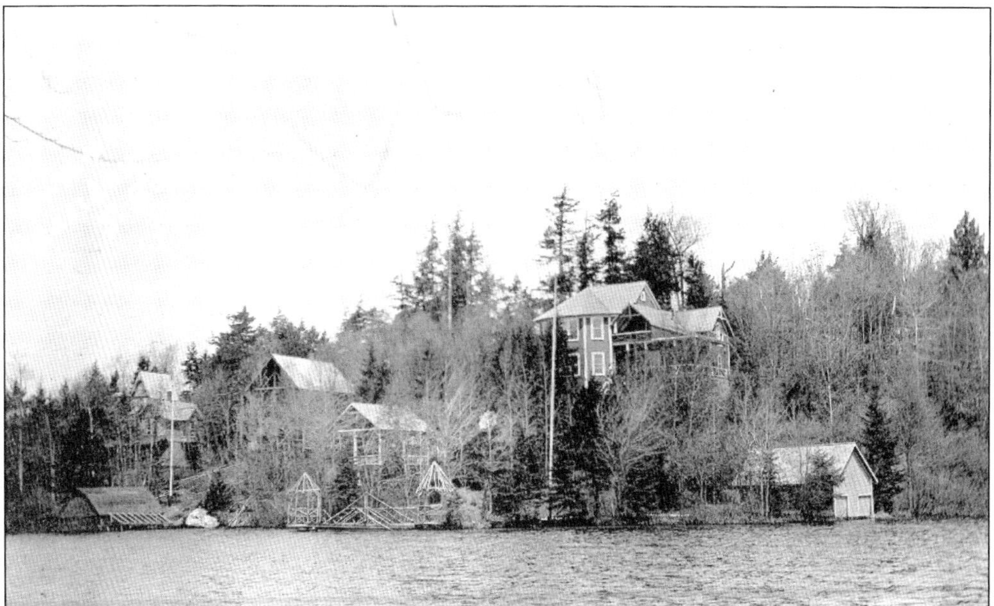
Joseph Bondy's cottage was located just to the west of the Star lake Inn property. The inn can be seen on the far right. Although Bondy's cottage was torn down and rebuilt by Dr. Perrson, almost all of the other cottages along this stretch of shoreline are still standing.

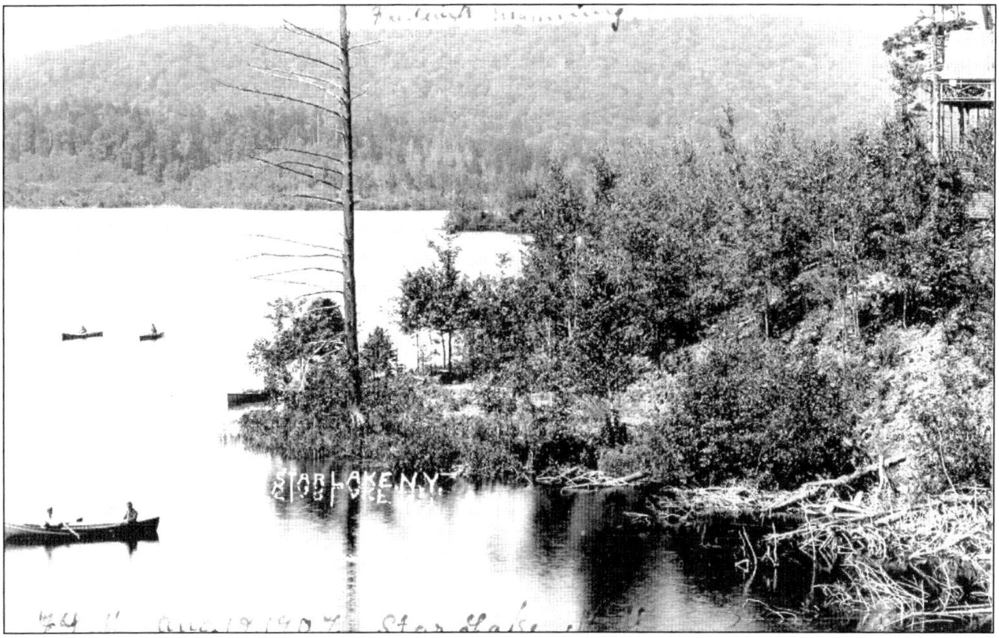

This c. 1905 view shows Joseph Bondy's Point. This photograph was most likely taken from one of the top balconies at the Star Lake Inn. Much of the lake was undeveloped at the time.

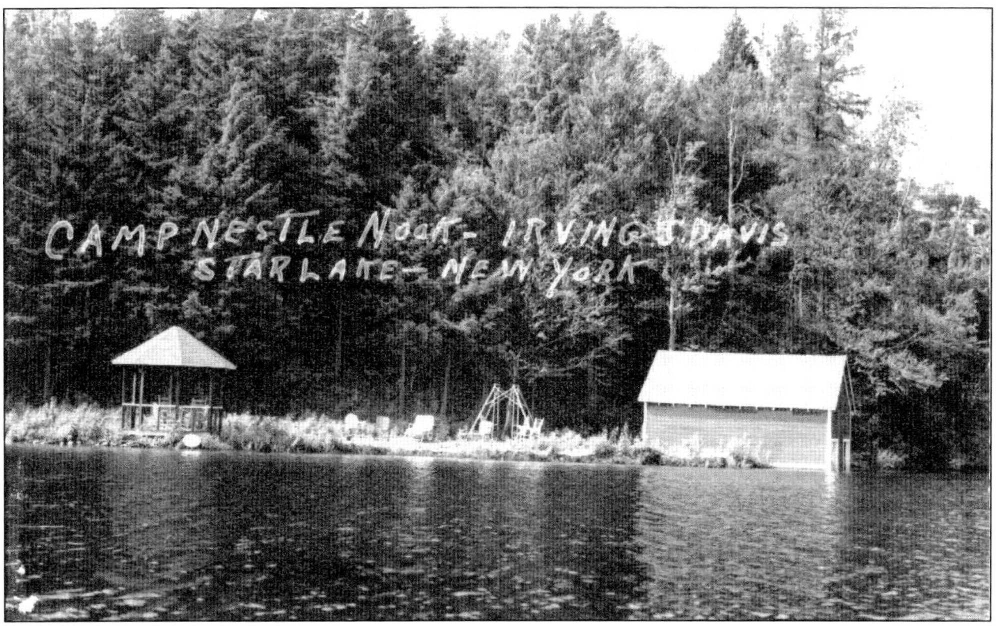

Irving J. Davis bought Joseph Bondy's cottage and renamed it Camp Nestle Nook around 1930. The wooden pavilion is still standing on the point, just to the west of the Star Lake Inn property.

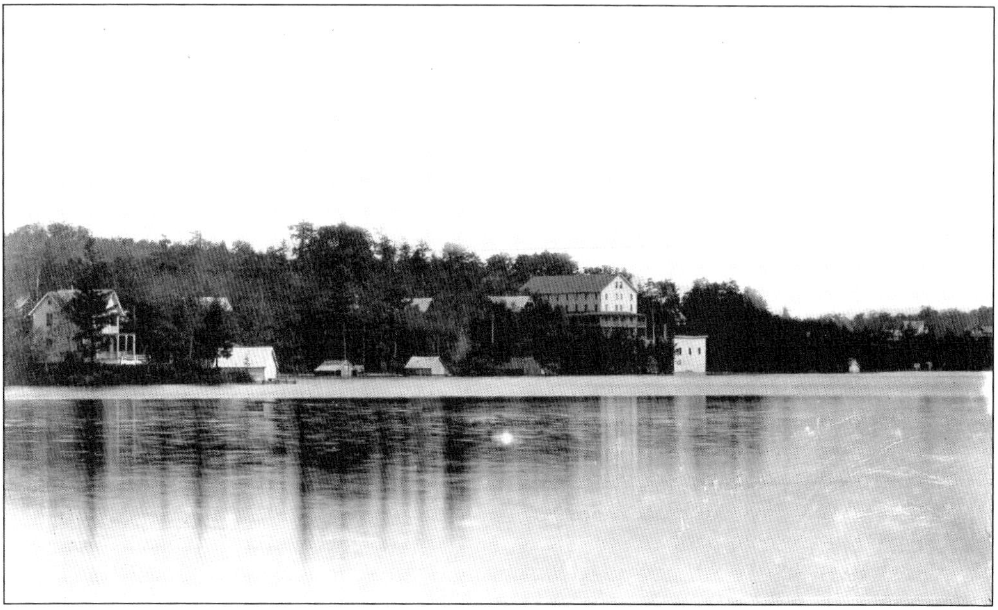

This lakeshore view was taken around 1910. The island camp Hiawatha can be seen on the far left, and the Star lake Inn can be seen in the distance.

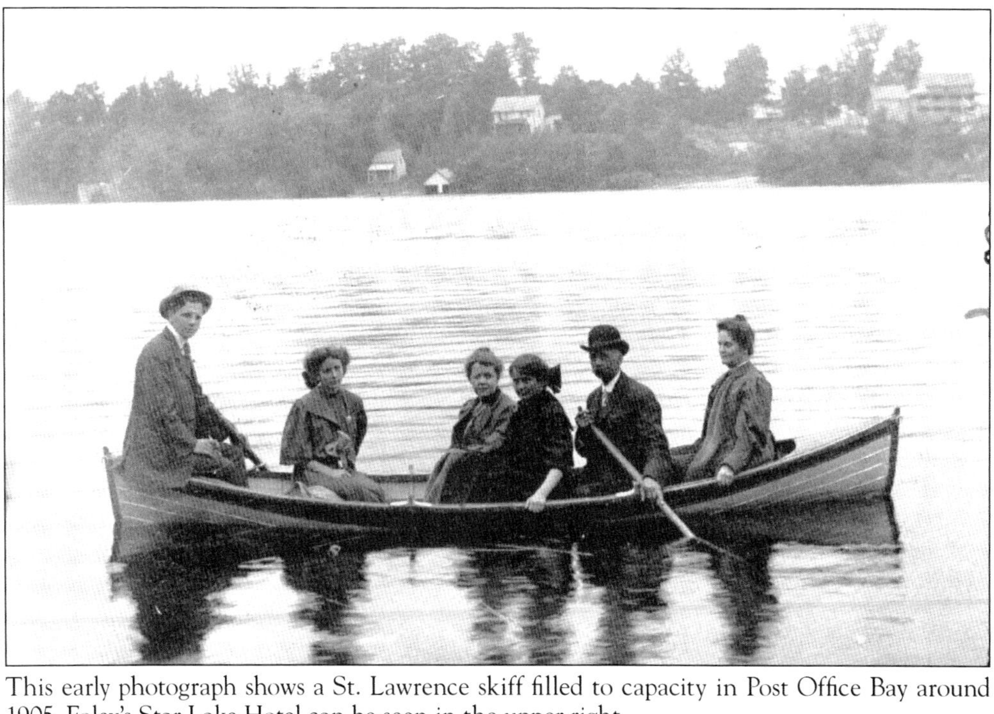

This early photograph shows a St. Lawrence skiff filled to capacity in Post Office Bay around 1905. Foley's Star Lake Hotel can be seen in the upper right.

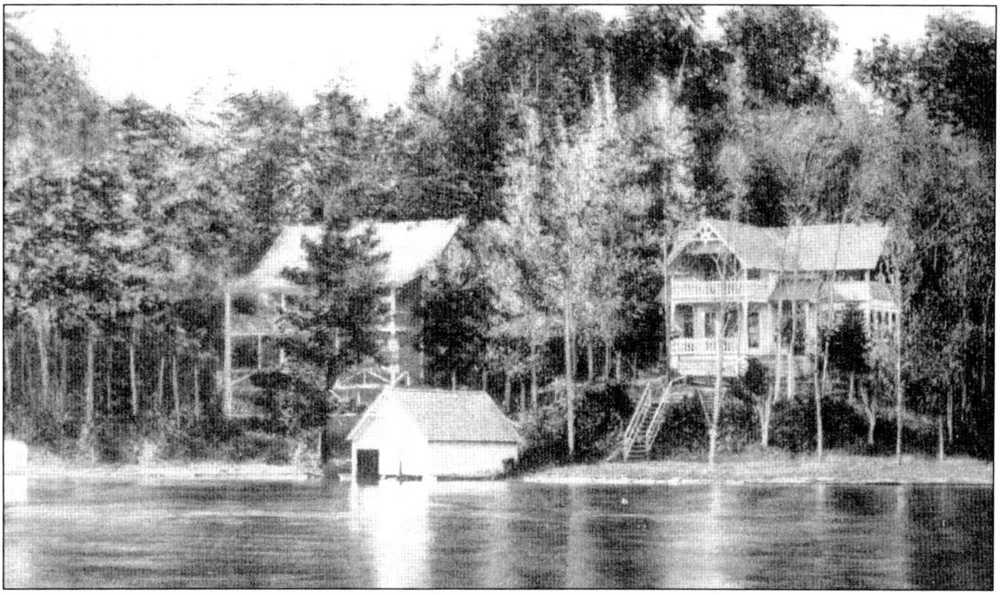

Built by C. C. Burns, this large camp has undergone many design changes through the years. It is located on a small point just before entering Post Office Bay on the north shore. The camp was sold to Richard Witter, owner of the local pharmacy in the village for many years. To the left of Witter's camp and boathouse is Just In Villa cottage.

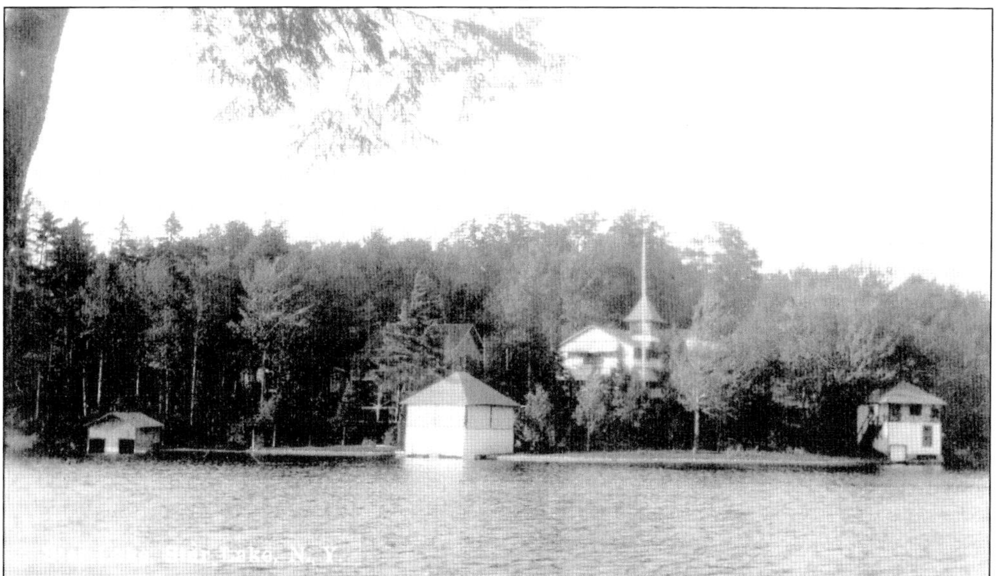

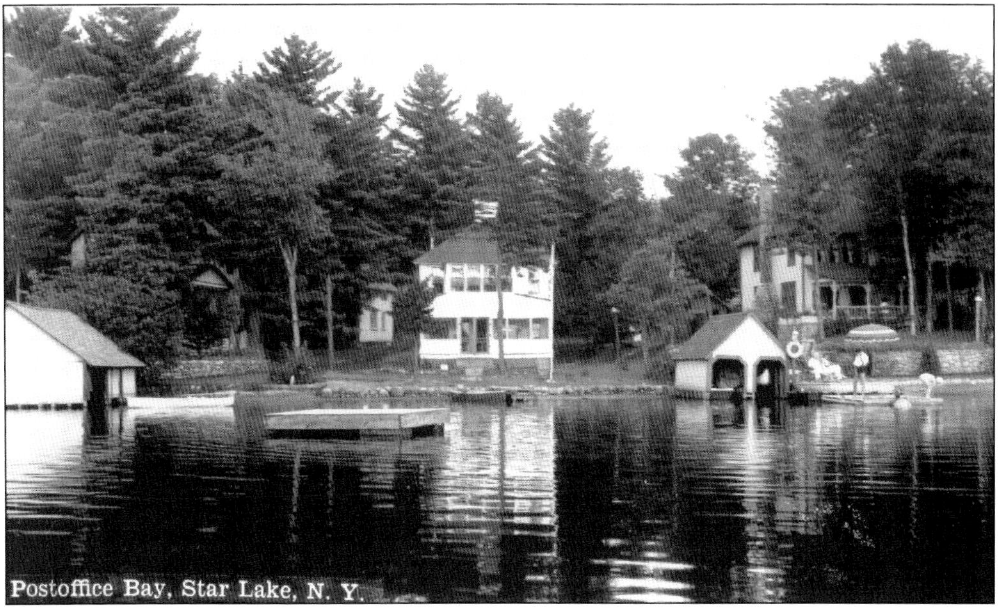

These three cottages are located at the end of Post Office Bay. From left to right are what were originally know as Benson camp, Sayers, and Greene's cottage.

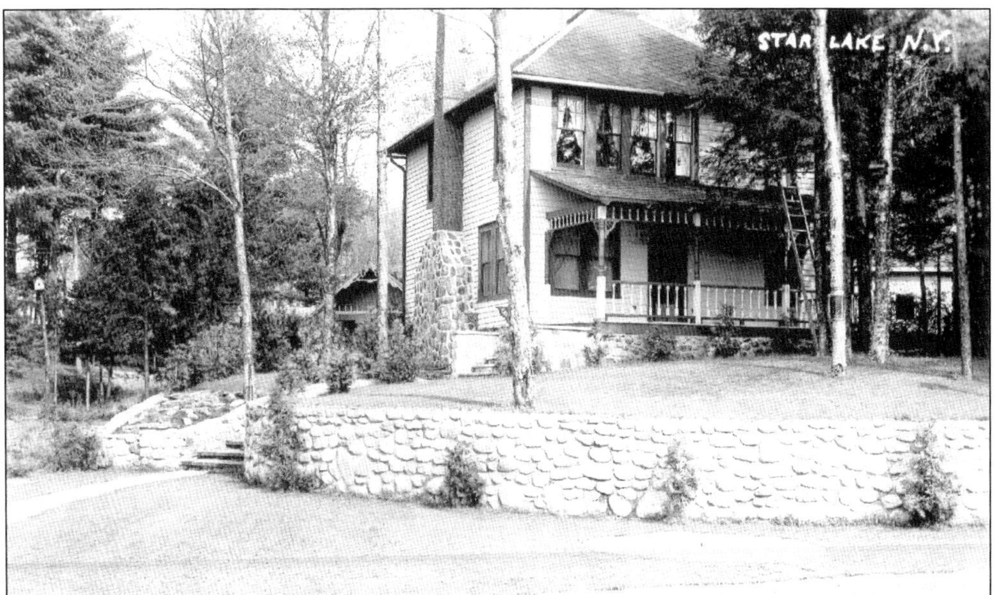

This cottage, located on Post Office Bay, was originally owned by John Greene. The guest cabin can be seen behind the cottage. The front porch was later enclosed.

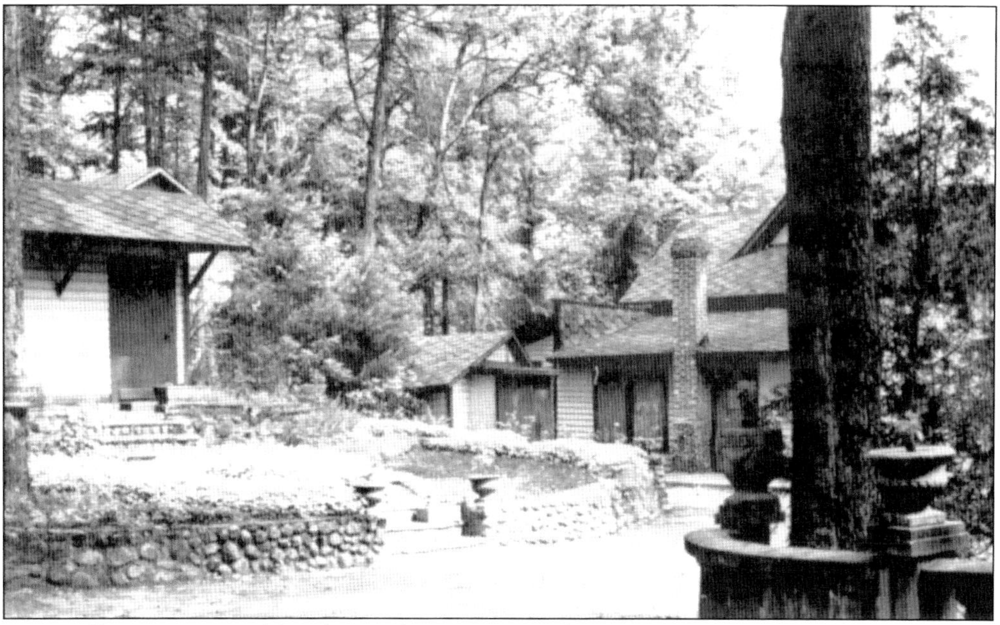

Dr. Mueller's cottage and boathouse, later Gertz-Croft, are seen along the south shore in this view looking toward Post Office Bay. The second floor of the boathouse was a dance hall. Mueller was a well respected physician from New York City who also researched and patented many medicines. He briefly owned a white mice farm near Colton Lane. The mice were used in his research facility. This boathouse burned down shortly after this photograph was taken. The fancy stone chimney and concrete railings can still be seen along the shoreline.

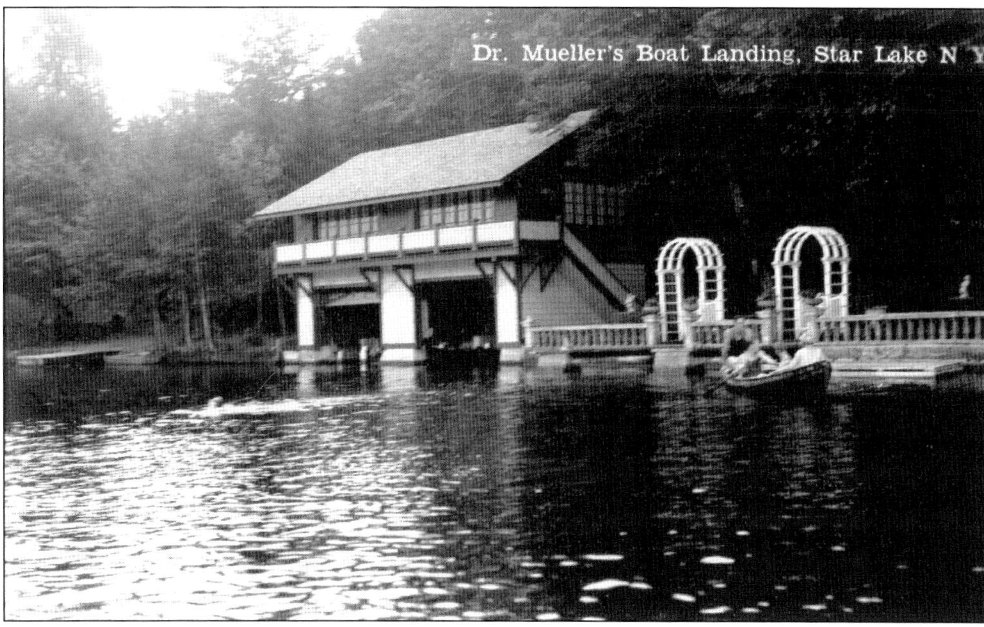

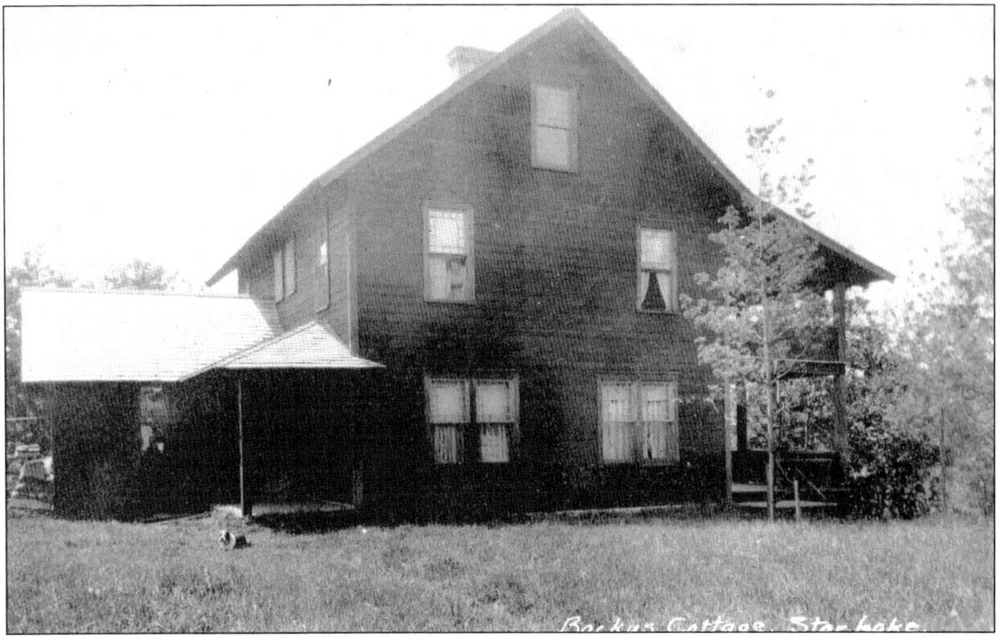

Pictured around 1910, the Backus family cottage was located on Youngs Road. The Backuses were one of the earliest families to settle in Star Lake. Christopher Backus built many of the early Victorian-era cottages and boathouses on the lake, along with much of the stonework that can be seen around town.

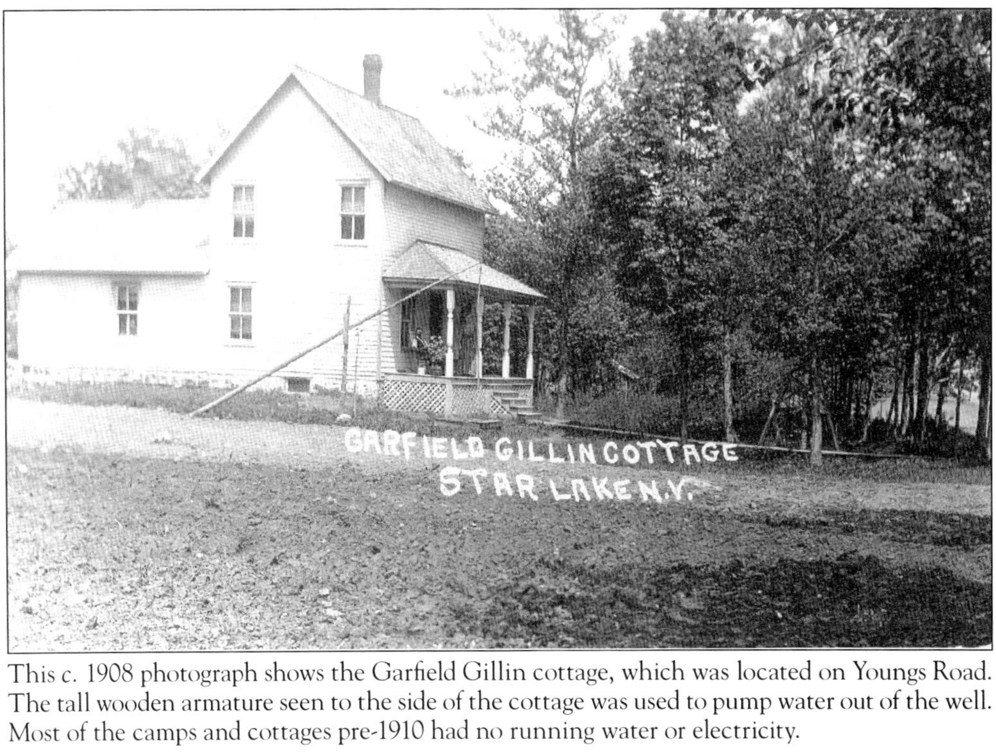

This c. 1908 photograph shows the Garfield Gillin cottage, which was located on Youngs Road. The tall wooden armature seen to the side of the cottage was used to pump water out of the well. Most of the camps and cottages pre-1910 had no running water or electricity.

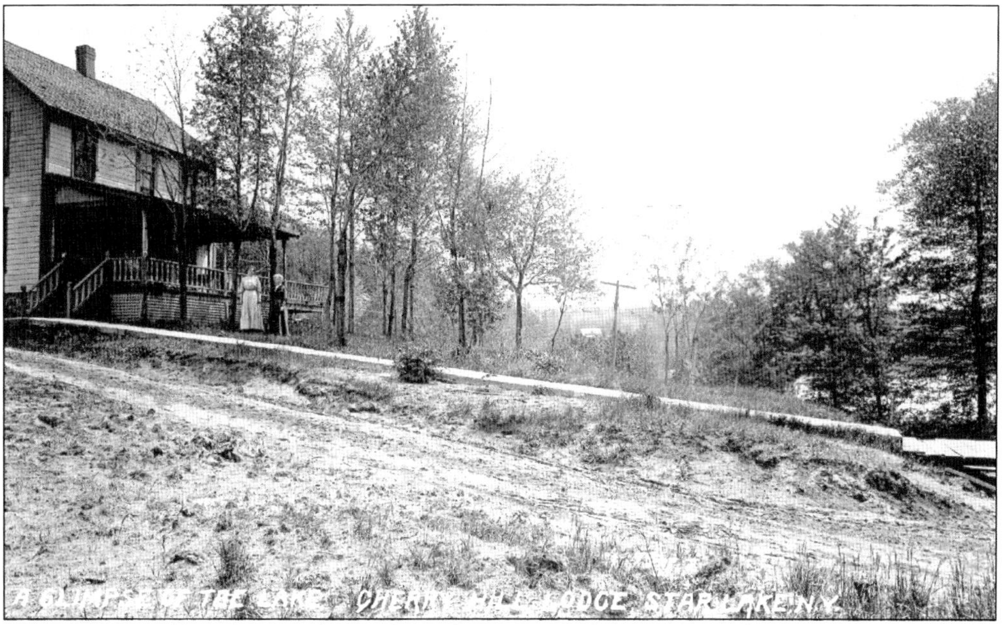

The Cherry Hill Lodge was located on the Oswegatchie Trail Road and served as a small boardinghouse for travelers seeking a night's shelter. It was owned for many years by Mrs. Van Camp. The lodge is now used as a summer cottage.

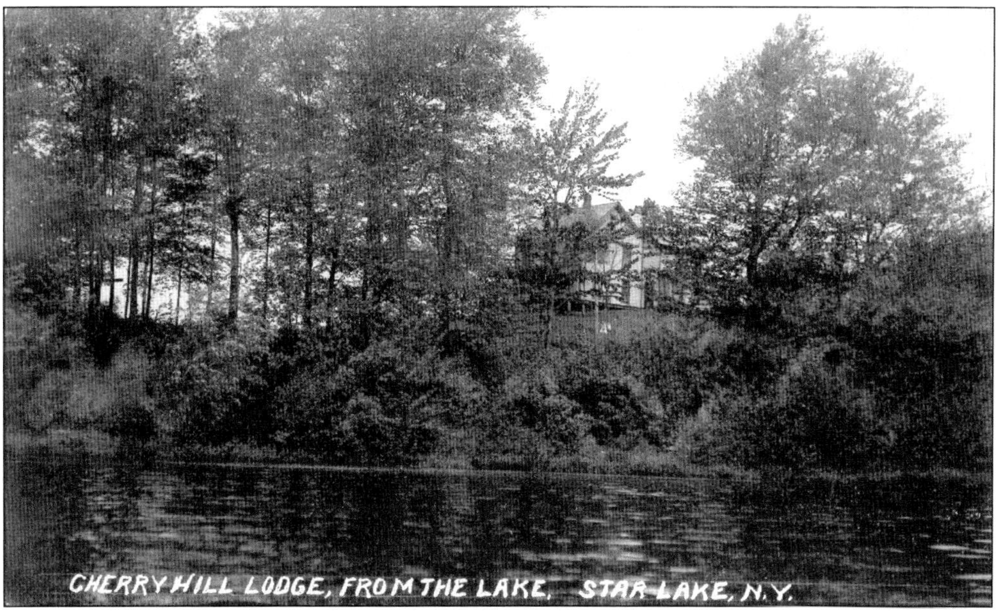

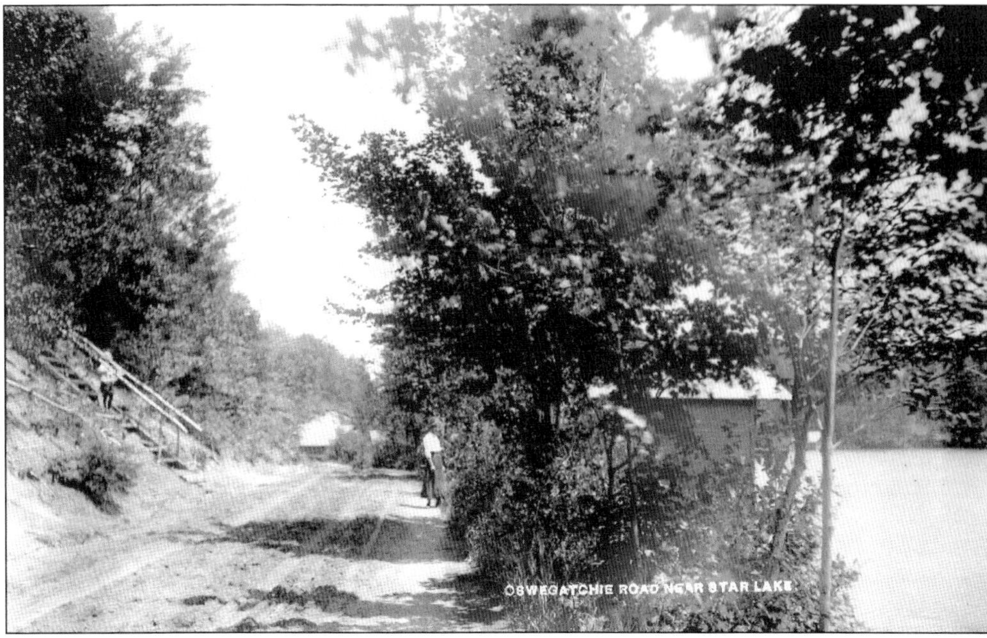

This is a scene along the Oswegatchie Trail Road around 1910. Many of the boathouses were demolished or moved during the 1920s to make room for an expansion to the roadway. In some areas along the shoreline, over 20 feet of lakefront was backfilled to widen the road for two-lane automobile traffic.

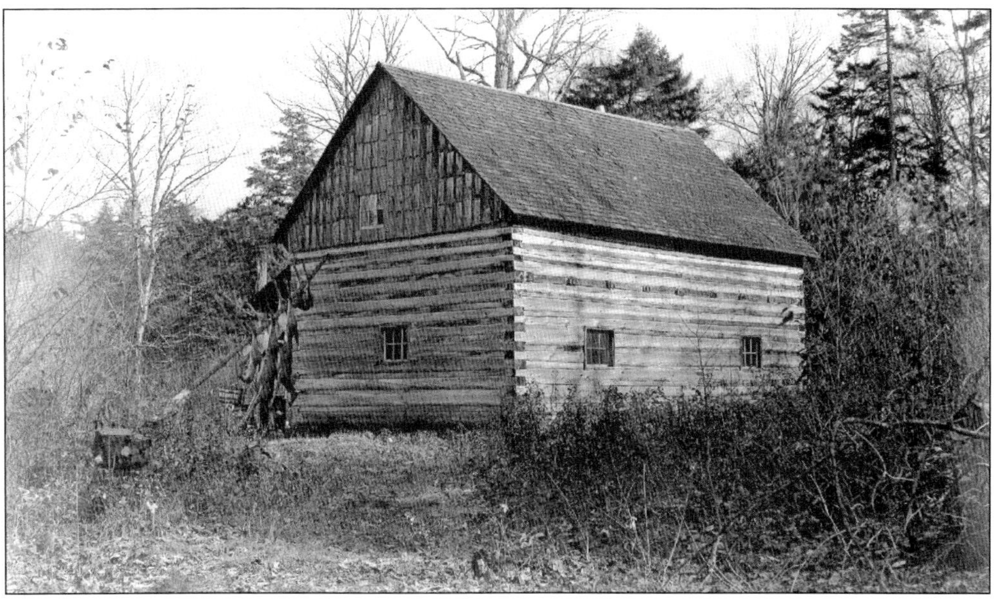

The True Williams cabin was built during the summer of 1897 and was located somewhere in lower Star Lake, most likely near the hospital. True Williams was Mark Twain's illustrator for his books *Tom Sawyer* and *Huckleberry Finn*. Williams died in 1897 and reportedly never spent a single night at his newly built summer retreat. His cabin was left to his niece Bertha Sherman and was referred to often as the Sherman log cabin.

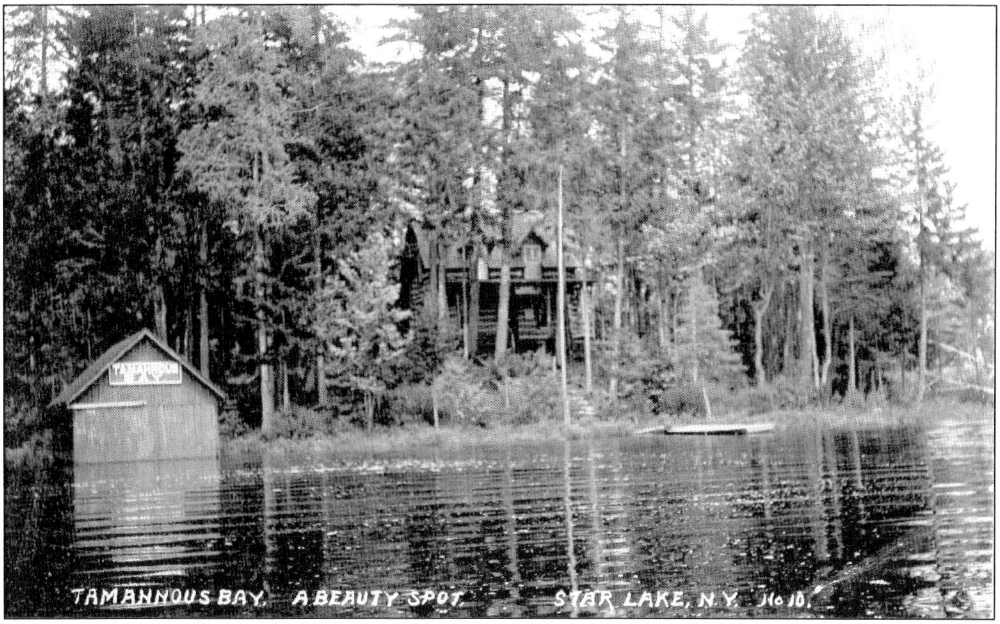

These two views of Tamahnous Bay date from around 1910. Tamahnous is Native American for "magic." The early log cabin and boathouse still stand and are owned by descendants of the original family. Schuler's camps were also located in this bay.

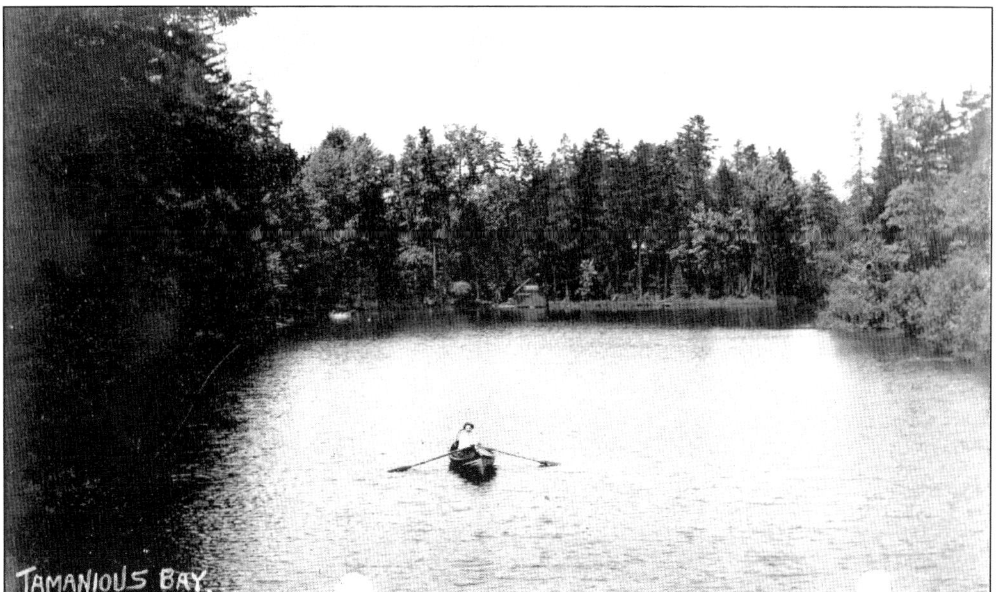

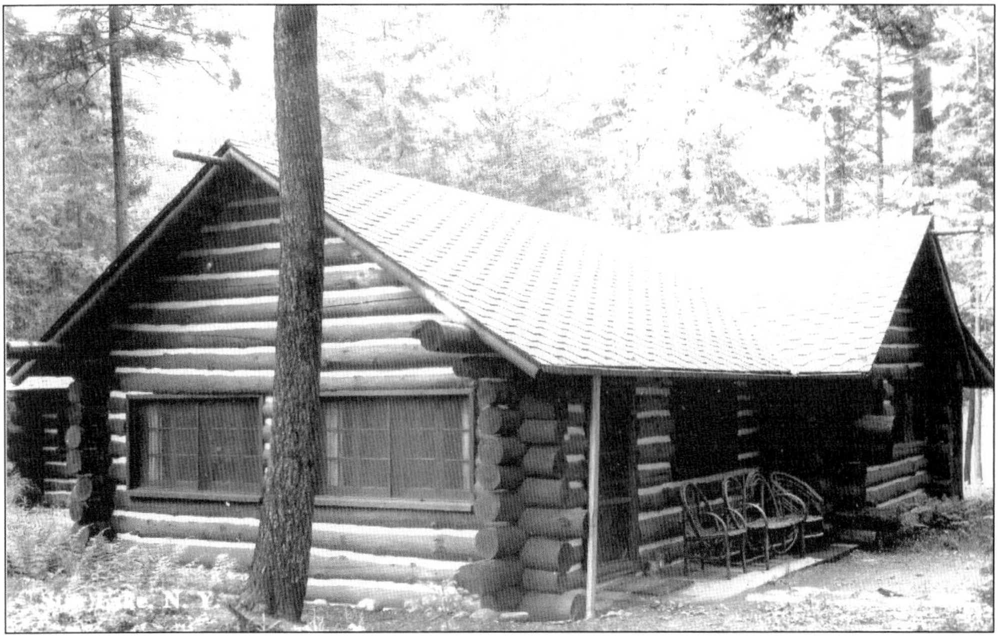

Both of these camps, located next to each other on Tamahnous Bay, were built by Andy Schuler, owner of the well-known Schuler's Potato Chips and vice president of the Sunshine Biscuit Company. Schuler also grew experimental potatoes for potato chips on his land near Streeter Lake, which is now referred to as the Potato Patch. The Schuler Mausoleum is located near Streeter Lake, and Crystal Lake and is a popular hiking destination.

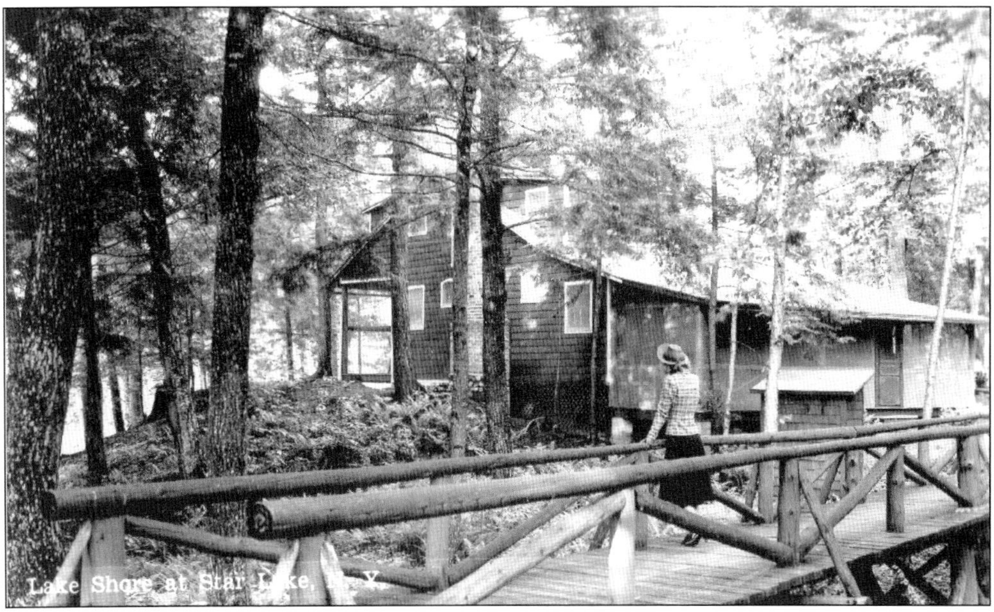

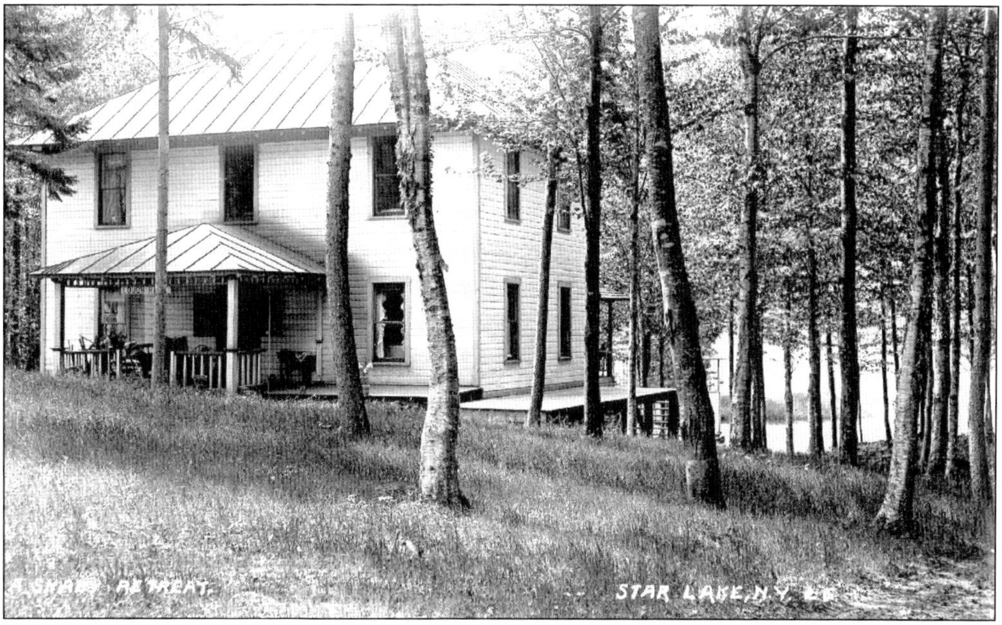

These two views of the Buena Vista cottage date from around 1908 and 1920. Buena Vista is Latin for "beautiful views." The camp was originally named Lough Hill and later renamed Buena Vista by Flora Scharch. Scharch was a schoolteacher from Syracuse who spent the summer months in Star Lake renting out rooms in her cottage for $15 to $18 per week. The cottage is located on the west side of the lake near where St. Huberts church stands today.

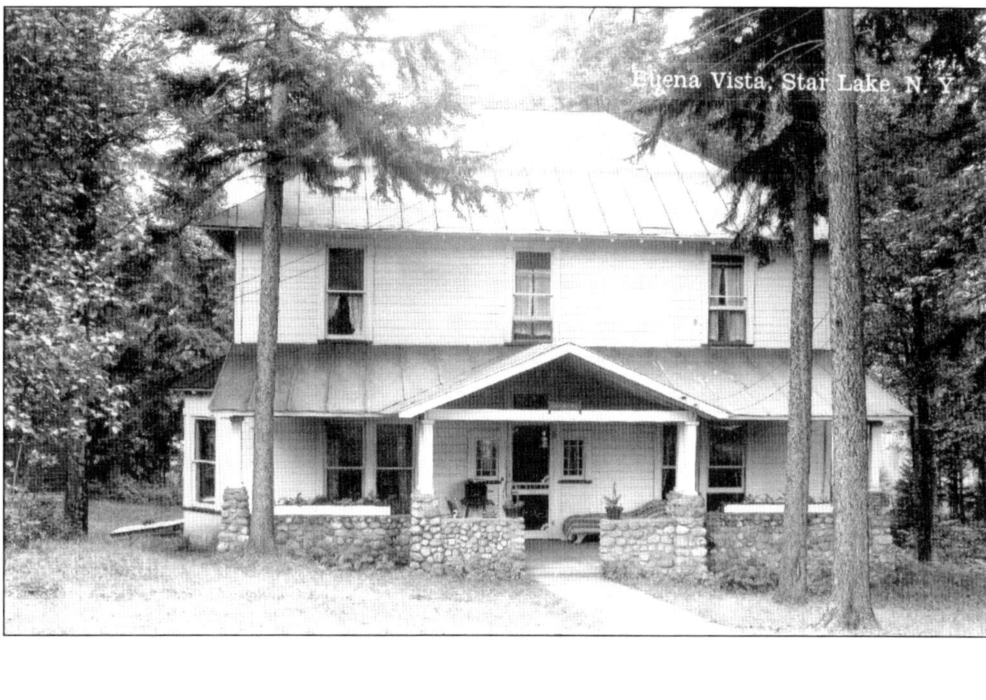

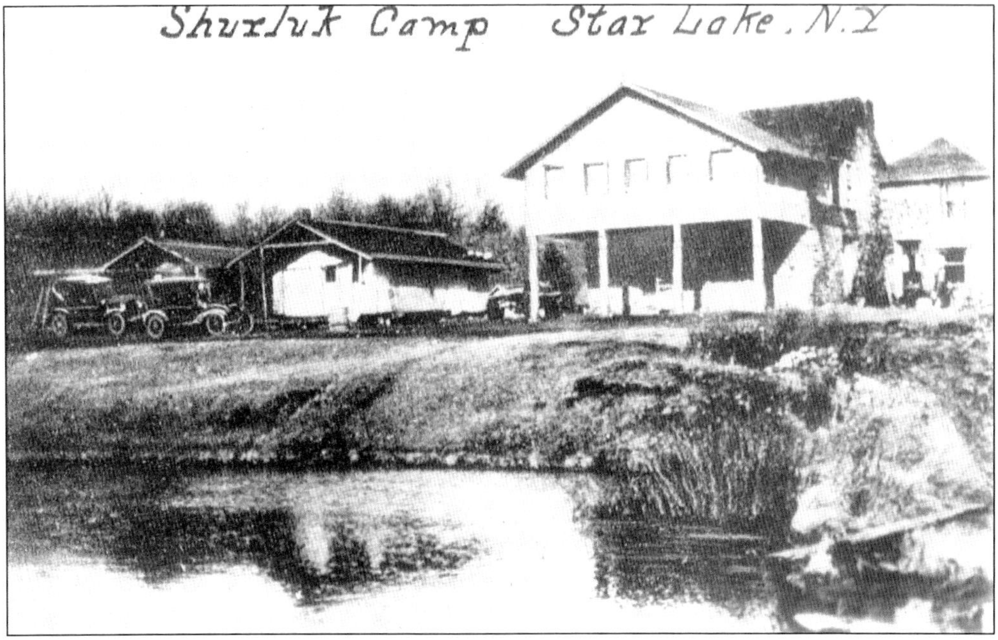

The Shurluk camp was built by Edwin Young Jr. and his brother Robert Young at the very end of what is now Youngs Road. The Youngs' hunting camp became well known for its hunting and fishing guide services. It was also a silver fox ranch for a brief time period. This property is now known as the Twelve Cedars Hunting Club.

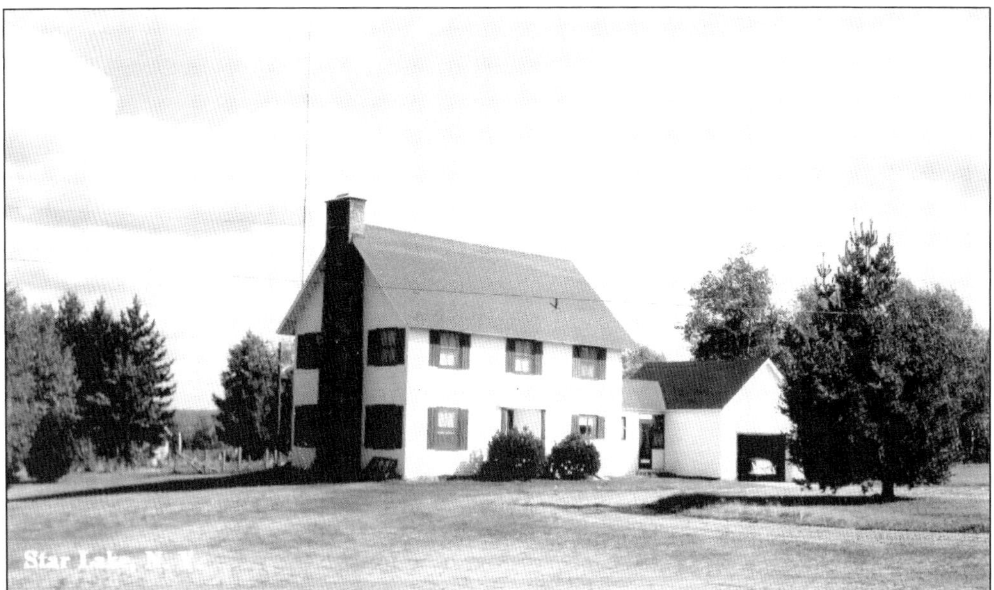

This home was built just outside the village of Star Lake on Route 3 for the plant manager of Jones & Laughlin Company in Benson Mines. A total of 14 homes were built in Star Lake for the mining company employees. They are all now privately owned residences.

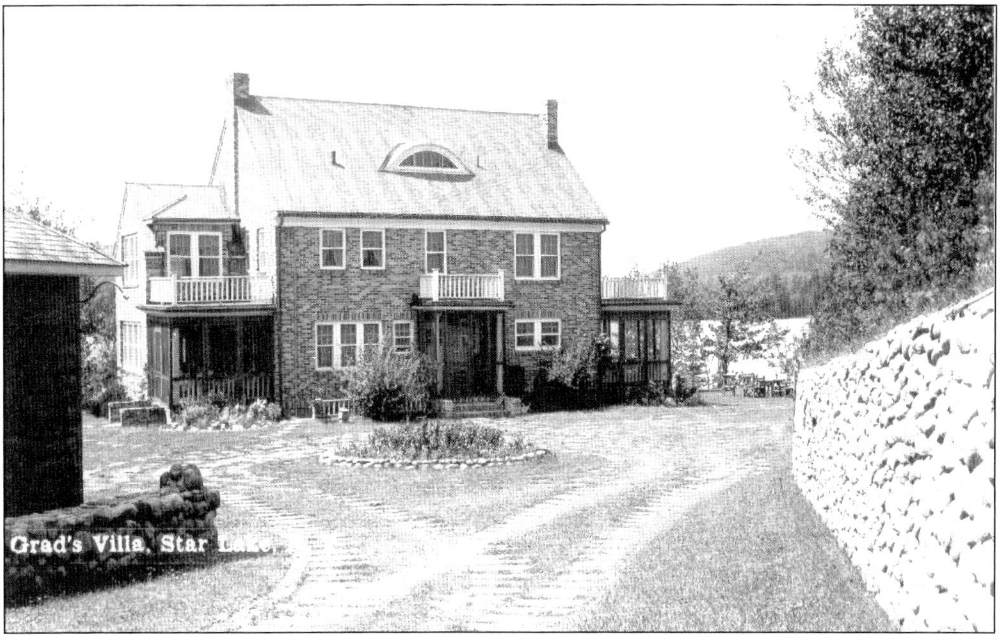

These 1930s views show Dr. Grad's Villa, which is sometimes referred to as Grad's Shaw. This was one of the only brick cottages built on the lake at this time. The interior of the cottage was ornately painted with landscape scenery by Italian artists. Dr. Grad, a pediatrician from New York City, would often be seen arriving in Star Lake in his chauffer-driven car.

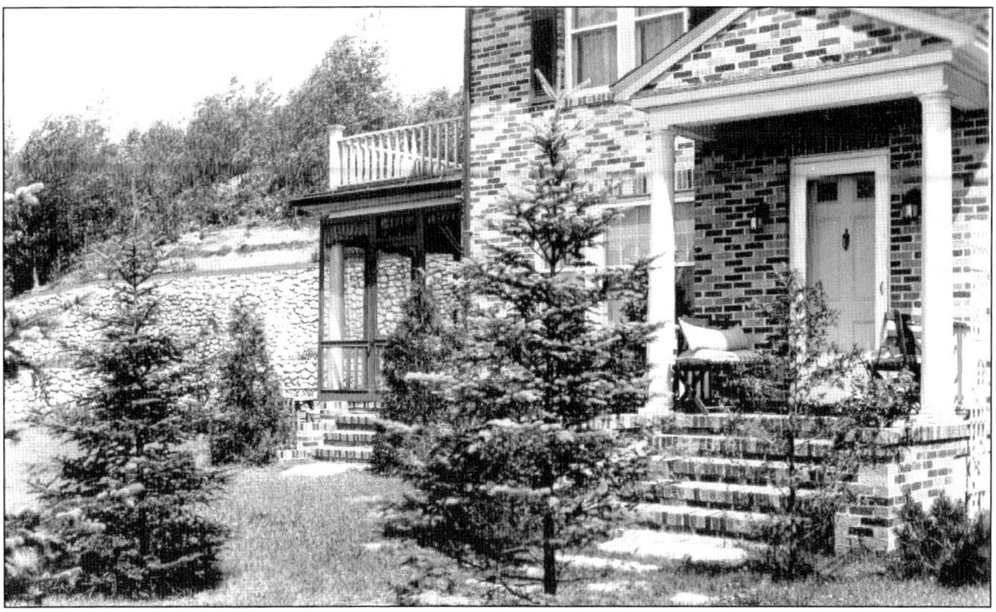

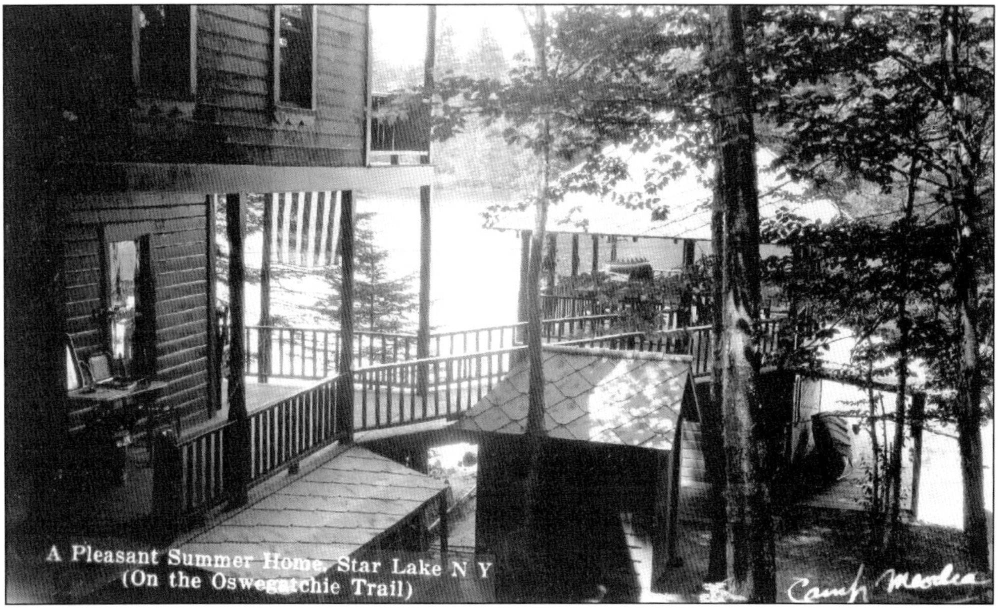

A summer camp on the Oswegatchie Trail is featured in this view, dating from around 1920.

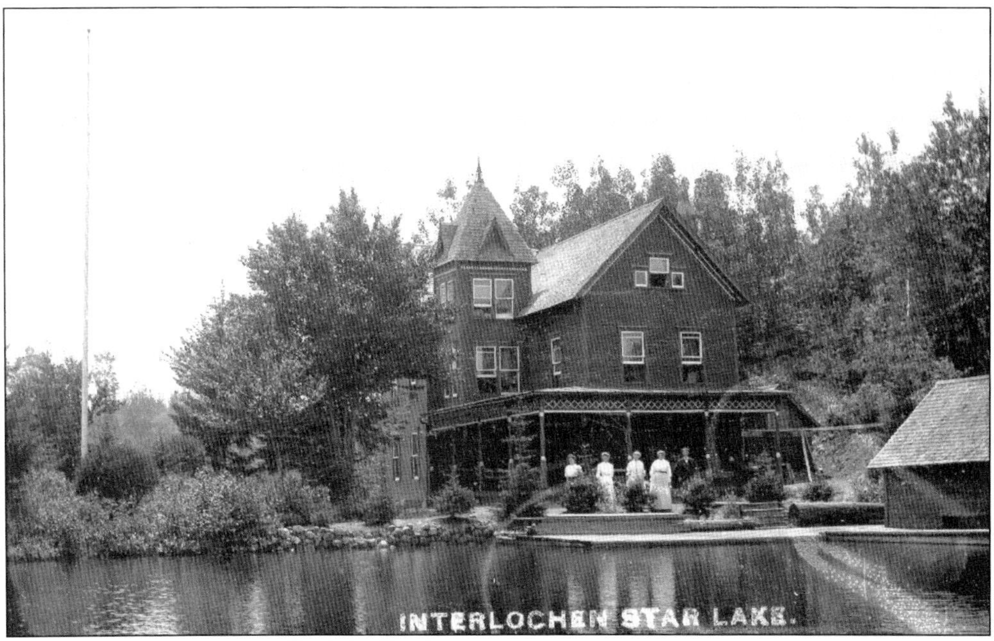

Preston Moody and his family stand in front of their Interlochen cottage around 1910. This cottage, still named Interlochen, or "between the lakes," is located on the Ridge Point peninsula, which separates Second and Third Lakes. Moody was a well-known shirt and collar manufacturer from New York City.

Six

Recreation and Personalities

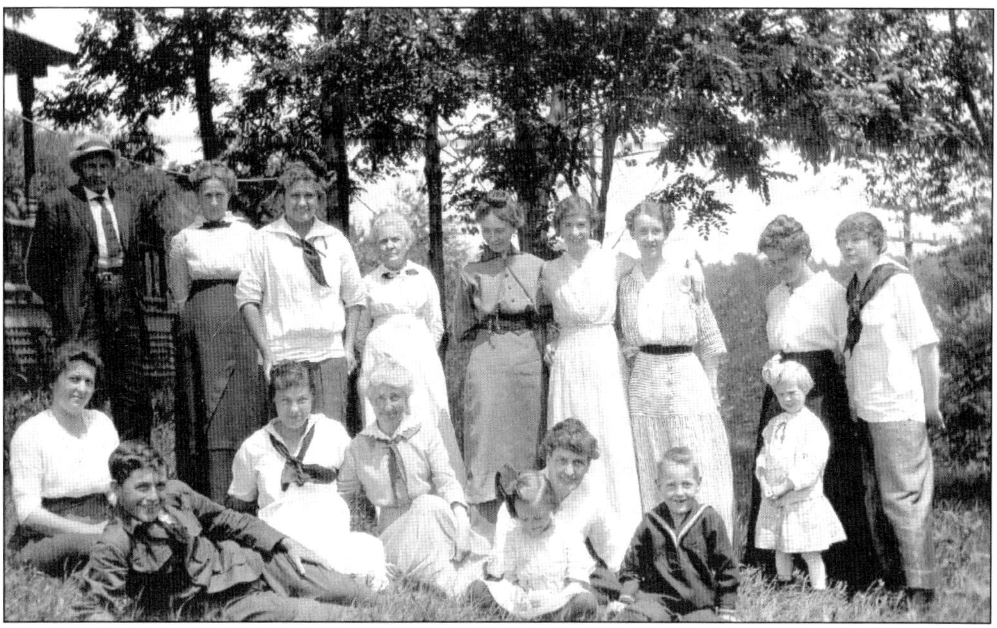

Dressed in their best clothes, family members pose for a photograph at Star Lake in 1915. By that time, most people owned a Kodak Brownie box camera, and many family photographs were converted to postcards, either by taking negatives to a local studio or by developing the photo cards at home.

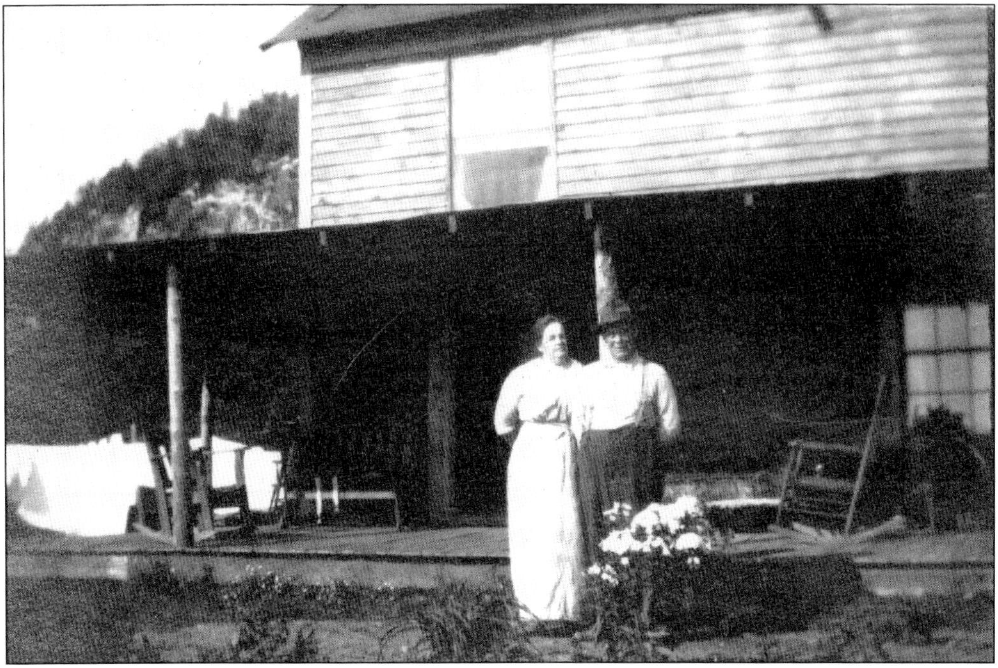

Well-known hunting and fishing guide John McBroom and his wife stand in front of their rustic home around 1920. Maple Mountain can be seen in the background. McBroom was often hired by the Star Lake Inn as a guide and was a personal friend of proprietor Charles Sayles.

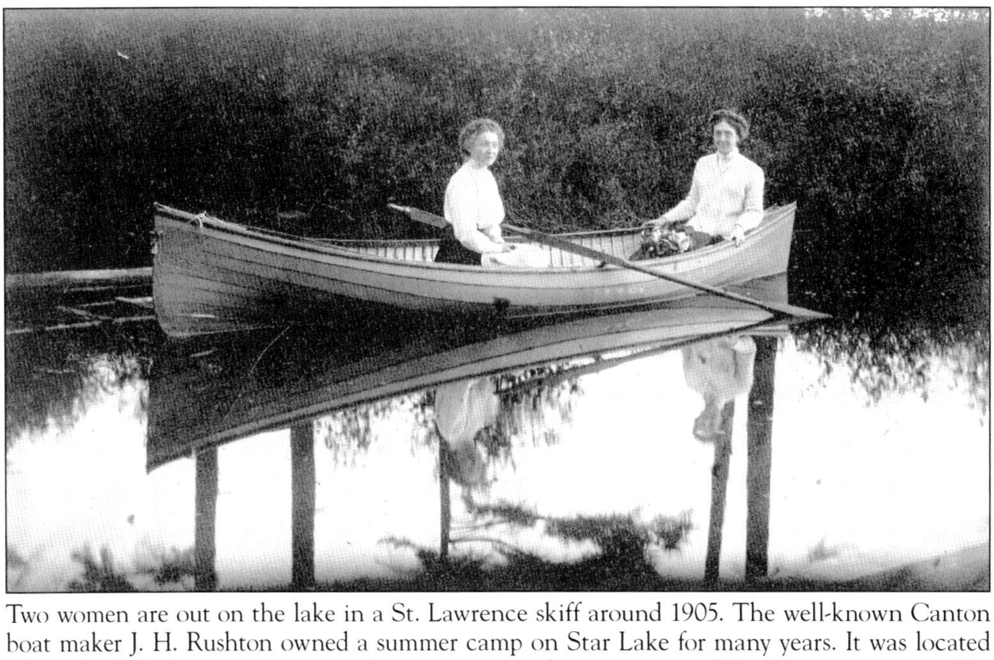

Two women are out on the lake in a St. Lawrence skiff around 1905. The well-known Canton boat maker J. H. Rushton owned a summer camp on Star Lake for many years. It was located where the Hillside cottage now stands. At one point, there were several Rushton canoes owned by cottage owners on the lake.

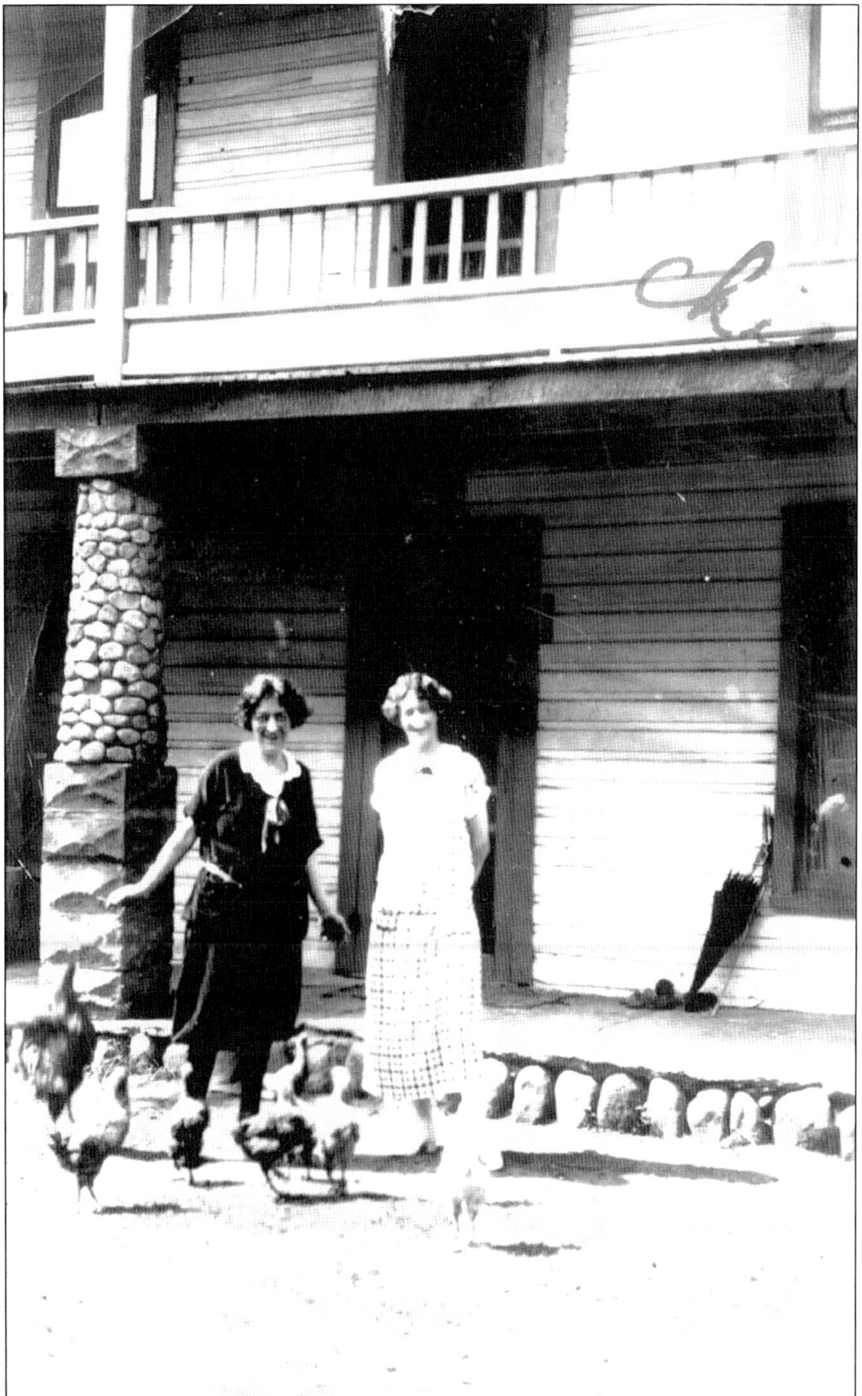

The Kilbourne women stand in front of the Peacock Lodge around 1915. The Kilbourne family was involved in many business ventures during the early days of Star Lake, running a taxi service, selling blocks of ice to cottages via boat, and renting several of the cottages they owned during the summer months.

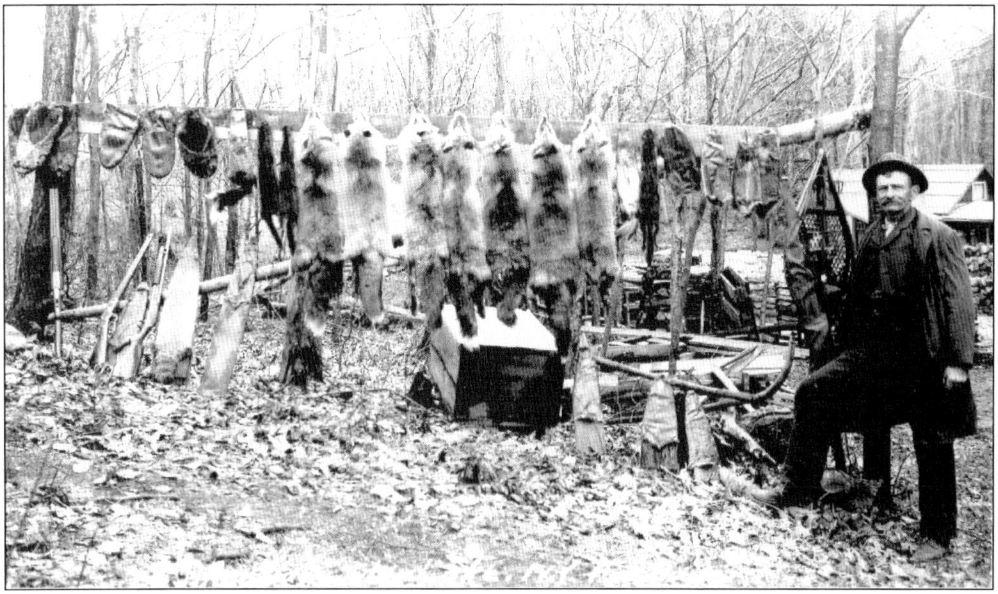

Frank J. Redway was the local fur buyer of Star Lake. Along with being a fur trader, Redway was a hotel owner, surveyor, and one of the first postmasters of Star Lake.

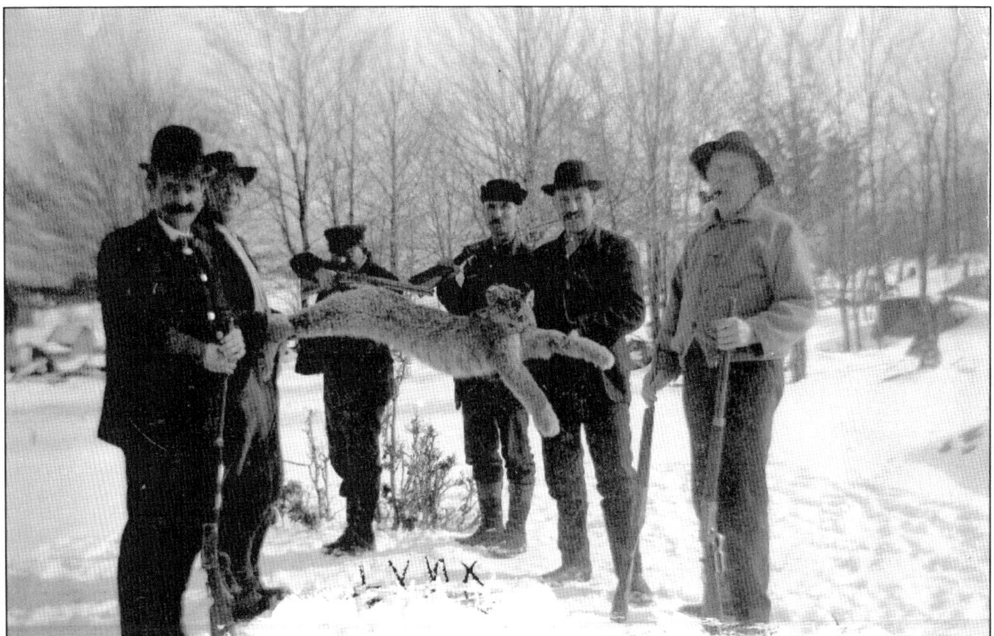

Six men proudly display a rare Adirondack lynx they killed in the Star Lake area around 1905. The Adirondack lynx disappeared when the more aggressive bobcats expanded into the region when logging operations increased the populations of deer, a primary food source for bobcats.

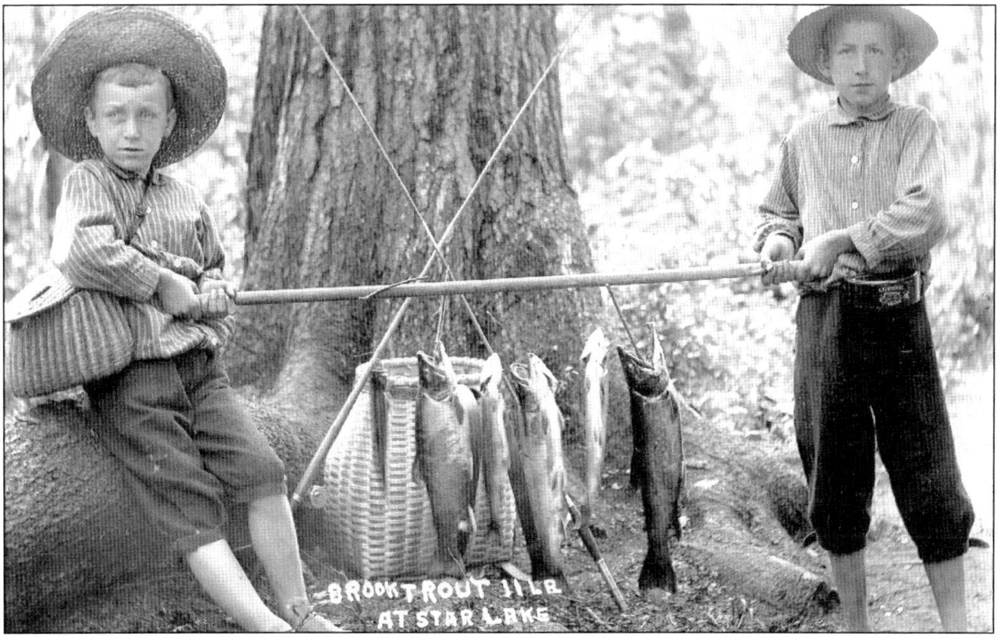

Two boys hold up 11 pounds of brook trout caught in Star Lake around 1910. Star Lake was the first lake in New York State to be stocked on application with 40,000 brook trout fry from the Caledonia Hatchery in 1889.

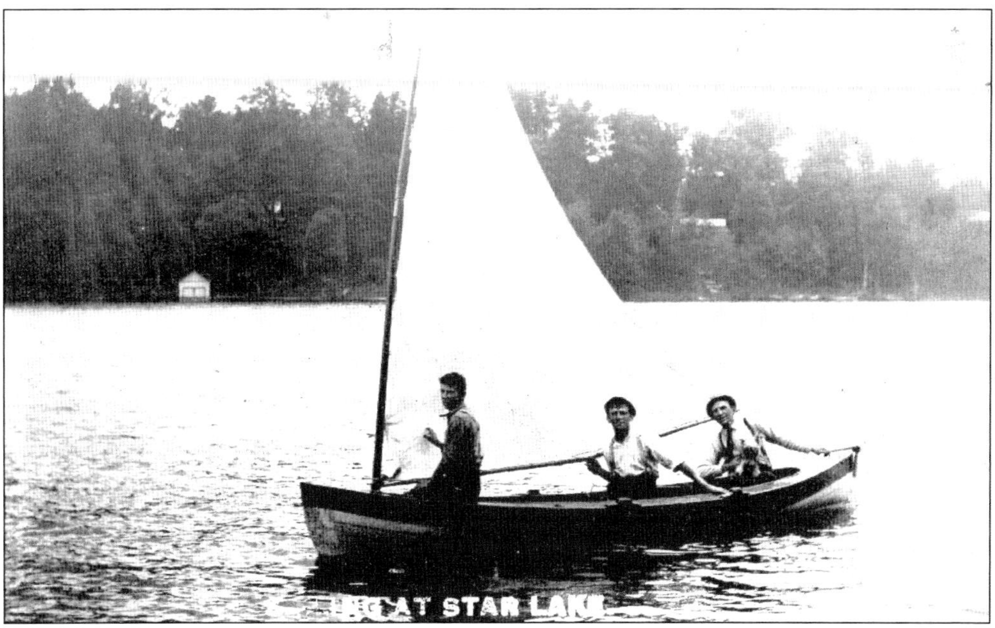

Three men and a dog enjoy the day on the water in a St. Lawrence sailing skiff. The photo postcard is postmarked 1906.

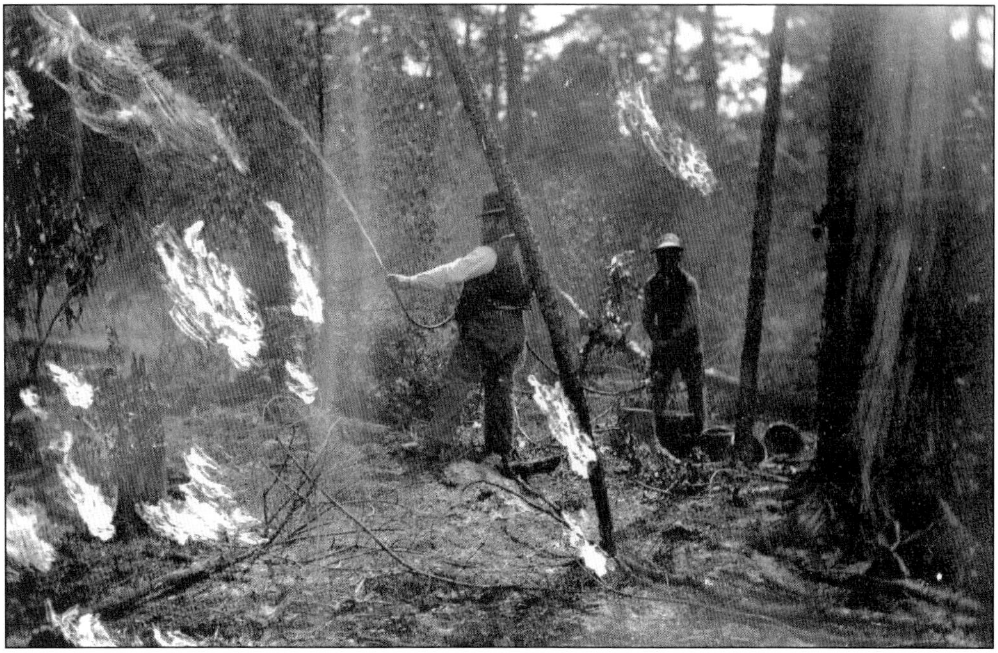

As the raging forest fire of 1909 fast approached the village of Star Lake, more than 200 townspeople armed with hand pump water tanks and buckets of water took to the outskirts of town to try and prevent its encroachment. The fire roared for almost a week and swept in to within a half-mile of the village. Luckily, there was no loss of life or dwellings.

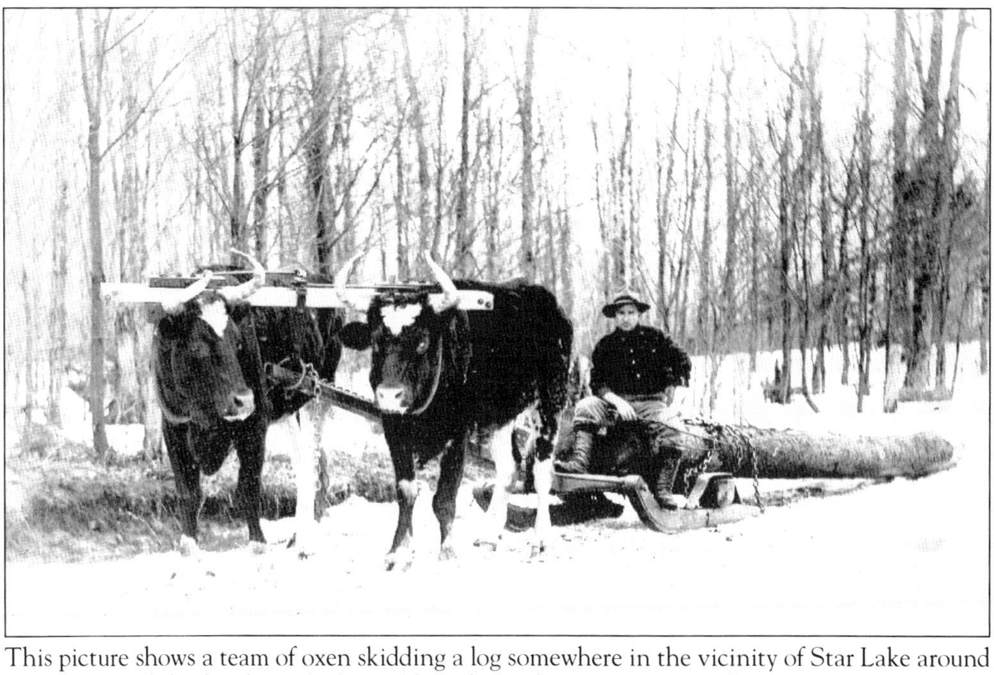

This picture shows a team of oxen skidding a log somewhere in the vicinity of Star Lake around 1910. Some of the locals worked as jobbers for Perley Waite's Sawmill in Star Lake, the Rich Lumber Company in Wanakena, and the Emporium Lumber Company in Cranberry Lake.

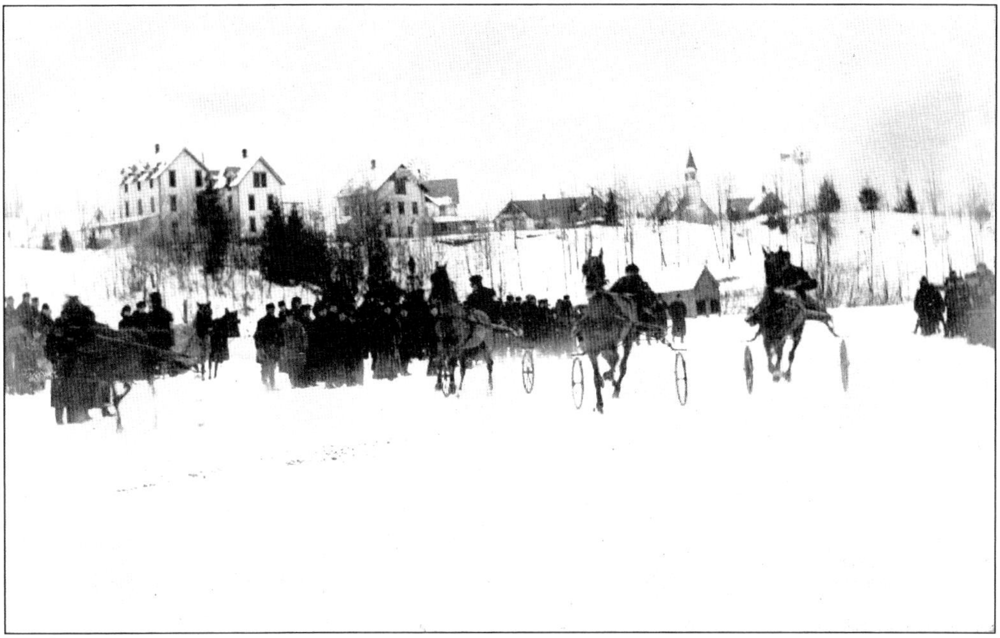

Horse racing on the ice in Post Office Bay was a major annual event for Star Lake, attracting hundreds of spectators. Horses from many of the surrounding counties were entered in the races, as the prize money totaled $1,000—a huge sum at the time. The card is postmarked 1908.

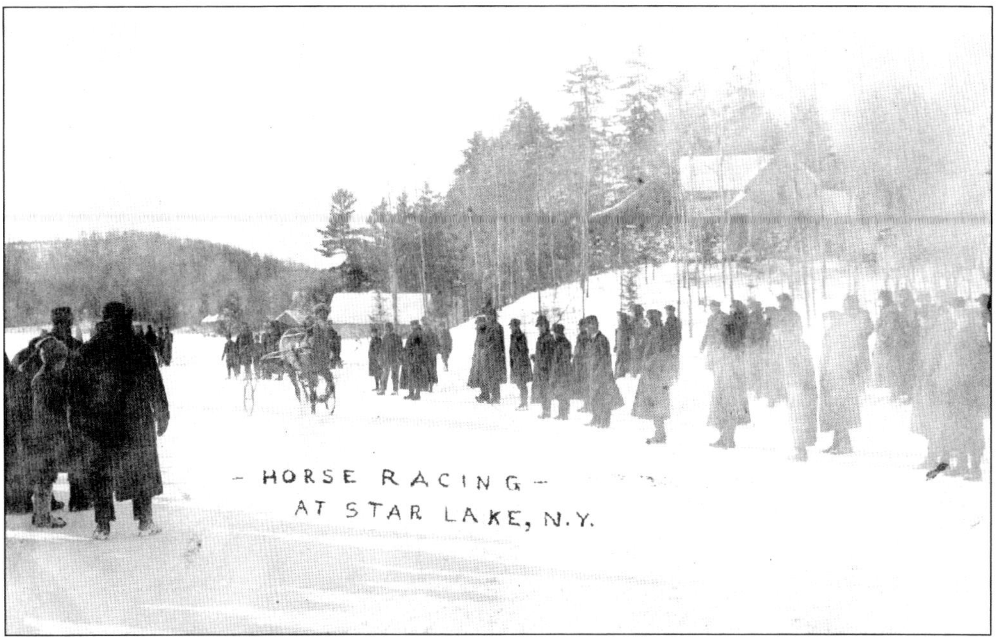

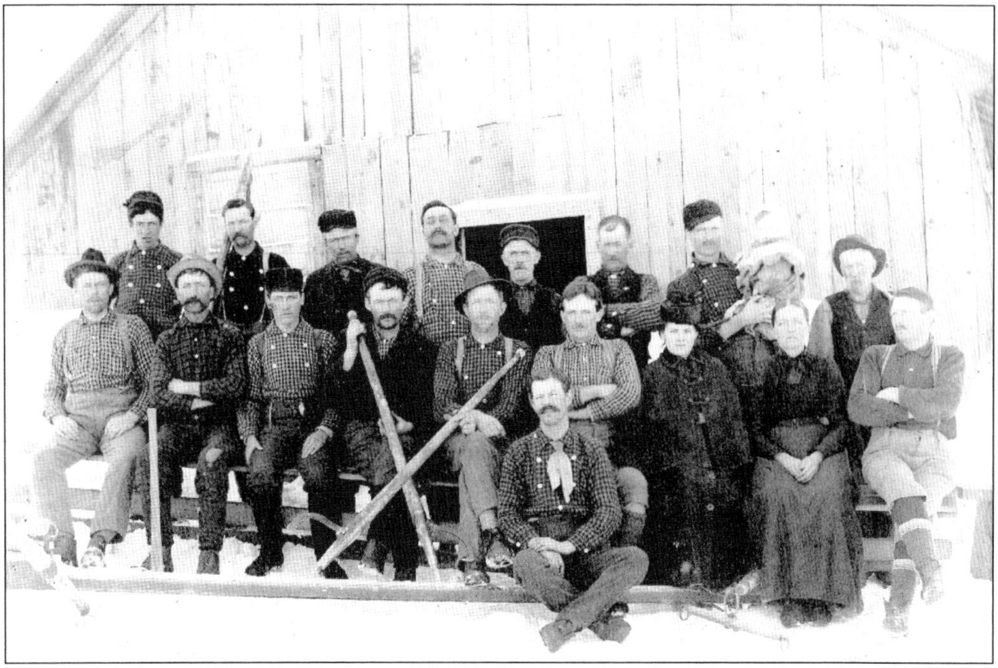

A group of lumberjacks stands in front of Perley Waite's sawmill in Star Lake around 1885. The sawmill was located at the base of Maple Mountain, near the Oswegatchie Trail Road.

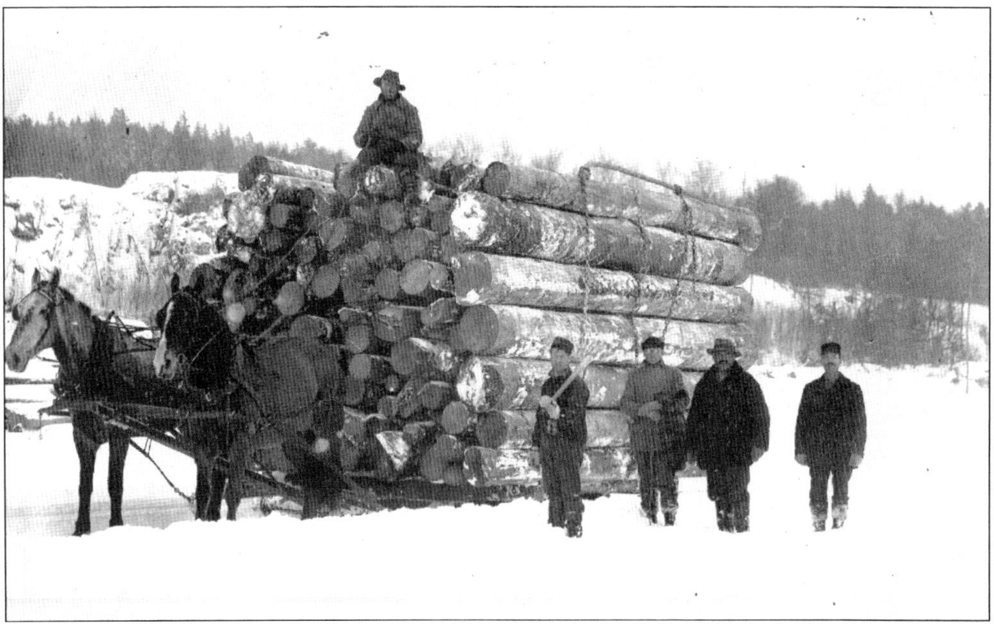

This early photograph, taken by Runions photo studio in Star Lake, shows logs being hauled by sled on an iced road. The destination was most likely the Emporium Lumber Company in Cranberry Lake or Perley Waite's sawmill in Star Lake, which was located at the foot of Maple Mountain.

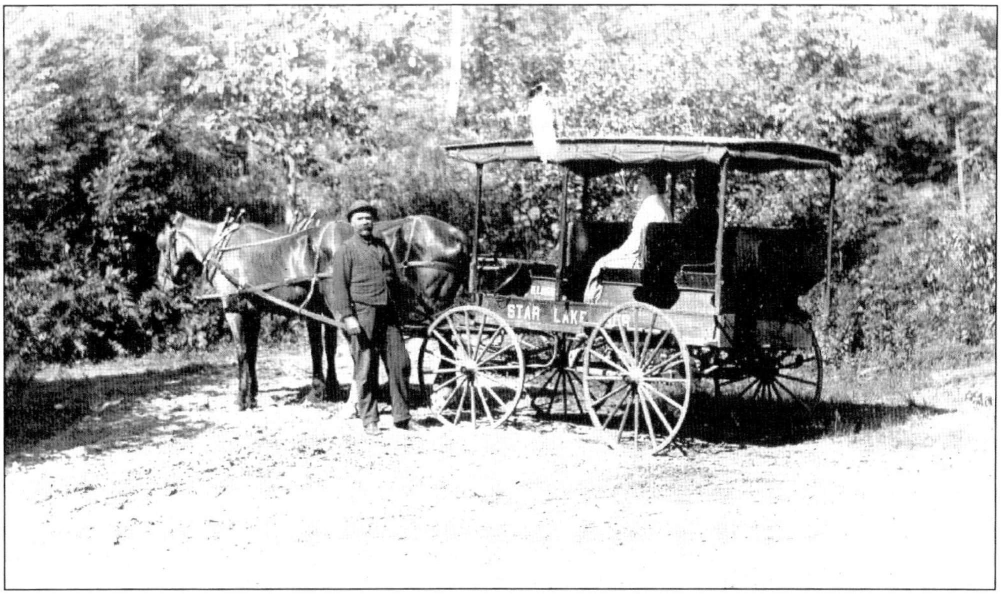

Winfred Backus stands alongside his Star Lake bus around 1910. Backus drove his passenger coach from the railroad stations of Oswegatchie and Benson Mines to Star Lake. His private work ledger from 1897 to 1906 shows that he charged 25¢ for a one-way trip per passenger and 25¢ per trunk. He also worked with his brother Christopher Backus on building many of the early cottages around the lake, hauling boats, hauling lumber, removing unwanted tree stumps, and selling firewood for $1.50 per cord.

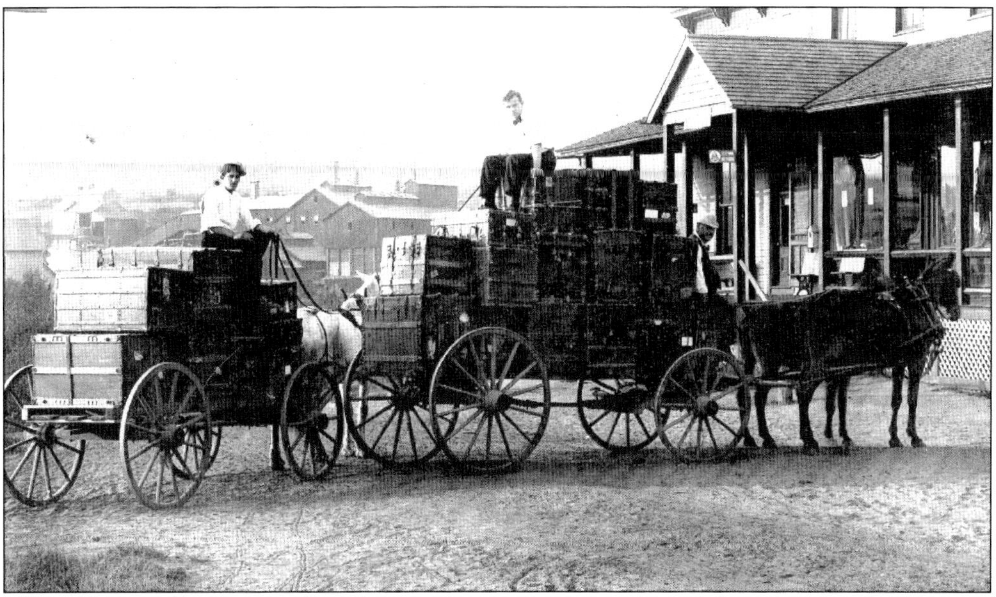

These two horse-drawn wagons are loaded with wardrobe trunks destined for one of the Star Lake hotels around 1905. Winfred Backus can be seen driving the front wagon. Benson Mines can be seen in the distance. Women often traveled with multiple trunks, each packed with dresses, hats, and other personal effects. Around this time, Benson Mines became the preferred railroad station for arrivals and departures when traveling to Star Lake. A round-trip ticket from New York City to Benson Mines was $14.10 in 1905.

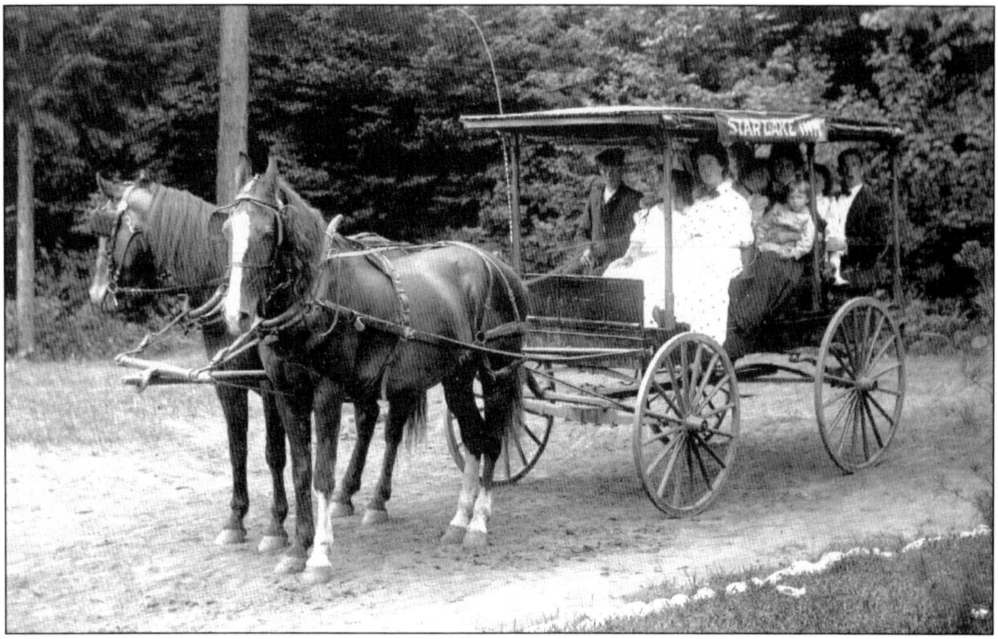

Charley Burley of Oswegatchie and Winfred Backus of Star Lake operated the local coaches delivering passengers to the local hotels and cottages. The Star Lake Inn also operated its own service, charging guests 25¢ for fare plus an additional 25¢ per trunk.

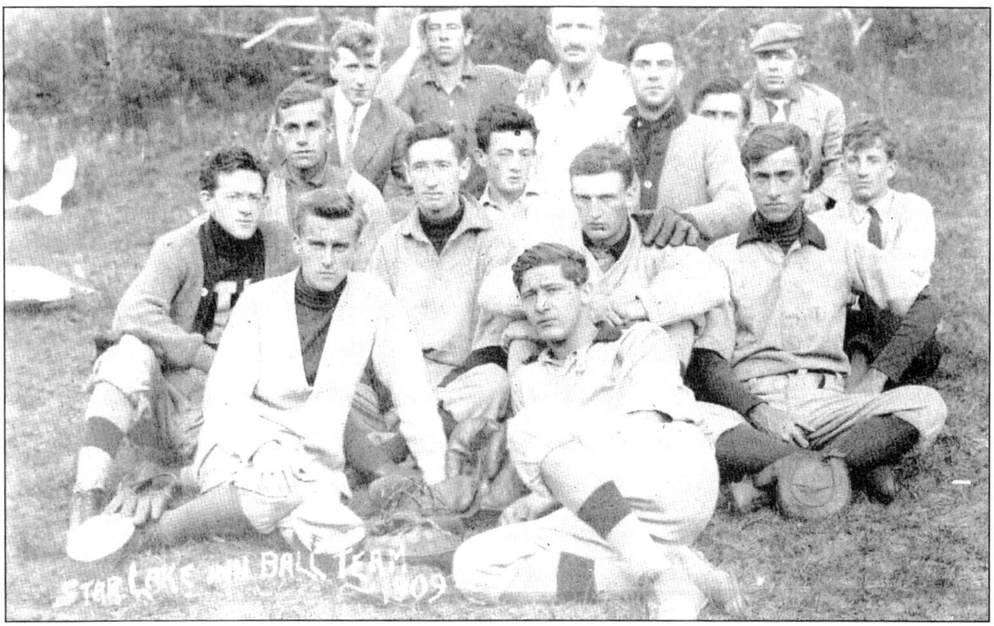

This team photograph shows the Star Lake Inn baseball team around 1909. The team manager can be seen in the middle of the back row, wearing the white sweater and tie. Many of the neighboring towns also had ball teams, including Harrisville, Newton Falls, Benson Mines, and Wanakena.

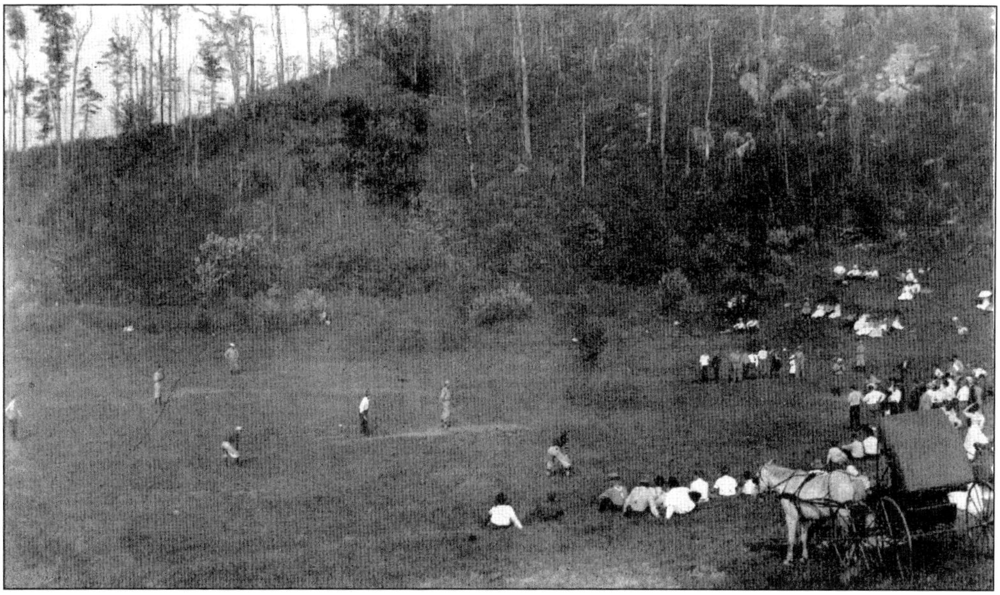

This baseball game between Star Lake and Wanakena ended with a 5-1 hometown win on August 21, 1909. The game was played on the old McFarrin farm, which is now the first and ninth holes of the Clifton-Fine golf course. The large rock formations of Bald Mountain can be seen in the outfield. McFarrin's white horse and buggy can be seen in the lower photograph.

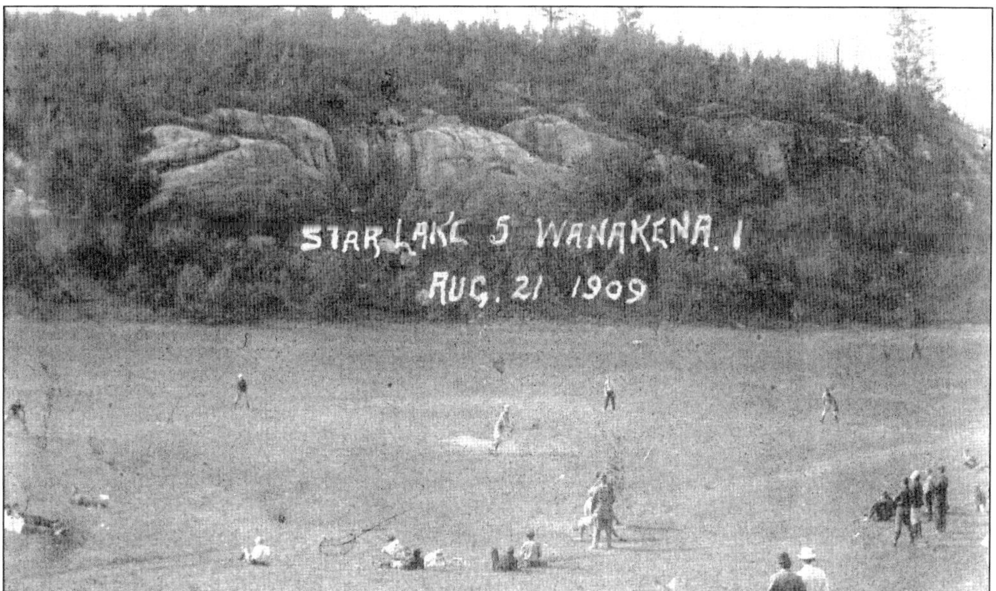

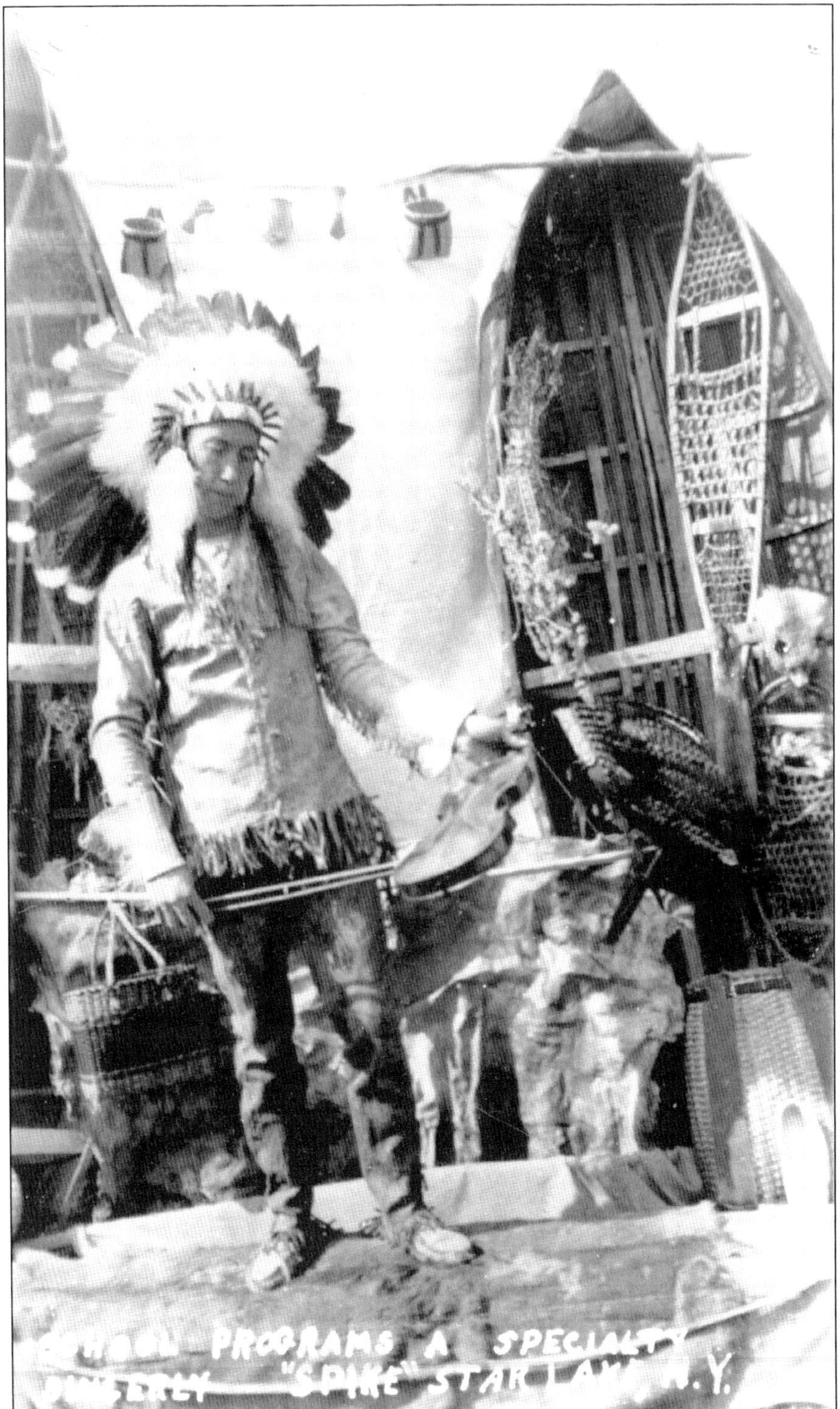

Alton Draper, better known as Spike the Indian, is pictured outside of his souvenir stand, playing the violin.

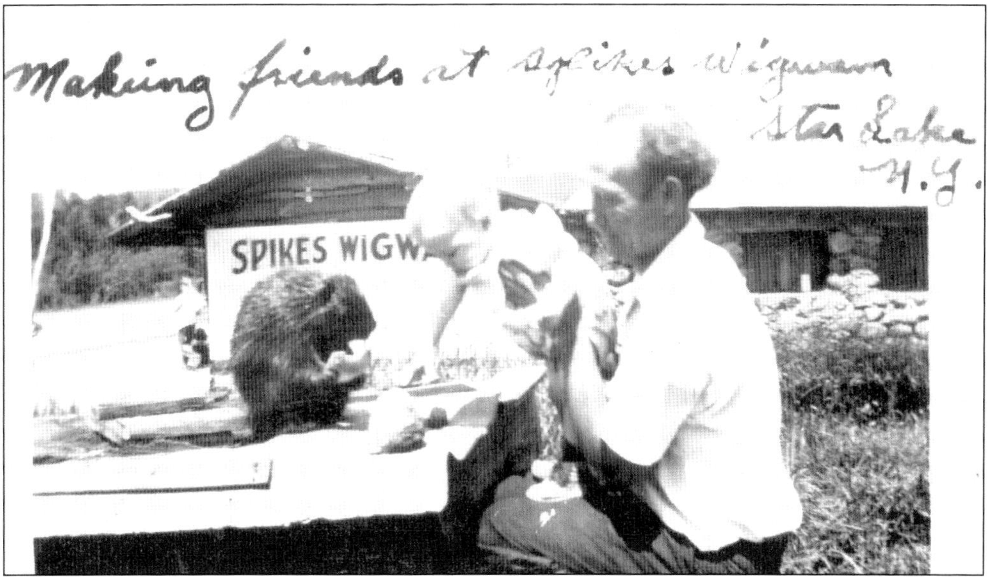

Spike was a local legend, catering not only to the tourists passing through but also to the many schoolchildren in the surrounding towns who often would take field trips to meet a genuine Native American Indian. In January 1938, he made a bet with the locals that he could survive in the woods for a month without any food or shelter. He took only his hunting knife and the clothes on his back. Miraculously, he pulled off the feat, surviving on porcupine meat, fish that he caught with a bone hook, roots, berries, and yellow birch bark. An article about his success was published in the *New York Times*.

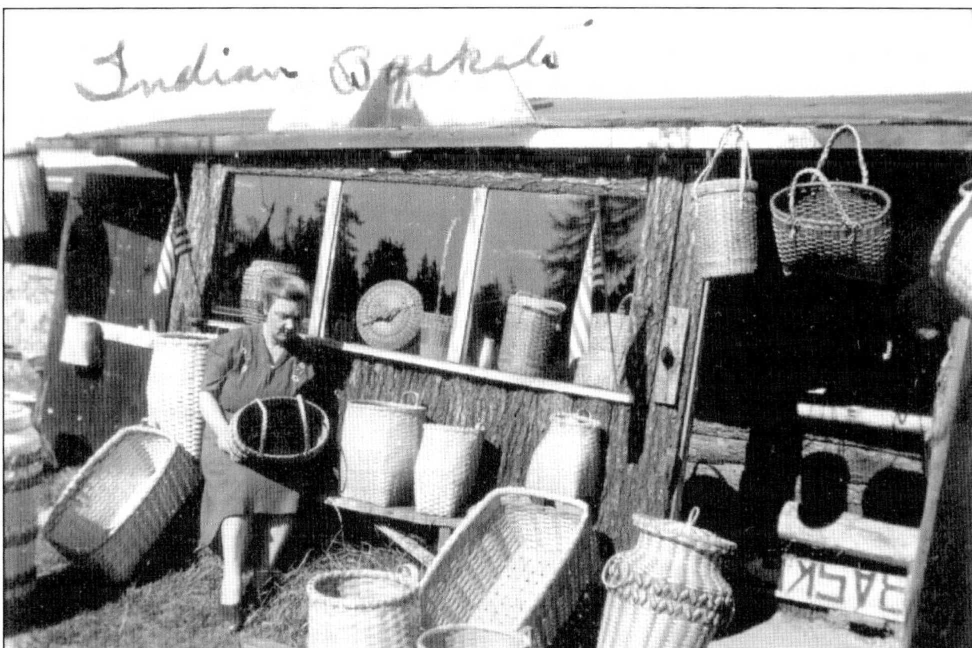

Spike Draper's wife, Lorene, poses in front of the family's wigwam roadside souvenir store around 1930. Pack baskets, decorative Indian baskets, moccasins, and handmade trinkets were sold to tourists traveling on the Oswegatchie Trail Road to Star Lake and beyond.

ADIRONDACK BUS LINES

Star Lake, N. Y.

Phone 5F31, Benson Mines

READ DOWN					READ UP			
		Leave			Arrive			
Miles	Fare	P. M.*	A. M.		P. M.	A. M.*	Fare	Miles
0	.00	6:20	8:27	Gouverneur	5:50	9:40	$3.70	74
2	.25	6:30	8:40	Hailesboro	5:40	9:30	3.60	72
6	.30	6:40	8:50	Fowler	5:25	9:22	3.40	68
9	.45	6:47	8:58	Fullerville	5:15	9:15	3.25	65
15.5	.80	7:03	9:14	Edwards	4:55	8:50	2.95	58.5
20	1.00	7:12	9:26	South Edwards	4:42	8:35	2.70	54
25	1.25	7:25	9:39	Fine	4:30	8:22	2.45	49
27	1.35	7:32	9:44	Scott's Bridge	4:22	8:16	2.35	47
29	1.45	7:36	9:49	Flat Rock	4:17	8:10	2.25	45
32	1.60	7:42	10:07	Oswegatchie	4:05	8:00	2.10	42
35	1.75	7:52	10:16	Star Lake	3:55	7:50	1.95	39
37	1.85	8:00	10:22	Benson Mines	3:40	7:42	1.85	37
41	2.05	8:12	10:34	Newton Falls	3:25	7:30	1.65	33
48	2.40	8:35	10:55	Windfall	2:57	7:10	1.30	26
51	2.55	8:45	11:05	Cranberry Lake	2:45	7:00	1.15	23
54	2.70	8:53	11:14	Brandy Brook	2:33	6:42	1.00	20
57	2.85	9:00	11:20	Shurtleff	2:24	6:35	.85	17
60	3.00	9:10	11:27	Sevey	2:15	2:25	.70	14
63	3.15	9:25	11:36	Jock Pond	2:03	6:10	.55	11
64	3.20	9:3[illegible]	11:40	Childwold P. O.	1:57	6:05	.50	10
67	3.35	9:45	11:52	Gale	1:45	5:50	.35	7
73	3.65	10:15	12:15	Piercefield	1:20	5:22	.15	1
74	3.70	10:20	12:20	Piercefield R. R.	1:15	5:17	.00	0

Regular Service Starts May 1, 1927

*Schedule in Effect from June 1 to October 1.

Alfred L. Kilbourne started the Adirondack Bus Lines in May 1927 upon completion of the Star Lake-Cranberry Lake cement road. His route between Gouverneur and Piercefield was 71 miles long, and he made two trips daily.

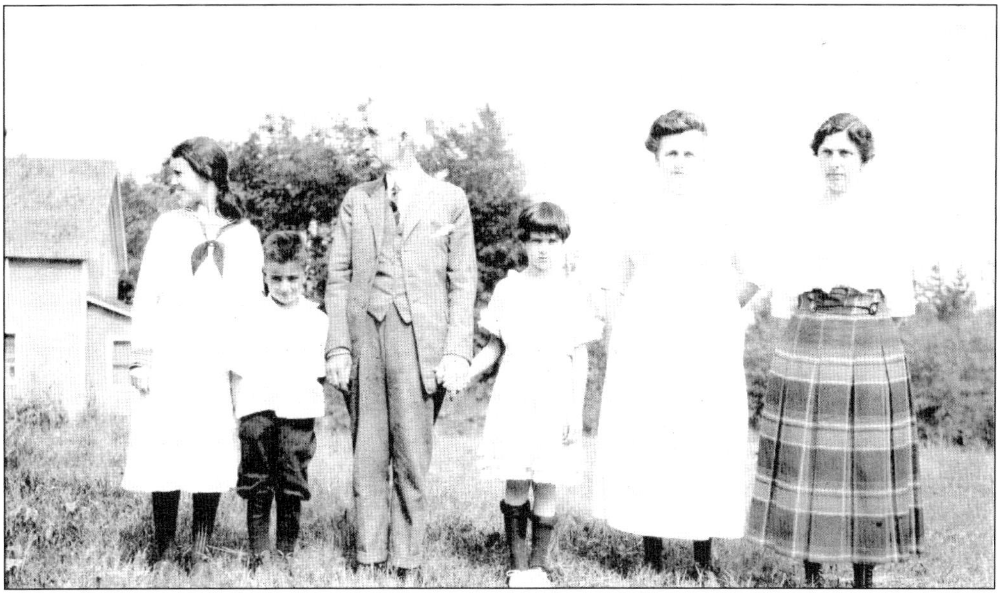

Members of the Forney family of Star Lake stand near Youngs Road around 1925. Edmund Pendleton, third from the left, was the third postmaster of Star Lake, serving from 1899 to 1905, and was also the secretary of the Benson Mines Iron Ore Company around 1890.

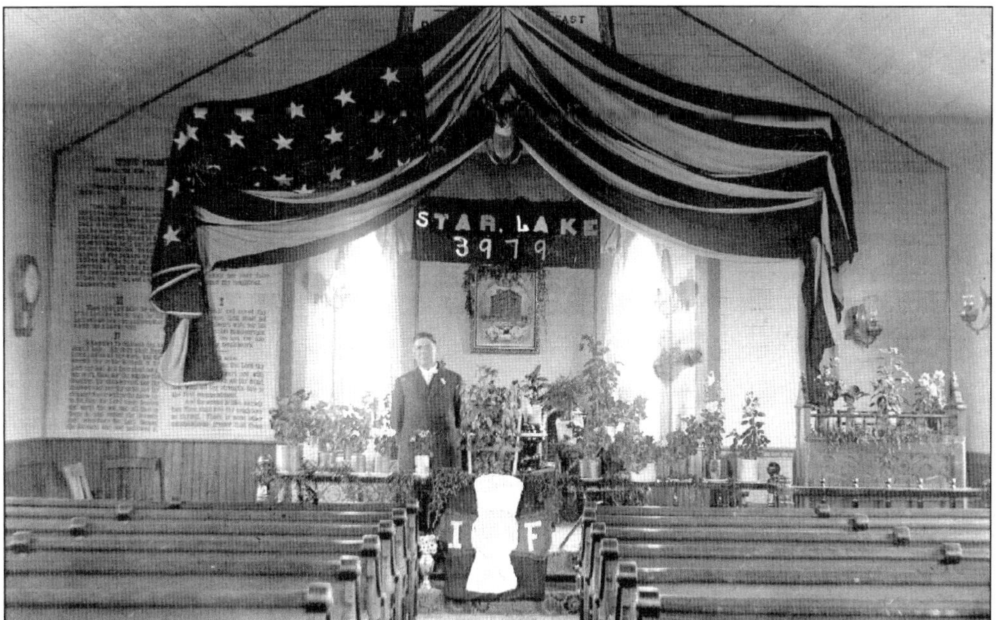

This *c.* 1905 view shows the Star Lake Chapter of the Independent Order of Foresters (IOF). The IOF was a national fraternal organization that helped other members during times of need.

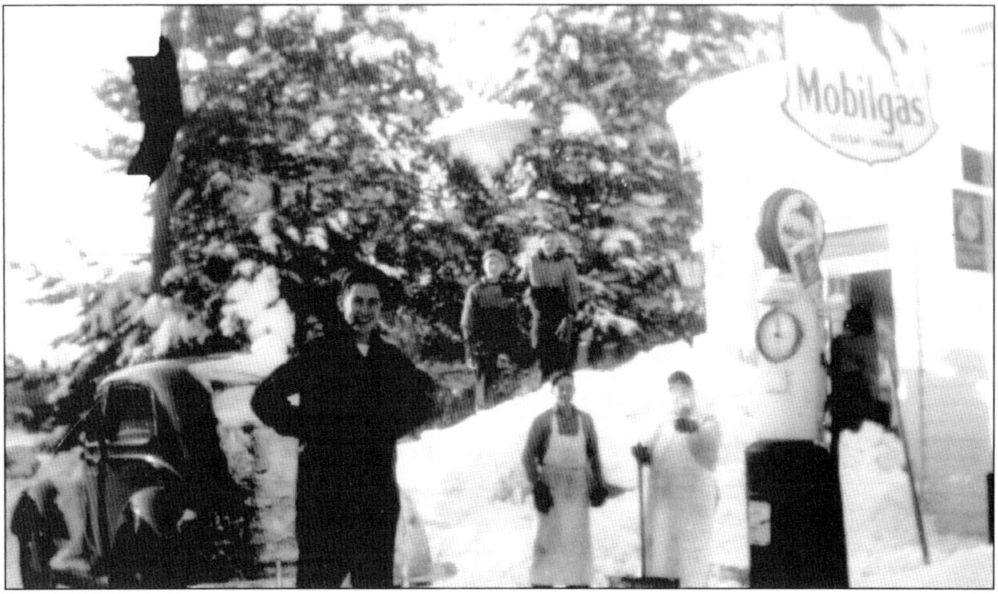

A group stands in front of Tears Store around 1930. The store and gas station were owned by Maurice and Claude Tears and managed by Howard Clark. Clark can be seen on the far right, holding the shovel.

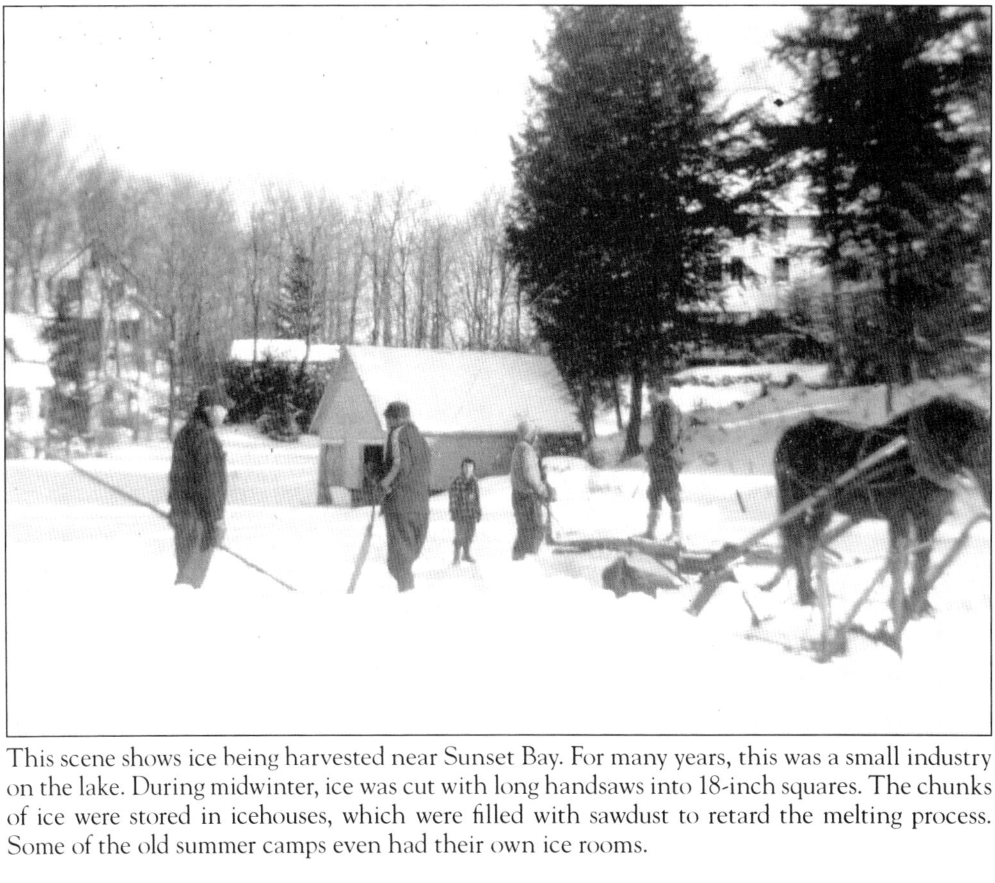

This scene shows ice being harvested near Sunset Bay. For many years, this was a small industry on the lake. During midwinter, ice was cut with long handsaws into 18-inch squares. The chunks of ice were stored in icehouses, which were filled with sawdust to retard the melting process. Some of the old summer camps even had their own ice rooms.

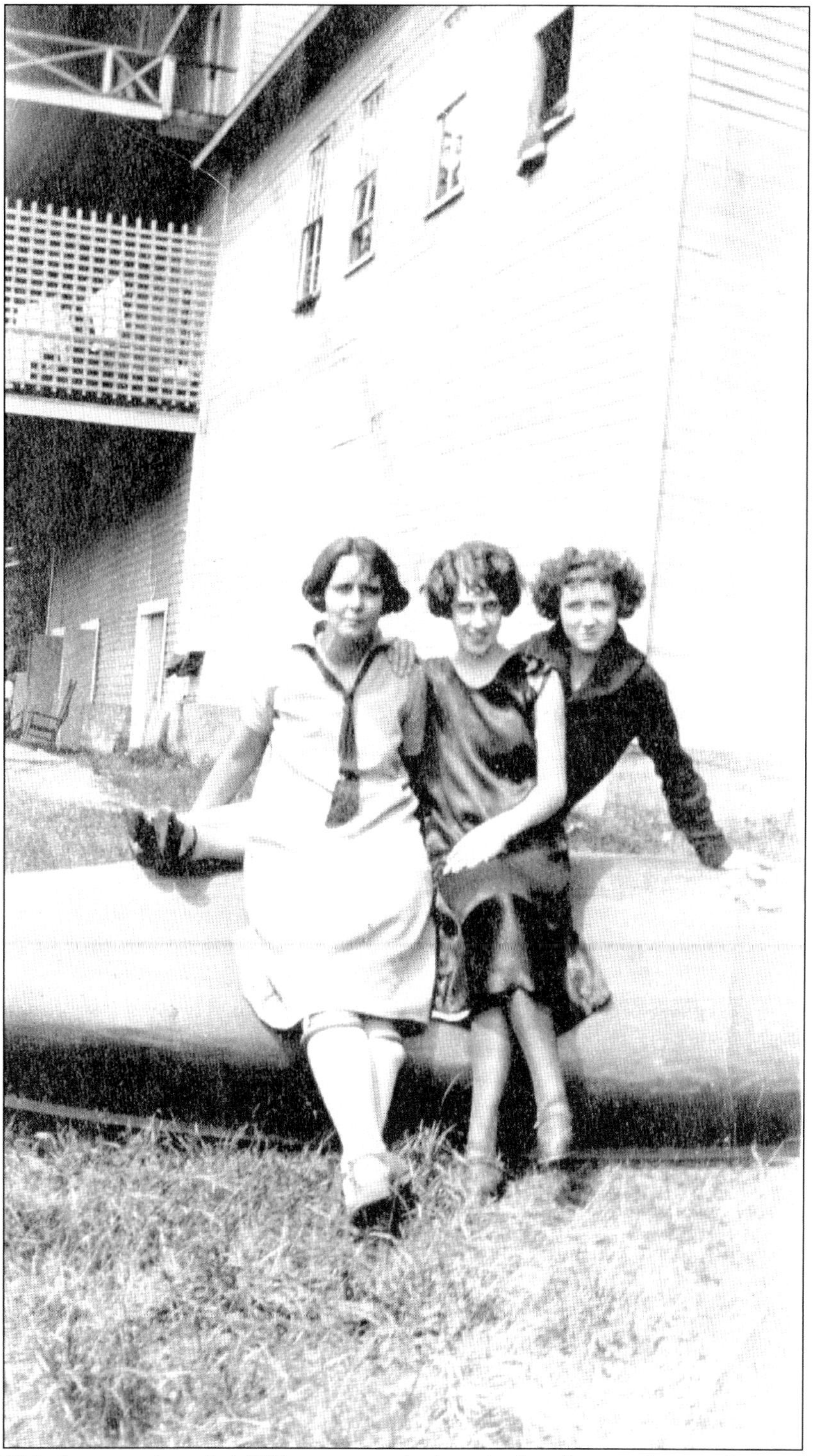

This c. 1920 photograph, titled "When we worked at the Inn," was taken in front of the Star Lake Inn near the shore. Evelyn Amey, on the left, and Edna Marshall, in the center, were just a few of the local townspeople who worked at the inn during the summer months.

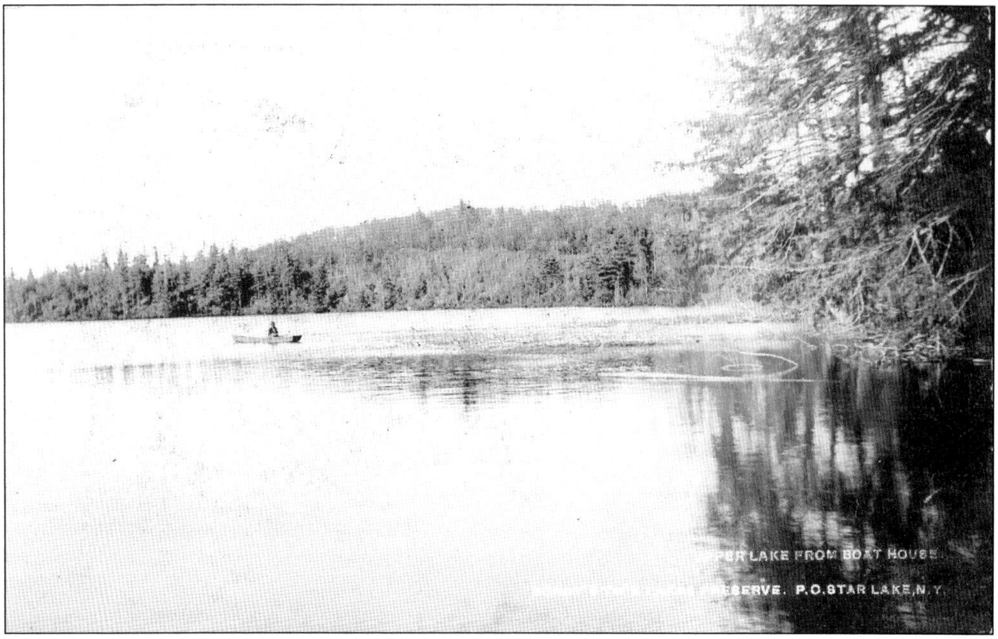

In 1911, Joseph Bondy, the wealthy attorney from Syracuse, purchased a 135-acre tract of land known as Twin Lakes from E. G. Gustin of Carthage. His intentions for this land were to keep it as a private wildlife preserve and build a small cabin on the property. In 1918, with the spread of the disease tuberculosis on the rise, state and county health officials looked to purchase the Twin Lakes property from Bondy for a huge tuberculosis hospital. It was thought to have been the ideal location for such a hospital in St. Lawrence County. The Carthage and Adirondack Railroad passed through a corner of the property, as well as telephone and telegraph lines, and electricity was available from nearby Benson Mines. After much debate, the proposal was denied for lack of convenience and accessibility for friends and family of the patients.

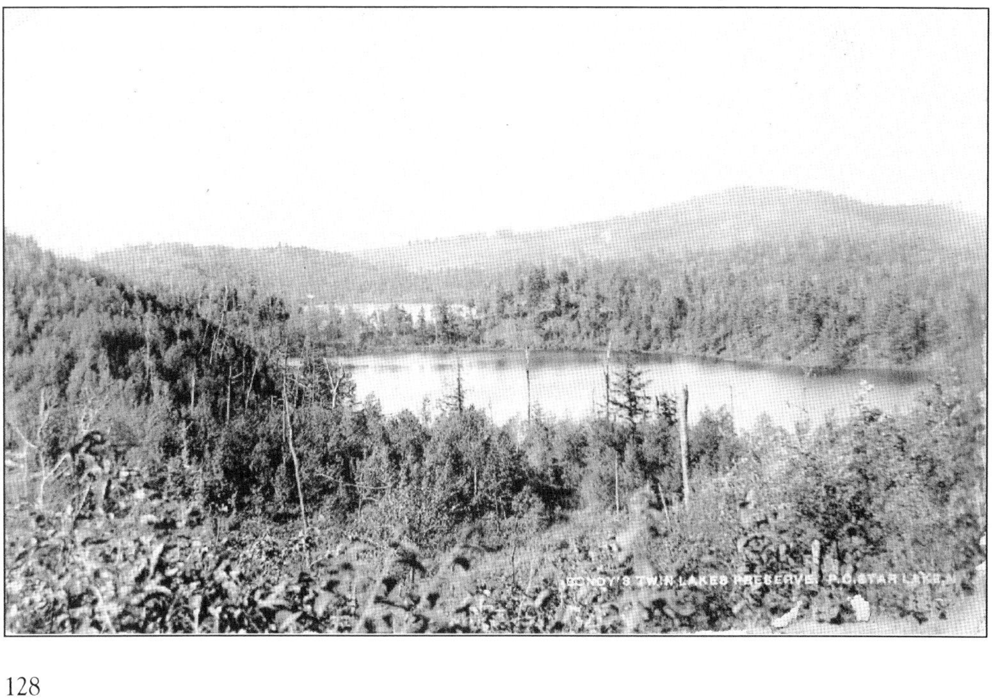